T0132539

Soft Computing in Materials Development and its Sustainability in the Manufacturing Sector

This book focuses on the application of soft computing in materials and manufacturing sectors with the objective to offer an intelligent approach to improve the manufacturing process, material selection and characterization techniques for developing advanced new materials. This book unveils different models and soft computing techniques applicable in the field of advanced materials and solves the problems to help the industry and scientists to develop sustainable materials for all purposes. The book focuses on the overall well-being of the environment for better sustenance and livelihood. First, the authors discuss the implementation of soft computing in various areas of engineering materials. They also review the latest intelligent technologies and algorithms related to the state-of-the-art methodologies of monitoring and effective implementation of sustainable engineering practices. Finally, the authors examine the future generation of sustainable and intelligent monitoring techniques beneficial for manufacturing and cover novel soft computing techniques for effective manufacturing processes at par with the standards laid down by the International Standards of Organization (ISO). This book is intended for academics and researchers from all the fields of engineering interested in joining interdisciplinary initiatives on soft computing techniques for advanced materials and manufacturing.

Edge AI in Future Computing

Series Editors:
Arun Kumar Sangaiah, SCOPE, VIT University, Tamil Nadu
Mamta Mittal, G. B. Pant Government Engineering College,
Okhla, New Delhi

**Soft Computing in Materials Development and its Sustainability
in the Manufacturing Sector**
*Amar Patnaik, Vikas Kukshal, Pankaj Agarwal, Ankush Sharma,
Mahavir Choudhary*

**Soft Computing Techniques in Engineering, Health,
Mathematical and Social Sciences**
Pradip Debnath and S. A. Mohiuddine

**Machine Learning for Edge Computing: Frameworks,
Patterns and Best Practices**
Amitoj Singh, Vinay Kukreja, Taghi Javdani Gandomani

**Internet of Things: Frameworks for Enabling and
Emerging Technologies**
*Bharat Bhushan, Sudhir Kumar Sharma, Bhuvan Unhelkar,
Muhammad Fazal Ijaz, Lamia Karim*

For more information about this series, please visit: https://www.routledge.com/
Edge-AI-in-Future-Computing/book-series/EAIFC

Soft Computing in Materials Development and its Sustainability in the Manufacturing Sector

Edited by
Amar Patnaik, Vikas Kukshal,
Pankaj Agarwal, Ankush Sharma,
Mahavir Choudhary

CRC Press
Taylor & Francis Group
Boca Raton London New York

CRC Press is an imprint of the
Taylor & Francis Group, an **Informa** business

MATLAB® is a trademark of The MathWorks, Inc. and is used with permission. The MathWorks does not warrant the accuracy of the text or exercises in this book. This book's use or discussion of MATLAB® software or related products does not constitute endorsement or sponsorship by The MathWorks of a particular pedagogical approach or particular use of the MATLAB® software

First edition published 2023
by CRC Press
6000 Broken Sound Parkway NW, Suite 300, Boca Raton, FL 33487-2742

and by CRC Press
4 Park Square, Milton Park, Abingdon, Oxon, OX14 4RN

CRC Press is an imprint of Taylor & Francis Group, LLC

© 2023 selection and editorial matter, Amar Patnaik, Vikas Kukshal, Pankaj Agarwal, Ankush Sharma, Mahavir Choudhary; individual chapters, the contributors

ISBN: 978-0-367-72358-3 (hbk)
ISBN: 978-0-367-72360-6 (pbk)
ISBN: 978-1-003-15451-8 (ebk)

DOI: 10.1201/9781003154518

Typeset in Times
by codeMantra

Contents

Preface

The book entitled "Soft Computing in Materials Development and Its Sustainability in the Manufacturing Sector" embraces innovations in the area of soft computing in mechanical, materials and manufacturing processes, proposed by various researchers, scientists, professionals, and academicians. Through this book an attempt has been made to overcome numerous problems faced by the students related to soft computing and engineering, ultimately to bestow sound knowledge. The drafted book's presentation is basic, clear and simple to comprehend. This book emphasizes the application of numerous soft computing techniques in various engineering materials including metals, polymers, composites, biocomposites, fiber composites, ceramics, etc. along with their property characterizations and potential applications of these materials. Despite this however, a significant gap exists between the actual theories and software systems therefore, this book is motivated from the scarcity of wider aspects relating to advanced materials, materials manufacturing and processing, optimization and sustainable development, tribology for industrial application and diverse engineering applications. All the chapters were subjected to a peer-review process by the researchers working in the relevant fields. The chapters were selected based on their quality and their relevance to the title of the book. This book will result in an excellent collection of current technical strategies and enable the researchers working in the field of advanced material and manufacturing processes to explore current areas of research and educate future generations.

This book is a result of several people's hard work and efforts which has brought forth this successful record. It is very imperative to acknowledge their contribution in shaping the structure of the book. Hence, all the editors would like to express special gratitude to all the reviewers for their valuable time invested in reviewing process and for completing the review process in time. Their valuable advice and guidance helped in improving the quality of the chapters selected for the publication in the book. Finally, we would like to thank all the authors of the chapters for the timely submission of the chapter during the rigorous review process.

MATLAB® is a registered trademark of The MathWorks, Inc. For product information, please contact:

The MathWorks, Inc.
3 Apple Hill Drive
Natick, MA 01760-2098 USA
Tel: 508-647-7000
Fax: 508-647-7001
E-mail: info@mathworks.com
Web: www.mathworks.com

Acknowledgements

This book would not have been possible without the kind support and efforts of many people. It has been great honour and privilege for the kind association with all the authors, reviewers and the concerned Institutes of the editors. First, all the editors would like to express a deep sense of gratitude to all those whose work, research and support have helped and contributed to this book. We gratefully express gratitude to all the authors of the accepted chapters for transforming their work into the chapters of the book. We are highly indebted to all the authors for their continuous support during the rigorous review process.

We would like to acknowledge all the reviewers who have invested a huge amount of their precious time in the review process of all the book chapters. Their continuous support and timely completion of the review process have helped the editors to complete the book within the stipulated time. Their exemplary guidance and advice helped in improving the quality of the chapters selected for the publication in the book.

It's very difficult to thank everyone associated with this book. Therefore, we owe our gratitude to all the persons who have lent their helping hand in the completion of the book directly or indirectly. Last but not least, we would like to thank our family members for their unceasing encouragement and support in allowing us to successfully complete this book.

Editors

Dr. Amar Patnaik is an Associate Professor of Mechanical Engineering at Malaviya National Institute of Technology Jaipur, India. Dr. Patnaik has more than 10 years of teaching experience and has taught a broad spectrum of courses at both the undergraduate and graduate levels. He also served in various administrative functions, including Dean International Affairs, and coordinator of various projects. He has guided twenty PhDs and several M.Tech theses. He has published more than 200 research articles in reputed journals, contributed five book chapters, edited one book and filed seven patents. He is also the guest editor of various reputed International and National journals. Dr. Patnaik has delivered more than thirty Guest lecturers in different Institutions and Organizations. He is a life member of Tribology Society of India, Electron Microscope Society of India and ISTE.

Dr. Vikas Kukshal is presently working as an Assistant Professor in the Department of Mechanical Engineering, NIT Uttarakhand, India. He has more than 10 years of teaching experience and has taught a broad spectrum of courses at both the undergraduate and postgraduate levels. He has authored and co-authored more than twenty-six articles in Journals and Conferences, and has contributed seven book chapters. Presently, he is a reviewer of various national and international journals. He is a life member of Tribology Society of India, The Indian Institute of Metals and The Institution of Engineers. His research area includes material characterization, composite materials, high entropy materials, simulation and modelling.

Mr. Pankaj Agarwal is presently working as Assistant Professor at the Department of Mechanical Engineering at Amity University Rajasthan, Jaipur, India. He received his M.Tech degree in Mechanical Engineering specialization from Jagannath University, Jaipur, India in 2013 and B.E. in Mechanical Engineering from the University of Rajasthan, Jaipur, India in 2007. He has published more than twenty research articles in national and international journals as well as conferences and two book chapters for international publishers. He has handled/handling journals of international repute such as Taylor & Francis, Taru Publication, etc. as guest editor. He has organized several International Conferences, FDPs and Workshops as a core team member of the organizing committee. His research interests are optimization, composite materials, simulation and Modelling and Soft computing.

Dr. Ankush Sharma is presently working as a scientific officer in the Centre of excellence for composite materials at ATIRA, Ahmedabad. He has completed Ph.D. in composite material from Malaviya National Institute of Technology Jaipur. He has more than 6 years of teaching as well as research experience and taught a broad spectrum of courses at both the undergraduate and graduate levels. He has published more than fifteen research articles in national and international journals as well as conferences and three book chapters for international publishers. Dr. Sharma has also filed one patent. He has received the best research award from the Institute of Technical and Scientific Research (ITSR Foundation Award-2020), Jaipur in the year 2020. His research interests are optimization, composite materials and tribology. He is a life member of The Institution of Engineers (India).

Dr. Mahavir Choudhary is Director of Vincenzo Solutions Private Limited incubated at MNIT Innovation & Incubation Centre, Jaipur, India. He received his Masters of Engineering from SGSITS Indore in Production Engineering with a specialization in computer integrated manufacturing (CIM). He has more than 10 years of teaching experience and has taught a broad spectrum of courses at both the undergraduate and graduate levels. He has published more than five research articles in national and international journals as well as conferences. His research interests are optimization, composite materials, numerical simulation and soft computing.

List of Contributors

Reeya Agrawal
Department of Computer Engineering
and Applications
GLA University
Mathura, Uttar Pradesh, India

Shivprakash B. Barve
School of Mechanical Engineering
Dr. Vishwanath Karad MIT World
Peace University
Pune, Maharashtra, India

Sahil Bendure
School of Mechanical Engineering
Dr. Vishwanath Karad MIT World
Peace University
Pune, Maharashtra, India

V. Phanindra Bogu
Department of Mechanical Engineering
Vidya Jyothi Institute of Technology
Hyderabad, Telangana, India

Locherla Daloji
Department of Mechanical Engineering
Vishnu Institute of Technology
Bhimavaram, Andhra Pradesh, India

K. Dhakar
Industrial and Production Engineering
Department
G.S. Institute of Technology and
Science
Indore, Madhya Pradesh, India

Satwik Dudeja
Department of Mechanical Engineering
Delhi Technological University
New Delhi, India

Aniket kumar Dutt
CSIR-National Metallurgical
Laboratory
Jamshedpur, Jharkhand, India

Mohd Faizan
Netaji Subhash Engineering College
Kolkata, West Bengal, India
Department of Mechanical Engineering
MMMUT
Gorakhpur, Uttar Pradesh, India

Neetu Faujdar
Department of Computer Engineering
and Applications
GLA University, India
Mathura, Uttar Pradesh, India
National Institute of Technology
Pune, Maharashtra, India

Srinu Gangolu
Department of Mechanical Engineering
National Institute of Technology Calicut
Calicut, Kerala, India

Swati Gangwar
Department of Mechanical Engineering
NSUT
New Delhi, India

Shaswat Garg
Department of Mechanical Engineering
Delhi Technological University
New Delhi, India

Navriti Gupta
Department of Mechanical Engineering
Delhi Technological University
New Delhi, India

P.K. Gupta
Mechanical Engineering Department
Malaviya National Institute of
    Technology
Jaipur, Rajasthan, India

Rahul Jagtap
School of Mechanical Engineering
Dr. Vishwanath Karad MIT World
    Peace University
Pune, Maharashtra, India

Swati Kamble
Manufacturing Engineering &
    Industrial management department
College of Engineering Pune (COEP)
Pune, Maharashtra, India

Vikas Kukshal
Department of Mechanical Engineering
National Institute of Technology
    Uttarakhand
Srinagar (Garhwal), Uttarakhand, India

Pawan Kumar
Department of Engineering Metallurgy
University of Johannesburg
Johannesburg, South Africa

Sanjeev Kumar
Automation Development Centre
TATA Steel
Jamshedpur, Jharkhand, India

Satish Kumar
Department of Applied Mechanics
Motilal Nehru National Institute of
    Technology Allahabad, India
Prayagraj, Uttar Pradesh, India

Sneham Kumar
Department of Mechanical Engineering
Delhi Technological University
New Delhi, India

Hare Shankar Kumhar
Department of Mechanical Engineering
National Institute of Technology
    Uttarakhand
Srinagar (Garhwal), Uttar Pradesh,
    India

Mamookho Elizabeth Makhatha
Department of Engineering Metallurgy
University of Johannesburg
Johannesburg, South Africa

Ishan Mishra
Department of Mechanical Engineering
Delhi Technological University
New Delhi, India

Sanjeev Mishra
Department of Management Studies
Rajasthan Technical University
Kota, Rajasthan, India

V. Murari
Department of Applied Mechanics
Motilal Nehru National Institute of
    Technology Allahabad, India
Prayagraj, Uttar Pradesh, India

Malaykumar Patel
School of Mechanical Engineering
Dr. Vishwanath Karad MIT World
    Peace University
Pune, Maharashtra, India

Rajesh V. Patil
School of Mechanical Engineering
Dr. Vishwanath Karad MIT World
    Peace University
Pune, Maharashtra, India

Vinay Polimetla
Department of Mechanical Engineering
Indian Institute of Technology Madras
Chennai, Tamil Nadu, India
National Institute of Technology Calicut
Calicut, Kerala, India

Bangaru Babu Popuri
Department of Mechanical Engineering
National Institute of Technology
  Warangal, India
Warangal, Telangana, India

Rajiv B.
Manufacturing Engineering &
  Industrial management department
College of Engineering Pune (COEP)
Pune, Maharashtra, India

Kumari Sarita
Department of Electrical Engineering
Indian Institute of Technology (BHU)
Varanasi, Uttar Pradesh, India

Sandeep Sharda
Department of Management Studies
Rajasthan Technical University
Kota, Rajasthan, India

Harinarayan Sharma
Department of Mechanical Engineering
Netaji Subhas Institute of Technology
Bihta, Bihar, India

Aquib Ahmad Siddiqui
Department of Applied Mechanics
Motilal Nehru National Institute of
  Technology Allahabad, India
Prayagraj, Uttar Pradesh, India

A. Singhai
Industrial and Production Engineering
  Department
G.S. Institute of Technology and
  Science
Indore, Madhya Pradesh, India

Abhishek M. Thote
School of Mechanical Engineering
Dr. Vishwanath Karad MIT World
  Peace University
Pune, Maharashtra, India

Ninad Vaidya
School of Mechanical Engineering
Dr. Vishwanath Karad MIT World
  Peace University
Pune, Maharashtra, India

1 Predictive Maintenance of Industrial Rotating Equipment Using Supervised Machine Learning

Hare Shankar Kumhar and Vikas Kukshal
National Institute of Technology Uttarakhand

Kumari Sarita
Indian Institute of Technology (BHU)

Sanjeev Kumar
TATA Steel

CONTENTS

DOI: 10.1201/9781003154518-1

1

1.1 INTRODUCTION: NEED FOR CONDITION MONITORING

The degradation of life and quality of industrial equipment is caused due to increased vibration, temperature, and other parameters like pressure. Condition monitoring is done to avoid the rapid degradation of equipment life by giving appropriate maintenance at an equal interval of time or when it is required. Condition monitoring is also useful for the diagnosis of the device. Now, most of the industries are moving towards the preventive and predictive monitoring of machines for the proper functioning of processes and reliable system operation. Predictive maintenance is something that helps in predicting the future status of the equipment knowing its current and past status [1–3]. This makes the system more reliable than traditional condition monitoring after fault occurrence. The use of data of the equipment using data analysis techniques and predictive algorithms is discussed by Horrell et al. [3] for achieving predictive maintenance of the equipment. Various time-domain (current, voltage, vibration trends with time and their amplitudes and phase) and frequency-domain techniques (Fast Fourier Transform (FFT) and Wavelet Transform (WT)) are used for the diagnosis of equipment faults [4–6]. These are helpful in the diagnosis of faults but the diagnosis is done at the time of occurrence of a fault or after the occurrence of faults, not before the occurrence of the fault. The authors [6] have observed that the vibration parameter is very effective to monitor the health status of rotating equipment. The traditional method of vibration-based condition monitoring used in industries is based on the concept of the threshold value, which is set as a target. Once the equipment vibration reaches the threshold value, the maintenance team plans the maintenance schedule. The fault is diagnosed by looking at the peak value and corresponding frequency of peak amplitude, which indicate the type of faults like unbalance, misalignment, looseness, or any damage. This method is not reliable as it may cause a sudden stop of the process and a huge loss to be faced. Various cost-effective and reliable monitoring systems are proposed by various researchers [7–9], which are focused on condition-based monitoring systems. The role of machine learning in predictive maintenance is discussed by Toh et al. [10]. The concept of predictive maintenance and its advantages for industries to move towards industry 4.0 is explained by various authors [11–14]. The big data analysis and development in recent technologies of data collection, its storage, pre-processing, and Internet of Things (IoT) have helped a lot the industries to move towards digitalization of processes [15, 16].

With the development in machine learning and data science, preventive and predictive maintenance are now feasible to forecast when equipment problems may occur in the future and prevent them with appropriate action, which makes the system more reliable and helps to achieve better performance of the working equipment. There are various supervised and unsupervised machine learning techniques, which are useful in predicting the target parameter based on the historical data of the equipment [17–19]. The unsupervised machine learning techniques are used when one does not have the data on different fault conditions of the equipment. On the other side, supervised machine learning techniques are useful in predicting the future health status when previous condition data are available as historical data. The most commonly used unsupervised techniques are Principal Component Analysis (PCA) and Clustering, whereas the supervised techniques are Regression, Classification, and Curve fitted model, which helps to model the predictive algorithm for the predictive maintenance of the machine [17–19]. There are three types of maintenance, which are generally implemented in industries: (i) reactive maintenance, (ii) preventive maintenance and (iii) predictive maintenance [20]. Reactive maintenance is when the maintenance is done after the fault has occurred; preventive maintenance is the one in which the maintenance is done within a fixed time interval like once in a month, 6 months or in a year; and predictive maintenance is the one in which the fault condition is predicted and the maintenance schedule is forecasted using that prediction. The predictive maintenance is advantageous as compared with the other two [21]. It helps in scheduling the maintenance only when the equipment needs it. This results in saving maintenance costs by avoiding unnecessary maintenance and also makes the condition monitoring system more reliable. Proper maintenance scheduling can be achieved if the monitoring system can estimate the remaining useful life of the equipment. The remaining useful life estimation gives an indication of life left for the equipment when any of its health indicators will reach the threshold value of breakdown condition. There are various regression-based techniques available, which are suitable for different applications [22]. Among them, the most commonly used and affordable method is Gaussian Process Regression. To predict the health condition and the remaining useful life of a gyroscope, the author has used an improved Gaussian Process Regression with a physical degradation model which predicts the gyroscope drift and also estimates the remaining useful life [22]. In the available literature [23], the independent effect of the indicators is used to predict the target variable for condition monitoring and ignoring the coupling effect between different signals or parameters, which is the reason for not getting the accurately predicted result. This problem can be solved by implementing Multi-signal and Multi-feature Fusion (MSMFF) which will improve the prediction accuracy. Along with the predictive model and algorithm, signal processing plays an important role in predictive maintenance and fault diagnosis. The Ding et al. has explained the signal-processing scheme in detail. In a research article, the authors have explained the procedure systematically through filtering of noise from the raw signal, features extraction and selection and manifold learning-based features fusion and finally ended with the regression model for Remaining Useful Life (RUL) estimation considering the coupling effects between the variables and their relationship with the RUL estimator [23]. By condition monitoring of the equipment, one can find the equipment wear and the remaining useful life in time. A researcher has proposed an integrated prediction model based on trajectory similarity and support vector regression, which is also a commonly used regression technique [24]. Along with the predictive model, the authors have explained the results in the time domain and also carried out wavelet analysis.

In this chapter, a regression model-based algorithm is proposed for predictive maintenance and remaining useful life estimation. The proposed algorithm is validated using the historical data of the fan-motor system used in the industry. Section 1.2 covers the methodology used to implement the concept and procedure carried out. The computation procedure is carried out using MATLAB software and discussed in Section 1.3. The results obtained are discussed in Section 1.4. Finally, the observation of the considered case study of the fan-motor system is concluded along with some future scopes of the proposed work.

1.2   METHODOLOGY: APPROACHES FOLLOWED
FOR PREDICTIVE MAINTENANCE

This section discusses the steps followed in developing the predictive maintenance algorithm, useful life estimating models and introduction to the case study considered in this chapter.

1.2.1   Steps for Predictive Maintenance

The following are the steps involved in predictive maintenance:

- **Collect sensors data of Induced Draft (ID) fan-motor system.**
  The sensors data are exported and collected from IBA Analyzer which helps to export the dat type file into another form like txt or csv. The dat type data file is opened in IBA and then exported in the desired signals with a desirable time gap of data in txt or csv file.
- **Predict and fix failures before they arise.**
  - Import and analyze historical sensor data.
  - Train model to predict when failures will occur.
  - Deploy model to run on live sensor data.
  - **Predict failures in real-time.**

The methodology starts from exporting various sensors data from IBA Analyzer software to the data standardization in WEKA software, feature selection and ends with the predictive maintenance algorithm using MATLAB software.

During data collection, it should be known whether the collected data is of normal operating condition or fault condition. If we get only normal data, it means that scheduled maintenance is done regularly and no failure has occurred. In another case, if we are getting failure data, it means that the system has faced failures; the data is collected to train the model to avoid such faults in the future by predicting them before they occur.

1.2.2   A Brief Introduction to Fitting Model

In the curve fitting toolbox in MATLAB, one can define custom linear equations that use linear least-squares fitting. Linear least-squares fitting is more efficient and usually faster than non-linear fitting. Curve Fitting Toolbox™ is a programme that lets us fit curves and surfaces to data using a tool and functions. The toolkit can be used to perform exploratory data analysis, pre- and post-process data, compare possible models, and eliminate outliers. Regression analysis can be done using the given library of linear and non-linear models, or we may create unique equations. To increase the quality of our fits, the library includes optimal solver settings and starting circumstances. Non-parametric modelling techniques such as splines, interpolation, and smoothing are also supported by the toolkit. Several post-processing methods can be used to display, interpolate, and extrapolate data, estimate confidence intervals and calculate integrals and derivatives after creating a fit.

1.2.3 ESTIMATION OF REMAINING USEFUL LIFE

Typically, the Remaining Useful Life (RUL) is estimated for a system by developing a model that can perform the estimation based upon the time evolution or statistical properties of condition indicator values. Predictions based on these models are statistical estimates with a margin of error. They give a probability distribution for the test machine's RUL. After finding potential condition indicators, the next stage in the algorithm-design process is to create a model for RUL prediction. This phase is frequently iterative with the process of selecting condition indicators since the model we create uses the time evolution of condition indicator values to forecast RUL.

1.2.4 CASE STUDY: INDUCED DRAFT (ID) FAN-MOTOR SYSTEM

The vibration sensors are connected to the bearings of fans and motors to measure the vibration level on the horizontal axis only. If there is a problem with the fan-motor system, the vibration level will rise which can be observed in the online monitoring system. The measurement points of vibration in the ID fan-motor system are shown in Figure 1.1, which are Motor Driving End (MDE), Motor Non-driving End (MNDE), Fan Driving End (FDE), and Fan Non-driving End (FNDE). There are lots of sensors data coming from the equipment that are analyzed in IBA Analyzer to see the real-time values of the data and check whether these are under the normal operational limit or not. Few sensor signals are shown in Figure 1.2, which are the sensor data of the selected ID fan-motor system. This way of monitoring the equipment is not reliable as it is very complex and time-consuming to see the plot of each sensor data. The monitoring system needs to be reliable and simple.

When the condition monitoring system can anticipate the health status of the monitoring equipment as well as the requirement for maintenance, it will become reliable. Machine learning algorithms are useful for preventative maintenance of the equipment.

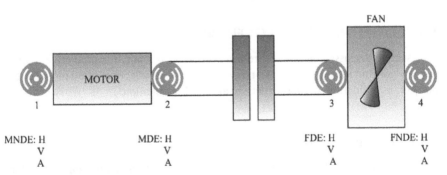

1-4: Vibration Measurement Points

FIGURE 1.1 Schematic diagram of the fan-motor system and measurement points of vibrations. The vibrations in three orthogonal directions are measured — horizontal, vertical, and axial directions. The vibrations of four ends are measured — MNDE, MDE, FDE, and FNDE — as shown here by numbers 1, 2, 3, and 4, respectively (a–d).

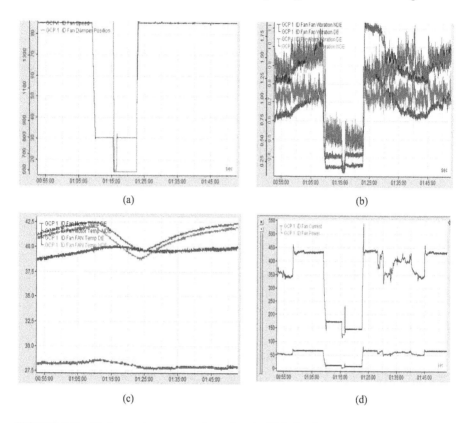

FIGURE 1.2 ID fan-motor sensors data plots in IBA Analyzer: (a) speed and damper position of ID fan, (b) vibrations of fan and motor at driving and non-driving ends, (c) temperatures of fan and motor at driving and non-driving ends, (d) current and power of fan

1.3 COMPUTATIONAL PROCEDURE

This section discusses the procedure followed for developing the predictive maintenance algorithm including data pre-processing, features selection, fitted model development, its validation, outlier detection, and RUL estimation.

1.3.1 DATA PRE-PROCESSING

It is very necessary to know the data variables, which will help in knowing the working condition and characteristics of equipment with its parameters. The correlation between the parameters of any equipment before doing any physical or data-based modelling of the equipment is to be known first. The selected parameters are given in Table 1.1, and the correlation diagram between parameters is shown in Figure 1.3.

TABLE 1.1

Selected Sensor Data (Parameters) for Predictors

	Parameters
FanSp	Fan Speed
DP	Damper Position
FVDE	Fan Vibration of Driving End
FVNDE	Fan Vibration of Non-driving End
FCur	Fan Current
FPower	Fan Power
MTDE	Motor Temperature Driving End
MTNDE	Motor Temperature Non-driving End
FTDE	Fan Temperature of Driving End
FTNDE	Fan Temperature of Non-driving End
MVDE	Motor Vibration of Driving End
MVNDE	Motor Vibration of Non-driving End

1.3.2 FEATURE SELECTION FOR PREDICTIVE MAINTENANCE

First, the highly correlated variables are selected for the feature selection process. Figure 1.3 shows the correlation matrix of the different variables (sensors data).

The highly correlated parameters observed from Table 1.2 are tabulated in Table 1.3.

1.3.3 VARIATION OF VIBRATION WITH OTHER SELECTED VARIABLES

At this stage, out of five parameters, four can be the predictors for the predictive model and the fifth one (i.e., vibration) is taken as the target parameter. Now, it is

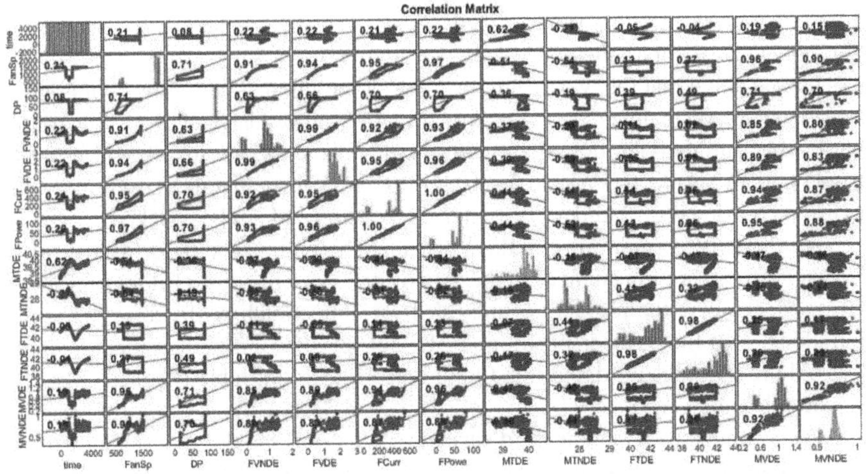

FIGURE 1.3 Correlation matrix of the fan-motor parameters (sensors data) — *x*-axis: parameters; *y*-axis: parameters

TABLE 1.2

The Correlation Coefficients Between the Variables. It Ranges from 0 to 1, Where 0 Means Unrelated Variables and 1 Means Highly Correlated Variables.

Parameters	Correlation Coefficients
current-power	1
vib-speed	0.9–1.0
temp-speed	0.1–0.3
current/power-speed	0.97–1.0
DP-speed	0.7
vib-DP	0.7
temp-DP	0.3–0.5
current/power-DP	0.7

TABLE 1.3

The Highly Correlated Parameters with Units. The Parameters, Which Have High Correlation Coefficient, Are As Follows.

Current	Ampere
Power	Kilowatt
Vibration	mm/sec
Speed	RPM
Damper position	%

checked which parameters fit as predictors. Then, the vibration signal is plotted with other parameters to get some useful information regarding predictors. The nature of variation shows whether the parameter fits as a predictor or not. The variation of vibration with other parameters is shown in Figures 1.4–1.8.

It can be noted that the two different values of vibration at the same damper position are obtained. To understand this situation, we need to correlate the third variable that is affecting the vibration along with the damper position. So, we will move to the 3D plot for getting this problem solved. It is also known that the current/power is highly proportional to Damper Position (DP), so this need not be checked.

Note that current and power values are not giving any specific or useful information for the vibration change, so these two variables are not useful for prediction purposes. To solve the problem of the third variable, which is affecting the vibration along with the damper position, a 3D plot of vibration with respect to other selected predictors is used and it is found that the third variable is speed, which is shown in Figure 1.9.

It is now understood that the third variable (i.e., speed) should be considered along with the damper position to study the variation in vibration. The DP, speed and vibration are correlated and this is the reason why the two different vibration values at the same DP are obtained because in those cases the speed was different. Now, we can move to our prediction model taking these variables as selected features.

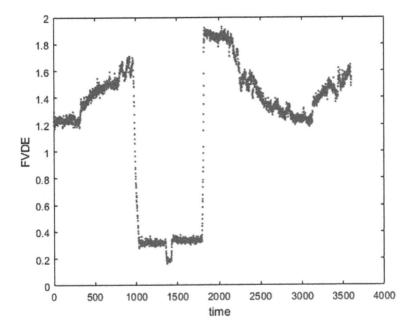

FIGURE 1.4 Fan vibration driving end versus time — *x*-axis: Time (seconds); *y*-axis: Fan vibration driving end (mm/sec)

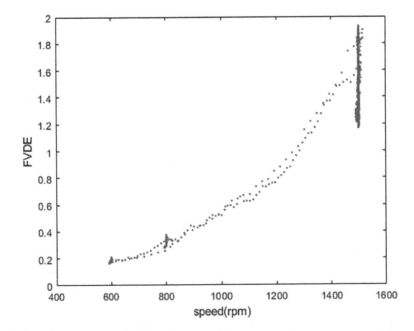

FIGURE 1.5 Fan vibration driving end versus fan speed — *x*-axis: Fan speed (rpm); *y*-axis: Fan vibration (mm/sec)

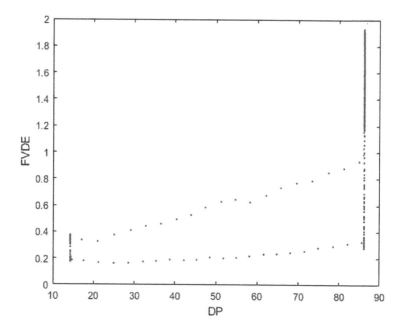

FIGURE 1.6   Fan vibration driving end versus damper position — *x*-axis: Damper position (%); *y*-axis: Fan vibration (mm/sec)

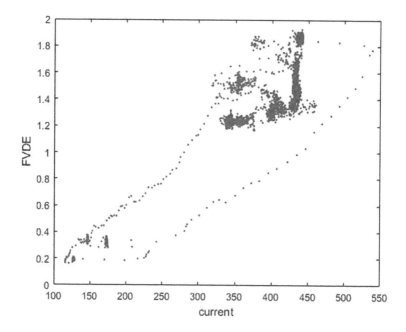

FIGURE 1.7   Fan vibration driving end versus current. These parameters are giving an almost linear curve showing a proportionality nature.

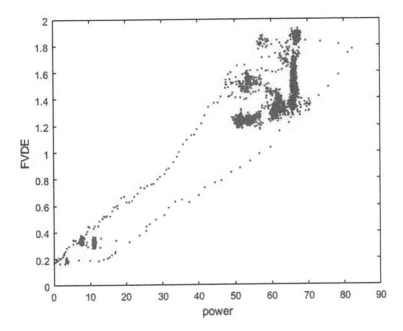

FIGURE 1.8 Fan vibration driving end versus power. These are also proportional and give almost linear relationships.

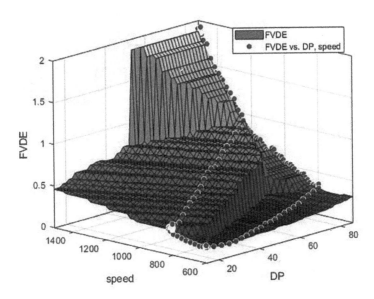

FIGURE 1.9 3D plot of fan vibration, damper position, and speed. The damper position, the speed, and the vibration of the driving end of fan are shown on z-axis, x-axis, and y-axis, respectively. The three parameters show the reason for getting different vibrations at the same damper position.

TABLE 1.4

Details of Polynomial Fitted Model. A Quadratic Polynomial Is Fitted As Shown Below.

Linear Model Poly12; x = DP, y = Speed

$f(x, y)$ = p00 + p10 * x + p01 * y + p11 * x * y + p02 * y^2

Coefficients with 95% confidence bounds:

p00 = 0.3525(0.2318, 0.4733)

p10 = 0.001337(−0.001501, 0.004176)

p01 = −0.001025(−0.001353, −0.0006971)

p11 = −2.032e-06(−5.565e-06, 1.516e-06)

Goodness of fit:

R-square = 0.9399, RMSE = 0.1459

1.3.4 FITTED MODEL

The details of the fitted polynomial type model are given in Table 1.4. The type of polynomial is 1–2 that is a quadratic polynomial of variables x and y.

The fitted model and its residual plot are shown in Figure 1.10, in which the target parameter is FVDE (Fan Vibration of Driving End) and predictors are speed and damper position.

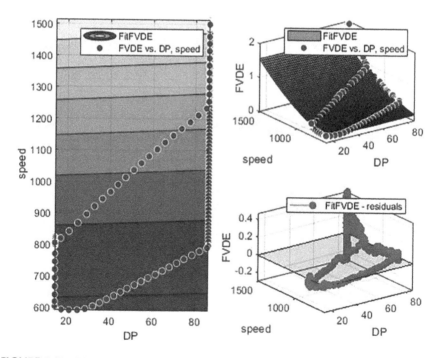

FIGURE 1.10 Plot of the fitted model and its residual. The quadratic model fitted is approximately the same as the actual data with minimum residual.

TABLE 1.5

Model Validation at Particular DP and Speed. The Fitted Model Is Validated with the New Data to Predict the Vibration at That Condition

DP (%)	Speed (rpm)	Predicted vib. (FVDE) (mm/sec)	Actual vib. (FVDE) (mm/sec)
70	1300	0.7868	0.78
80	1450	1.5776	1.57
86	1500	1.8832	1.87

1.3.5 MODEL VALIDATION

For validating our fitted model, we check the value of FVDE randomly for particular values of damper position and speed as given in Table 1.5.

As a conclusion, we are getting the perfect result from our fitted model. So, we will continue our prediction process with this model.

1.3.6 DETECTING OUTLIERS

In Figure 1.11, the fitted model is shown with the prediction intervals across the extrapolated fit range. This prediction interval is indicating that if the vibration points are going out of this range then there will be some problems.

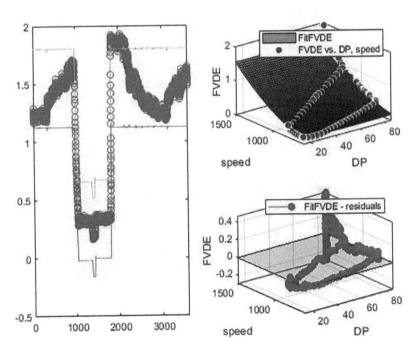

FIGURE 1.11 Prediction normal range. The prediction is done based on 95% of the confidence interval on the data. The actual data and the predicted data are approximately the same.

At full load, the maximum vibration value of FVDE under normal working conditions is found to be in the range of 1.34–1.65. From the data, it is found that the maximum vibration value of FVDE under full load conditions is less than or equal to 1.8. If the vibration value is greater than 1.8, then there may be some problems. We will try to find out these vibration points from the data using this model and, using these values, we will determine the time left to reach the threshold limit of vibration if the vibration is continuously increasing due to some faults.

First, we need to know the value of DP and speed at the high vibration points which are shown in Figure 1.12. The values of DP are found to be 86–86.08%. The values of speed are found to be 1495–1515 rpm.

1.3.7 REMAINING USEFUL LIFE ESTIMATION USING PCA

Using PCA and a suitable degradation model (linear or exponential), we can estimate the RUL of any equipment using at least 6 months of data on the equipment. The RUL technique is useful to predict the next similar fault condition to occur. We modelled a linear degradation model to monitor the health status of an ID fan and we used only 1-day data just to check our model. We set 1.8 as the threshold value of vibration in the worst case for checking our model in estimating the remaining useful cycle.

The component condition indicator is measured after 1000 seconds. Using the learned linear deterioration model, we can now forecast the component's remaining useful life at this moment. The RUL is the expected time for the degradation feature to reach the set threshold (1.8). The RUL is expected to be about 9916 seconds, implying a total predicted life duration of 9916 + 1000 seconds. We took 1000

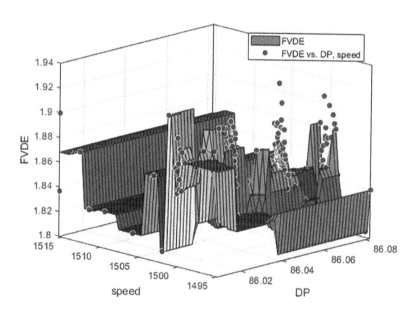

FIGURE 1.12 Damper position and speed at high vibration (> 1.8). These data points are helpful in finding the RUL of the equipment.

seconds to monitor the component condition and update the deterioration model after each observation. Using the current lifetime value contained in the model, we forecasted the component's RUL after 1000 cycles. This time the RUL is 5291, so the total RUL is 5291 + 1000 seconds.

This is not appropriate to calculate the RUL; we should calculate the time to be taken to reach the threshold limit of vibration because we have most of the data under normal conditions or under minor failure conditions but we don't have any major failure data. Here, we are going to find how many data points are outliers; if the vibration is increasing for a time range greater than 300 seconds (5 minutes), then these points should be considered for further estimation. So, firstly, we will plot the increased vibration points that are sustaining more than 5 minutes, as shown in Figure 1.13.

Figures 1.13 and 1.14 show the outlier vibrations and their histogram plot, respectively. These vibration points are sustaining more than 5 minutes; now, we need to estimate the time left for the vibration to reach its threshold value. The threshold value set for this is 3 mm/sec, which is changeable. The estimated time to reach the threshold value is discussed in the next section.

1.4   RESULTS AND DISCUSSION

The time left for the increased vibrations to reach the threshold value is found to be approximately 1600 minutes. The threshold value can be changed based on the vibration severity of the equipment. Here, the threshold value is set at 3 mm/sec. The time left to reach the threshold is shown in Figure 1.15.

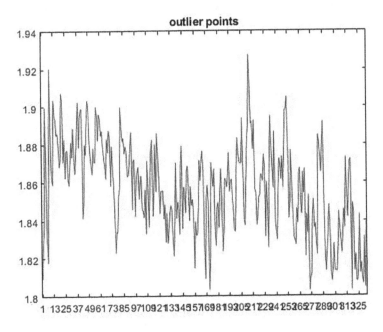

FIGURE 1.13   High vibration points (> 1.8). These outliers indicate the faulty condition of the equipment.

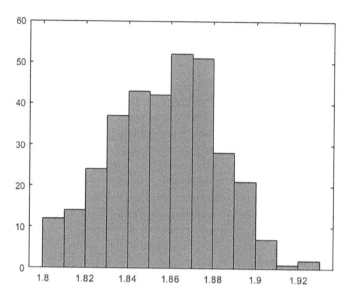

FIGURE 1.14 Histogram plot of high vibration points. This plot is helpful in knowing the number of times the peak vibration has occurred.

Now, we have to know the operating conditions — DP and speed at these increased vibration points. According to our predicted normal range, the value of vibration at max DP and speed is 1.5016; but, actually, the maximum vibration found is 1.9274.

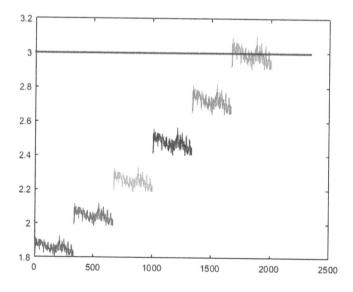

FIGURE 1.15 Time to reach the threshold value of vibration amplitude of 3. The number of cycles is indicated on *x*-axis, and the amplitude of the vibration is indicated on *y*-axis.

DP corresponding to max vibration = 86.08%

Speed corresponding to max vibration = 1495.5 rpm

The predicted normal value of vibration at these values of DP and speed = 1.4548

Actual max vibration = 1.9274

If the difference is negative, that means the actual value of vibration is larger than the predicted normal value, so we need to check the problem behind this. Since here the difference is negative, we confirmed that there is some problem; now, we need to check if we are going to decrease DP or speed or both then whether the vibration is decreasing or not. In this case, we will decrease both DP (by 3%) and speed (by 10 rpm) to see whether the vibration is decreasing or not.

With time, the threshold value of vibration increases because, for old equipment, 3 mm/sec vibration will be reached early. After successful maintenance and monitoring, the threshold value is again decreased. When the equipment is replaced, then also the threshold value is decreased because, for new and proper working equipment, the high vibration is not natural. The RUL is also affected according to the change in threshold value and condition of the equipment. If the equipment has not been properly maintained and 3 mm/sec vibration is natural, then the threshold will be increased.

1.4.1 PREDICTED SOLUTION TO DECREASE VIBRATION

In order to utilize the predicted solution to decrease the vibration, some steps are required to be followed. The steps are as mentioned below:

- Request the operator to follow the predicted solution given in Table 1.6 to decrease the vibration. In this case, we will decrease both DP (by 3%) and speed (by 10 rpm) to see whether the vibration is decreasing or not.
- If vibration is not decreasing by this method, then the maintenance team will go to the site for further diagnosis using FFT and orbit plot methods.

The RUL with respect to time is shown in Figure 1.15. The proposed model is validated by predicting the range of vibration for the next 3500 seconds and plotted with the actual vibration and found to be approximate to each other as shown in Figure 1.16.

TABLE 1.6

Predicted Solution to Decrease Vibration. This Table Suggests the Operator to Change the Damper Position and Speed to Get the Minimum Vibration and Time for Fault Diagnosis

Changing DP and Speed

Decrease in DP = 83.0822

Decrease in speed = 1485.5

Predicted vibration = 1.4338

Decrease in DP = 80.0822

Decrease in speed = 1475.5

Predicted vibration = 1.4130

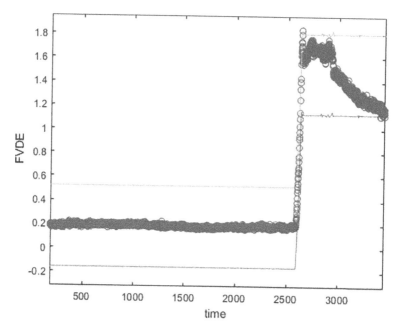

FIGURE 1.16 The plot of predicted vibration range and the actual vibration (FVDE) with time. The 95% confidence interval is used for prediction.

1.4.2 BENEFITS OF USING THE SUPERVISED MACHINE LEARNING TECHNIQUE

This chapter has introduced the supervised machine learning technique to diagnose the health status of ID fan-motor system. For using this type of technique, one must have the historical data of the target component or equipment. If the historical data is not available, one can use unsupervised machine learning techniques such as PCA, clustering, etc. In the case of the supervised learning technique, if one has a huge historical data set, it becomes very easy to prepare the fitted model. The whole data set is generally divided into three parts — one part for training the model, the second part for testing the fitted model, and the third one for validating the prepared model. This way one gets surety for the accuracy of the fitted model and gets accurate results of condition monitoring of the equipment. This is the main advantage of using the supervised machine learning technique.

1.5 CONCLUSION AND FUTURE SCOPE

Following the old condition monitoring technique, one cannot get reliable operation of equipment if they follow the fixed scheduled date for the maintenance of the equipment. The supervised machine learning-based condition monitoring method for the ID fan-motor system is more reliable since it can predict future problems and prevent equipment failure. It is also useful for predicting maintenance schedules well before a problem arises. As a result, supervised machine learning approaches enhance plant efficiency and performance. Other equipment monitoring can also benefit from these approaches. The only thing that differs is the features selection. If one can select the features, which are useful in indicating the target variable, then it is easy to implement the supervised learning techniques for every equipment of the plant.

The following are the future scopes of this project work:

- The supervised machine learning techniques can be useful in making a Digital Twin when they will be applied to any digital model of the equipment.
- The results of the proposed polynomial fitted model technique can be compared with other techniques like the Artificial Neural Network Model, etc.

REFERENCES

1. Kaparthi, Shashidhar, and Daniel Bumblauskas. "Designing predictive maintenance systems using decision tree-based machine learning techniques." *International Journal of Quality & Reliability Management* (2020). https://doi.org/10.1108/IJQRM-04-2019-0131.
2. Saidy, Clint, Kaishu Xia, Anil Kircaliali, Ramy Harik, and Abdel Bayoumi. "The application of statistical quality control methods in predictive maintenance 4.0: An unconventional use of Statistical Process Control (SPC) charts in health monitoring and predictive analytics." In *Advances in Asset Management and Condition Monitoring*, pp. 1051–1061. Springer, Cham, 2020. https://doi.org/10.1007/978-3-030-57745-2_87.
3. Horrell, Michael, Larry Reynolds, and Adam McElhinney. "Data science in heavy industry and the Internet of Things." *Harvard Data Science Review* (2020). https://doi.org/10.1162/99608f92.834c6595.
4. Gholap, Ananda B., and Jaybhaye, Maheshwar D. "Condition-based maintenance modeling using vibration signature analysis." In *Reliability and Risk Assessment in Engineering*, pp. 111–122. Springer, Singapore, 2020. https://doi.org/10.1007/978-981-15-3746-2_10.
5. Wang, Tianyang, Qinkai Han, Fulei Chu, and Zhipeng Feng. "Vibration based condition monitoring and fault diagnosis of wind turbine planetary gearbox: A review." *Mechanical Systems and Signal Processing*, vol. 126 (2019): 662–685. https://doi.org/10.1016/j.ymssp.2019.02.051.
6. Malla, Chandrabhanu, and Isham Panigrahi. "Review of condition monitoring of rolling element bearing using vibration analysis and other techniques." *Journal of Vibration Engineering & Technologies*, vol. 7, no. 4 (2019): 407–414. https://doi.org/10.1007/s42417-019-00119-y.
7. Li, Yang, Qirong Tang, Qing Chang, and Michael P. Brundage. "An event-based analysis of condition-based maintenance decision-making in multistage production systems." *International Journal of Production Research*, vol. 55, no. 16 (2017): 4753–4764. https://doi.org/10.1080/00207543.2017.1292063.
8. Quatrini, Elena, Francesco Costantino, Giulio Di Gravio, and Riccardo Patriarca. "Condition-based maintenance—An extensive literature review." *Machines*, vol. 8, no. 2 (2020): 31. https://doi.org/10.3390/machines8020031.
9. Fahmy, Muhamad Noval. "Implementation of maintenance method on steam turbine using Reliability-Centred Maintenance (RCM)." Ph.D. disscuss, Institut Teknologi Sepuluh Nopember, 2020. http://repository.its.ac.id/id/eprint/80589.
10. Toh, Gyungmin, and Junhong Park. "Review of vibration-based structural health monitoring using deep learning." *Applied Sciences*, vol. 10, no. 5 (2020): 1680. https://doi.org/10.3390/app10051680.
11. Bousdekis, Alexandros, and Gregoris Mentzas. "A proactive model for joint maintenance and logistics optimization in the frame of industrial Internet of Things." In *Operational Research in the Digital Era–ICT Challenges*, Springer, 2019, pp. 23–45. https://doi.org/10.1007/978-3-319-95666-4_3.

12. Gombé, B. O. et al. "A SAW wireless sensor network platform for industrial predictive maintenance." *Journal of Intelligent Manufacturing*, vol. 30, no. 4, pp. 1617–1628, 2019. https://doi.org/10.1007/s10845-017-1344-0.
13. Wan, J. et al. "A manufacturing big data solution for active preventive maintenance." *IEEE Transactions on Industrial Informatics*, vol. 13, no. 4, pp. 2039–2047, 2017. https://doi.org/10.1109/TII.2017.2670505.
14. Yu, Wenjin, Tharam Dillon, Fahed Mostafa, Wenny Rahayu, and Yuehua Liu. "A global manufacturing big data ecosystem for fault detection in predictive maintenance." *IEEE Transactions on Industrial Informatics* (2019). https://doi.org/10.1109/TII.2019.2915846.
15. Joyce, Jacob J., and W. Thamba Meshach. "Industrial Internet of Things (IIOT)—An Iot integrated services for Industry 4.0: A review." *International Journal of Applied Science and Engineering*, vol. 8, no. 1 (2020): 37–42. http://doi.org/10.30954/2322-0465.1.2020.5.
16. Munirathinam, Sathyan. "Industry 4.0: Industrial Internet of Things (IIOT)." *Advances in Computers*, vol. 117, no. 1 (2020): 129–164. https://doi.org/10.1016/bs.adcom.2019.10.010.
17. Amruthnath, Nagdev, and Tarun Gupta. "A research study on unsupervised machine learning algorithms for early fault detection in predictive maintenance." In *2018 5th International Conference on Industrial Engineering and Applications (ICIEA)*, 2018, pp. 355–361. https://doi.org/10.1109/IEA.2018.8387124.
18. Bakdi, Azzeddine, Abdelmalek Kouadri, and Abderazak Bensmail. "Fault detection and diagnosis in a cement rotary kiln using PCA with EWMA-based adaptive threshold monitoring scheme." *Control Engineering Practice*, vol. 66 (2017): 64–75. https://doi.org/10.1016/j.conengprac.2017.06.003.
19. Yiakopoulos, Christos T, Konstantinos C. Gryllias, and Ioannis A. Antoniadis. "Rolling element bearing fault detection in industrial environments based on a K-means clustering approach." *Expert Systems with Applications*, vol. 38, no. 3 (2011): 2888–2911. https://doi.org/10.1016/j.eswa.2010.08.083.
20. Sarita, Kumari, Ramesh Devarapalli, Sanjeev Kumar, Hasmath Malik, Fausto Pedro, García Márquez, and Pankaj Rai. "Principal component analysis technique for early fault detection." *Journal of Intelligent & Fuzzy Systems Preprint*, vol. 42, no. 2 (2021): 861–872.
21. Kumhar, Hare Shankar, Kumari Sarita, and Sanjeev Kumar. "Dynamic-balance monitoring scheme for industrial fans using neural-network based machine learning approach." In *Interdisciplinary Research in Technology and Management*, pp. 612–618. CRC Press, 2021 Editor: Satyajit Chakrabarti, Pub. Location: London.
22. Hassani, Seyed M. Mehdi, Jin, Xiaoning and Ni, Jun "Physics-based Gaussian process for the health monitoring for a rolling bearing." *Acta Astronautica*, vol. 154 (2019): 133–139.
23. Ding, Peng, Wang, Hua, Bao, Weigang, and Hong, Rongjing "HYGP-MSAM based model for slewing bearing residual useful life prediction." *Measurement*, vol. 141 (2019): 162–175.
24. Yang, Y. et al., "Research on the milling tool wear and life prediction by establishing an integrated predictive model." *Measurement*, vol. 145 (2019): 178–189.

2 Predictive Approach to Creep Life of Ni-based Single Crystal Superalloy Using Optimized Machine Learning Regression Algorithms

Vinay Polimetla and Srinu Gangolu
National Institute of Technology Calicut

CONTENTS

2.1 INTRODUCTION

Ni-based single crystal superalloys have been used widely at elevated temperature applications like gas turbine blades/vanes and isothermal forging dies, etc., where the materials have to be operated at almost 70% of their melting temperature (0.85–0.88 homologous temperature). Due to positive mechanical and creep properties even at high temperatures, these materials are generally known as "High Temperature

Materials". The major deformation mechanism during creep is responsible for the grain boundary sliding. Henceforth, the research focus has been shifted towards single crystal from polycrystalline creep resistance materials. The presence of intermolecular precipitated phases (γ') embedded into the matrix phase (γ) produces this impact. In general, the phases present in Ni-based superalloys like γ phase (Face Centered Cubic), γ' phase (Face Centered Cubic ordered L12 crystal structure), γ'' phase (Body Cubic Tetragonal ordered D022 crystal structure), Topological Closed Packed (TCP) phases and sometimes carbides and borides. The addition of alloying elements in different stoichiometric ratios leads to the evolution of these phases certainly (Long, Mao et al. 2018, Cui, Yu et al. 2018) [1,2].

Often, ten alloying elements, including Cobalt(Co), Chromium(Cr), Molybdenum(Mo), Niobium(Nb), Hafnium(Hf), Tungsten(W), Aluminum(Al), Titanium(Ti), Tantalum(Ta), Rhenium(Re) and Ruthenium(Ru), have been used in Ni-based superalloys to improve oxidation resistance and increase mechanical strength along with enhanced long-ranged microstructural stability. Upon adding Re, there forms a cluster of atoms within the matrix phase which hinders the dislocation motions and increases the phase stability. This results in two different generations of Ni-based superalloys with varying compositional percentages. However, considering the risk of formation of TCP phases by adding Re as alloying element leads to the addition of Ru in the next two different generations with invincible creep properties. Thus, the different generations of Ni-based superalloys evolve the new applications with different chemical compositions as shown in Table 2.1.

The impact on the microstructural parameters like critical flow stress of dislocations, stacking fault, volume fraction of secondary intermetallic phases, anti-phase boundary energy, etc., (Dang, Zhao et al. 2016, Bolton 2017) [1,3,4] upon addition of alloying element is significant and the effects produced by the addition of each individual alloying element can be seen from Table 2.2.

Maclachlan and Knowles (2001) [13] predicted stress fracture properties of different generations of superalloys considering the features relevant to creep deformation. Prasad (Prasad, Rajagopal et al. 2006) [14,15] estimated the creep behaviour based on dislocation motion between interfacial regions of phases and its damage caused under different load conditions. A better understanding of creep behaviour was done by Fedelich (Fedelich et al. 2012, Jiang et al. 2020, Perez prado et al. 2000) [5,6,7] with the help of γ' rafting during microstructural changes. For the low level to intermediate temperatures, a combination of Creep Constitutive Modelling techniques along with CALPHAD (Calculation of Phase Diagrams) calculations by Kim (Kim, Kim et al. 2016) [8] results in the best possible outcomes in creep properties estimations.

TABLE 2.1

Chemical Composition of Different Ni-based Superalloys Generations

Generation	Ni	Cr	Co	Al	Ti	Mo	W	Re	Ru
First	62.6	9	8	3.7	4.2	2	6	–	–
Second	61.8	7	8	6.2	–	2	5	3	–
Third	57.4	4.2	12.5	5.75	0.2	1.4	6	5.4	–
Fourth	66.9	3	6	6	–	3	6	5	2
Fifth	59.2	4.6	6.1	5.6	–	2.4	5	6.4	5

TABLE 2.2

Effects/Roles of Alloying Elements in Ni-based Superalloys

Effects/Roles	Alloying Elements
Formation of γ' phase	Al, Ti
Formation of topologically closed phases	Cr, Mo, W, Re, Co
Rise in lattice misfit between phases	Re, Ti, Mo, Ru
Solid solution strengthening	Cr, Mo, W, Re, Ta, Co
Increase in solvus temperature of γ' phase	Co

Being a recent trend subset of artificial intelligence, Machine Learning Algorithms (Liu et al. 2020) [9] stepped into the materials area in determining the combination of new alloys and their properties with less effort and expense (J. Wu et al. 2020, T Zhao et al. 2017, Long et al. 2018) [10,11,12]. The data-driven algorithms in Machine Learning predict the creep life of Ni-based superalloys concerning all the effecting factors and their relationship with creep behaviour (Liu, Wu et al. 2020) [12,16]. The effecting factors range in three specific domains like Chemical compositional parameters, Heat treatment environmental parameters and Microstructural evolution parameters (Ross et al. 1995, Royer et al. 1998, Snyder et al. 2012) [17,18,19].

Some of the milestones in this computational materials science include the work (Venkatesh and Rack 1999) [20] using Back-propagation Neural Network (BPNN) to predict the creep life of Inconel 690 and (Yamazaki et al. 1987, Yoo et al. 2002) [21,22] using Bayesian Neural Network with Markov chain Monte Carlo methods to estimate the creep mechanisms of Ni-based superalloy using specific relevant effecting factors as features.

2.2 CREEP MECHANISMS IN Ni-BASED SUPERALLOYS

The microstructural evolution of matrix and precipitated phases (γ/γ' phases) results in three different regimes of creep that would occur in Ni-SXs generally. The creep mechanisms involved within these regimes inherently correlate with the interactions between the dislocations and their movement inside the material. In principle, the dislocation-free zone of γ matrix experiences the multiplication of dislocations initially with respect to external temperature and stress. A short ordered interval exists where dislocations try to homogenize within those strained matrix channels and plasticity follows along the γ/γ' interfacial vicinity. As the shift of mechanical properties takes place from elastic to plastic behavior, the primary creep can be identified by the onset of plastic flow.

The creep/strain rate initially increases with the accumulation of dislocation-assisted strains, which are generated due to the activities associated with the dislocation, later decreases with the increase in dislocation density at the γ/γ' interfaces. The dislocation network hinders the motion of dislocations with the combinational hardening and softening effects produced by the multiplication of dislocation density forest and plastic flow of dislocation respectively. When the equilibrium point exists with the balancing of the hardening and softening effects, the decrease in strain rate is very significant up to a very low level and maintains near consistency which in return results in secondary creep initiation. Due to the lower creep strain, the secondary regime which is a steady state creep rate lasts long interval when the creep life is concerned. Furthermore, the increase in creep rate takes place with further inoculation of creep strains during steady state creep. This leads to the concentration of high stress fields which then propagates the shearing effect of dislocations into the precipitated γ' phase creating anti-phase boundary (a planar defect which is to be considered as most important fatigue defect) and disturbs the γ/γ' microstructure. Hence, within no specific time interval, the ultimate fracture of the alloy takes place with a drastic increase in strain rate with creep strain.

The phenomenon related to microstructure occurring within the three different creep regimes inside the alloy strongly rely on the dislocation movements and their interactions with the γ/γ' microstructure. This indicates the sensitiveness of temperature and applied stress towards the evolution of γ/γ' microstructure and reliability against the dislocation motion. In principle, diffusion plays a vital role in dislocation activities and temperature, a most important thermodynamical parameter involving the diffusion of solutes, has its prior influence by activating the slip systems for the motion to happen. At high temperatures (over 1100 °C), fast degradation of γ/γ' microstructure invokes with the multiplication of dislocations that generates the plastic strains. In order to have long order secondary creep rate, the low level applied stress can be accessed so that the activation barrier energy for the motion of dislocation is not enough to produce slip and rests inside the γ channels which in return would cause the creep deformation only by the adaptation of strains in the γ phase. Moreover, on the other hand, the shearing of γ' precipitates which causes the failure also results from the adaptation of strains in the γ phase. In certain cases, the creep life in every creep stage can be decreased by applying high level stresses but can accelerate the creep process, specifically in the secondary creep stage.

With the aid of high applied stress, the domination of the dislocation softening effect overweighs the hardening process while the creep deformation occurs under high temperature and high stress conditions. Hence, only continuous tertiary creep exhibits with accelerating creep in Ni-SX. The controversial proportion is observed against creep life with applied stress since no steady state creep is achieved and ends up in shorter creep life in case of high stress creep when compared with lower stress. Similar mechanisms can be achieved when considering temperature assists creep deformation. However, they would appear different at lower temperatures relatively (nearly 973 K). The experimental research works suggest that the plasticity is reduced due to less number of dislocations in microstructure at these temperatures. Henceforth, the accommodations of serrated creep strains are enough to generate the deformation at low stress and at high applied stresses, the creep deformation seems to be significant.

2.3 CREEP LIFE OF Ni-BASED SUPERALLOYS

Creep rupture life plays a vital role in determining the service life along with the mechanical and creep properties of Ni-based single crystal superalloy materials. The creep life of superalloys is the property that describes the sustainability of application and is most crucial to be determined to understand the creep behavior. However, the parameters that have their impact on the creep life are significant in number which ranges in three specific domains like Chemical compositional parameters, Heat treatment environmental parameters and Microstructural evolution parameters like lattice misfit, volume fraction of Ni_3Al, elastic constant like shear modulus, stacking fault energy and diffusion coefficient. In this study, focusing on lattice misfit and its impacts on creep life of different generations of Ni-based superalloys indicates the microstructural dependence on creep rupture life.

2.4 LATTICE MISFIT IN Ni-BASED SUPERALLOYS

The interfacial coherency, also known as the lattice misfit (δ), is what gives a superalloy its invincible creep qualities. It may be expressed as follows:

$$\delta = \frac{2\left[a_{\gamma'} + a_{\gamma}\right]}{\left[a_{\gamma'} - a_{\gamma}\right]} \tag{2.1}$$

where parameters $a\gamma'$ and $a\gamma$ denote the lattice constants of γ' phase and γ phase, respectively. The value of lattice constants of the two phases decides the sign of lattice misfit between those two phases. Certainly, there exists positive, negative and sometimes zero lattice misfit resulting in considerable impacts on creep properties. The site preference or the partition of alloying elements is the one that replicates the lattice misfit correlation with the alloying elements. Among the elements, Cr, Mo, Ru, Re, and W try to get into the matrix phase as their atomic radii are not much different from that of Ni. On the other hand, solutes such as Al, Ta and Ti, having larger atomic size than other elements in the matrix phase, settle in γ' phase and promote the ordered precipitated phases which thus increases the lattice constant. Replacement and occupying of the sites of basic Ni-Al structure can be relatively occurred by these large solute atoms and shows a positive impact on the lattice constant of γ' phase. However, some of the matrix phase partitioning elements with large atomic radius relative to Ni can increase the lattice constant of the matrix, but not greater than that of the precipitate phase. Thus at ambient temperature, most Ni-SXs show positive lattice misfits.

Meanwhile, due to the significant thermal expansion coefficient of γ phase, the transformation of the positive sign of lattice misfits to negative could be seen and this change in lattice misfit results in coarsening of the γ' precipitates because the stress concentration gradient near the interface between the two phases behaves like activation force which allows γ' precipitates to start growing. A decrease in lattice misfit indicates the loss of coherency and kinetics of coarsening. The formation of cuboids from the initial shape of spheres accounts for the expense of surface energy. To diminish the surface energy, almost closely spherical γ' precipitates can be produced by near zero lattice misfit. Compensating the elastic strain and the lattice distortion energy associated with it, the lattice misfit increases with the interfacial energy leading to the cubical change of γ' precipitation. The interfacial coherency will be constant with low lattice misfit and thus stabilizes the interface with low interfacial energy. However, the advantage behind having a cuboidal shape towards creep properties was shown in the minimization of elastic moduli of γ/γ' phases along $<1\ 0\ 0>$ direction. In the viewpoint of superalloy design, the enhancement of lattice misfit results from the larger atomic size elements like W and Mo. A threshold favourable lattice misfit value of around 0.4 was observed in many Ni-SXs, and it is noted that the medium level of lattice misfit seems to be advantageous to creep properties in the case of Ni-based superalloys. However, abnormal coarsening of γ' particles at the expense of inherent interface due to overdraft of lattice misfit results in the micro-structure instability. Therefore, the compositional impact of alloying elements should be optimized in adverse contents for most Ni-SXs.

2.5 MACHINE LEARNING ALGORITHMS FOR CREEP LIFE

Due to uncertainty in the evolution of microstructural coefficients of random phases, the creep mechanisms in each generation may vary accordingly and estimating creep life will be difficult in practice. The techniques used for estimating the creep life can be categorized into Time Temperature Parameter (TTP) method and Creep Constitutive Method (CCM), where TTP models like Larson Miller (LM) parameter (Bolton et al. 2017, Ciu et al. 2018) [1,2] estimate the creep life by extrapolating the short range order creep data onto the long range order creep master curves which lacks the invincible information of alteration in microstructural aspect. However, CCM techniques rely on crystallographic plasticity theory and internal continuous state mechanics for the best prediction.

The study includes the research effort in which a new model called Divide-and-conquer Self-adaptive (DCSA) has been introduced. The DCSA has indulged the art of using different regression algorithms like Random Forest (RF) algorithm, Support Vector Machine (SVM) algorithm, Linear Regression (LNR) algorithm, Ridge Regression (RR) algorithm, Lasso Regression (LR) algorithm onto the dataset containing all the effecting factors of three domains as input features and creep life as the dependent target variable. Using this approach, we can relate the correlation between the features to the creep life of different generations. Unfortunately, literature has not considered the microstructural effecting parameters like lattice misfit between coherent interfacial regions of phases and their impact on creep life. This study includes lattice misfit (constrained) along with all other effecting factors in previous work and correlates the sensitiveness of features on creep life.

2.6 MATERIALS AND METHODOLOGY

The dataset used in this prediction has been mined from several literatures and database warehouses (Long et al. 2018, D.M. Knowles et al. 2001, Ning et al. 2019, Prasad et al. 2006, Reed et al. 2006) [12,13,14,15,16] which was normalized using Standard Scaler algorithm before working on it. The resources have been using computational materials science platformed software like **VIEN ab initio, Quantum Expresso** which is based on first principle calculations with the aid of Density Functionality Theory (DFT) solving Schrodinger equation representing ground state atom energy. Kohn Sham's one electron equation is resolved by Green's Function technique. Coherent Potential Approximation (CPA) is used for calculating total energies through Exact Muffin Tin Orbitals (EMTO) methods with s, p, d and f orbitals in the basis set. Generalised Gradient Approximation (GGA) brings up the electronic exchange correlation potential parameter.

With 100 sample records of Ni-based superalloy generations containing effecting factors as features, the K means clustering algorithm been used to divide the dataset into clusters based on creep mechanisms. Each cluster, thereafter, is being split into train and test dataset, over cross fold technique, from sklearn module in ML. The training dataset of each individual cluster is operated by five regression algorithms to build a predictive model. The optimized predicted model is derived from the regression algorithm having precise R^2 values. To avoid overfitting of candidate models, we used Principle Component Analysis (PCA) in conjunction with k-fold cross-validation upon individual clusters to arrive at the best model selection as shown in the Figure 2.1

The dataset contains the effecting factors on the creep life as material attributes are shown in Table 2.3.

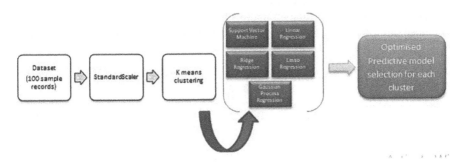

FIGURE 2.1 Ensemble method used for prediction of creep life of Ni based superalloy

TABLE 2.3
Symbols/Designation and Material Attributes in the Dataset

Designation	Material Attribute	Designation	Material Attribute
Ni	Mass percent of Ni	1lat	The first level aging time (h)
Re	Mass percent of Re	2lat	The second level aging time (h)
Co	Mass percent of Co	AtT	Alloy treatment temperature (°C)
Al	Mass percent of Al	1laT	The first level aging temperature (°C)
Ti	Mass percent of Ti	2laT	The second level aging temperature (°C)
W	Mass percent of W	T	Test temperature (°C)
Mo	Mass percent of Mo	S	Test stress (MPa)
Cr	Mass percent of Cr	r	Stacking fault energy (mJ/m²)
Ta	Mass percent of Ta	D_L	Diffusivity (m²/s)
C	Mass percent of C	G	Shear modulus (GPa)
B	Mass percent of B	L	Lattice constant (nm)
Y	Mass percent of Y	Ni_3Al	Molar percentage of γ' phase
Nb	Mass percent of Nb	Cn	Constrained lattice misfit
Hf	Mass percent of Hf		
Stt	Solution treatment time (h)		

2.7 RESULTS AND DISCUSSION

Being on random scales, the dataset is scaled upon to normalized scale and optimized by the Principle Component Analysis technique which leads to reducing the attributes/features errors and plots as shown in Figure 2.2. After dividing the dataset into different clusters based on their creep mechanisms, five regression algorithms have been passed over each cluster to check the best fit predictive model and thereafter split into training and testing dataset. The fitness value used here is R^2 validation to optimize the prediction for each individual cluster. The following Table 2.4 values indicate the selection of regression algorithms towards each cluster.

Clearly, we can conclude that except for cluster 3, the optimized regressor for the remaining clusters is the Gaussian Process regression algorithm whereas linear regression best fits with cluster 3 to predict the target variable. Based on the chemical composition of Re wt.%, the clusters represent the different generations of Ni-based superalloys as shown in Table 2.5.

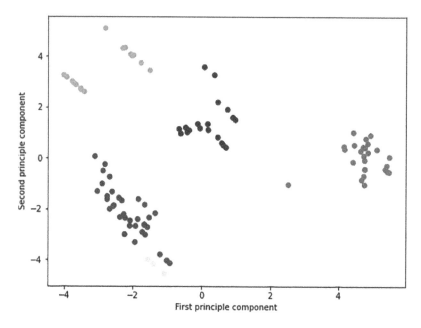

FIGURE 2.2   Principle component analysis of features

TABLE 2.4
R^2 Values of Each Cluster Onto Different Regression Algorithms

Method	Cluster-0	Cluster-1	Cluster-2	Cluster-3	Cluster-4
Linear regression	0.6808	0.7125	0.8988	0.8720	1.0000
Ridge regression	0.6432	0.5630	0.8794	0.7187	0.9999
Lasso regression	0.6808	0.7664	0.8799	0.8726	0.9999
SVM	0.9399	0.9998	0.9541	0.7881	0.9999
GPR	0.9999	0.9999	0.9999	0.9999	0.9999

TABLE 2.5
Generation Description of Each Cluster Based on Re wt.%

Cluster ID	Generation Description
0	Second generation 3% Re
1	Second generation 3% Re with Co % difference
2	Fifth and third generations 7.2% Re
3	First generation 0% Re
4	Fourth generation 4.5% Re

2.7.1 IMPORTANCE OF FEATURES

The creep mechanism of each Ni-based superalloy generation relies on several factors uniquely bringing the features which are important to be considered while determining the creep rupture/stress rupture life of the superalloy. The correlation coefficients of each effecting factor as a parameter onto the creep life imply the positive and/or negative impact. The following figures show the importance of features of each cluster (generations) that should be considered while fabrication and aging treatment.

The first two clusters (clusters 0 and 1) representing second generation Ni-based superalloy, with an addition of 3% of Re with a slight change in Co mass percent, mostly rely on the chemical composition of alloying elements when concerned with creep rupture life. As shown in Figures 2.3 and 2.4, the mole fraction of Ni_3Al, which is the precipitated phase, shows a negative effect on creep life along with the mass percent of Ni, Al, W, Mo, and Cr. This indicates the inverse proportion impact of these parameters onto the service life of superalloys. However, the impact of temperature and applied stress should also be considered into account with a slight negative correlation with respect to creep rupture life.

The solution treatment temperature with possible aging treatment temperature shows positive curvature which replicates the phase transformation and strengthening mechanisms regime onto the creep life. Upon adding Re alloying element, the hindering effect for dislocations occurs as the cluster formations took place in the matrix phase and the lattice parameter in the matrix phase changes towards positive sign. This leads to the lattice misfit, up to some extent, along the γ/γ' coherent interfacial region.

Temperature and applied stress in the orientation of slip planes play a vital role in the fifth and third generations as shown in Figure 2.5. To stabilize the phases and hinder the evolution of TCP, Ru is added in the case of fourth and fifth generations and this leads to an increase in lattice misfit between interfacial regimes which increases the creep life as it increases.

In the case of first generation Ni-based superalloys, the absence of Re element invokes the negative effect of constrained lattice misfit as shown in Figure 2.6. The aging temperature for the precipitate to be evolved has also negative correlation onto the creep life but has positive correlation with aging time.

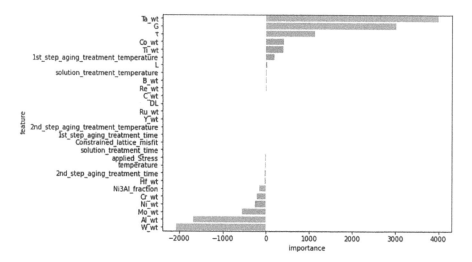

FIGURE 2.3 Feature importance of cluster 0 representing the second generation with 3% (wt.) Re

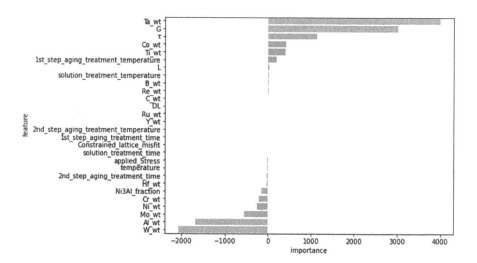

FIGURE 2.4 Feature importance of cluster 1 representing the second generation with modification in Co wt%

Overall, the above-shown graphs indicate that clusters 0 and 1 (i.e., second generation superalloy) have negative impact on the mole fraction of γ' phase, which in return increases with decreasing the creep life. With the addition of Re alloying element in the fifth and third generations, the constrained Lattice misfit improves drastically and leads to an increase in creep rupture life with a dense dislocation network around a coherent interface. However, the applied stress has a positive reliance on creep behavior in the fourth generation containing Re more than 4 wt.% and

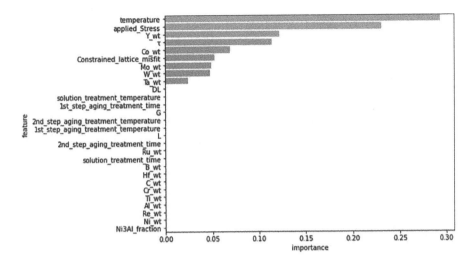

FIGURE 2.5   Feature importance of cluster 2 representing the fifth and third generations

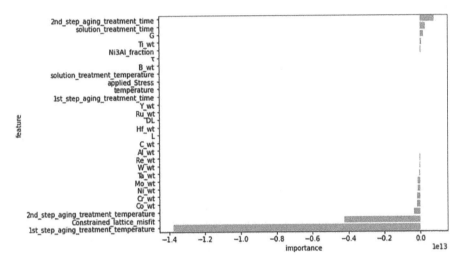

FIGURE 2.6   Feature importance of cluster 3 representing the first generation with no presence of Re

with slight impedance in other generations, as shown in Figure 2.7. The temperature dependence of creep life in the fifth and third generations shows highly advantageous towards increase in creep rupture life; whereas in the first, second, and fourth generations, it damages the creep life nature with increase. In addition, stacking fault energy and shear modulus of second generation expresses their impacts positively on creep life; whereas in the third and fifth generations, shear modulus plays a critical role. Furthermore, the alloying elements added in different generations have their unique identity and effect on different mechanisms, as shown in Table 2.2.

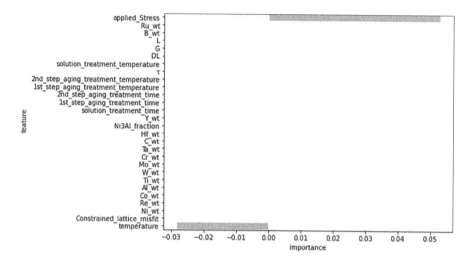

FIGURE 2.7 Feature importance of cluster 4 representing the fourth generation with 4.5% (wt.) Re. The ensemble method used in this study predicts the creep life of Ni based superalloys.

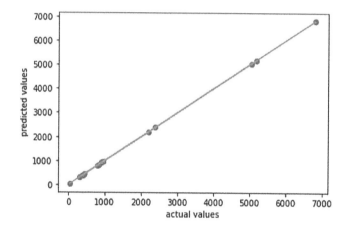

FIGURE 2.8 Prediction plot of ensemble method used on a new dataset.

When imposed on a test dataset of eight sample records containing the same features as the train dataset and plots, a linear curve graph with actual and predicted values on the x-axis and y-axis, respectively, is shown in Figure 2.8 as a validation.

2.8 CONCLUSIONS

The recent prediction approach of creep life of Ni-based single crystal superalloy effectively emphasizes the following conclusions:

1. Being the effecting factors of creep rupture life of Ni-based superalloys large in number significantly, creep constitutive models based on integrated computational materials science techniques have been absorbed to generate the material properties data.
2. Ensemble methods of machine learning have been implemented in order to characterize different generations of Ni-based superalloys with respect to parameter effecting their creep life and creep mechanisms.
3. The regression method used in this study possesses two basic steps from clustering the generations based on creep mechanisms to fitting the best optimized predictive model.
4. The validation of optimized model is done based on R^2 technique as a fitness model for the selection of the best predictive regressor upon each cluster.
5. With the addition of Re alloying element, the constrained lattice misfit increases which, in return, shows a positive impact on creep life, especially in the fifth and third generations. However, temperature and externally applied stress show invincible correlation with creep life in all the generations accordingly along with other parameters.
6. The predicted values on a new set of data points containing all the effecting factors as features give the precise values within the limit of actual values concluding further validation of the present ensemble technique.

2.9 FUTURE SCOPE

Comparatively, with the help of recent technology emerging in the trending world of engineering solutions, we established an effective technique for the prediction of creep life of Ni-based single crystal superalloys. There is a significant improvement, instead of relying on conventional experiments, where reduction in economic aspect and time effort can be achieved for alloy design. This machine learning assisted predictive approach can be imported to consider other relevant effects occurring inside the material during the creep deformation such as activation energy, site formation energy, etc., and this will be the focus of the future work.

2.9.1 DATASET AND CODE AVAILABILITY

The datasets and the code are available on github website using the following link: https://github.com/polimetl/Ensemble-Methods.git.

ABBREVIATIONS

ML	Machine Learning
DCSA	Divide-and-conquer self-adaptive
BPNN	Back-propagation neural network
CALPHAD	CALculation of PHAse Diagram
TTP	Time Temperature Parameter method
CCM	Creep Constitutive Method

RF	Random forest algorithm
SVM	Support vector machine algorithm
LNR	Linear regression algorithm
RR	Ridge regression algorithm
LR	Lasso regression algorithm
DFT	Density Functionality Theory
CPA	Coherent Potential Approximation
EMTO	exact muffin tin orbitals methods
GGA	Generalised Gradient Approximation

REFERENCES

1 Bolton, J. (2017). "Reliable analysis and extrapolation of creep rupture data." *International Journal of Pressure Vessels and Piping* **157**: 1–19.

2 Cui, L., J. Yu, J. Liu, T. Jin and X. Sun (2018). "The creep deformation mechanisms of a newly designed nickel-base superalloy." *Materials Science and Engineering: A* **710**: 309–317.

3 Dang, Y. Y., X. B. Zhao, Y. Yuan, H. F. Ying, J. T. Lu, Z. Yang and Y. Gu (2016). "Predicting long-term creep-rupture property of Inconel 740 and 740H." *Materials at High Temperatures* **33**(1): 1–5.

4 Elton, D. C., Z. Boukouvalas, M. S. Butrico, M. D. Fuge and P. W. Chung (2018). "Applying machine learning techniques to predict the properties of energetic materials." *Scientific Reports* **8**(1): 9059.

5 Fedelich, B., A. Epishin, T. Link, H. Klingelhöffer, G. Künecke and P. Portella (2012). "Experimental characterization and mechanical modeling of creep induced rafting in superalloys." *Computational Materials Science* **64**: 2–6.

6 Jiang, F., H. Yu, Q.-M. Hu, H. Wei, X. Sun and C. Dong (2020). "Effect of alloying elements on lattice misfit and elasticities of Ni-based single crystal superalloys by first-principle calculations." *Solid State Communications* **310**: 113852.

7 Kassner, M. E. and M. Pérez-Prado (2000). "Erratum to 'Five-power-law creep in single phase metals and alloys' [Progr. Mater. Sci. 45 (2000) 1–102]." *Progress in Materials Science* **45**: 273.

8 Kim, Y.-K., D. Kim, H.-K. Kim, C.-S. Oh and B.-J. Lee (2016). "An intermediate temperature creep model for Ni-based superalloys." *International Journal of Plasticity* **79**: 153–175.

9 Liu, Y., C. Niu, Z. Wang, Y. Gan, Y. Zhu, S. Sun and T. Shen (2020). "Machine learning in materials genome initiative: A review." *Journal of Materials Science & Technology* **57**: 113–122.

10 Liu, Y., J. Wu, Z. Wang, X.-G. Lu, M. Avdeev, S. Shi, C. Wang and T. Yu (2020). "Predicting creep rupture life of Ni-based single crystal superalloys using divide-and-conquer approach based machine learning." *Acta Materialia* **195**: 454–467.

11 Liu, Y., T. Zhao, W. Ju and S. Shi (2017). "Materials discovery and design using machine learning." *Journal of Materiomics* **3**(3): 159–177.

12 Long, H., S. Mao, Y. Liu, Z. Zhang and X. Han (2018). "Microstructural and compositional design of Ni-based single crystalline superalloys——A review." *Journal of Alloys and Compounds* **743**: 203–220.

13 Maclachlan, D. and D. M. Knowles (2001). "Modelling and prediction of the stress rupture behavior of single crystal superalloys." *Materials Science and Engineering: A* **302**: 275–285.

14 Ning, T., T. Sugui, Y. Huajin, S. Delong, Z. Shunke and Z. Guoqi (2019). "Deformation mechanisms and analysis of a single crystal nickel-based superalloy during tensile at room temperature." *Materials Science and Engineering: A* **744**: 154–162.

15 Prasad, S. C., K. R. Rajagopal and I. J. Rao (2006). "A continuum model for the anisotropic creep of single crystal nickel-based superalloys." *Acta Materialia* **54**(6): 1487–1500.

16 Reed, R. C. (2006). *The Superalloys: Fundamentals and Applications*. Cambridge, Cambridge University Press.

17 Ross, E. W., C. S. Wukusick and W. T. King (1995). Nickel-based superalloys for producing single crystal articles having improved tolerance to low angle grain boundaries, Google Patents.

18 Royer, A., P. Bastie and M. Veron (1998). "In situ determination of γ' phase volume fraction and of relations between lattice parameters and precipitate morphology in Ni-based single crystal superalloy." *Acta Materialia* **46**(15): 5357–5368.

19 Snyder, J. C., M. Rupp, K. Hansen, K.-R. Müller and K. Burke (2012). "Finding density functionals with machine learning." *Physical Review Letters* **108**(25): 253002.

20 Venkatesh, V. and H. J. Rack (1999). "A neural network approach to elevated temperature creep–fatigue life prediction." *International Journal of Fatigue* **21**(3): 225–234.

21 Yamazaki, M., T. Yamagata and H. Harada (1987). Nickel-base single crystal superalloy and process for production thereof, Google Patents.

22 Yoo, Y. S., C. Y. Jo and C. N. Jones (2002). "Compositional prediction of creep rupture life of single crystal Ni base superalloy by Bayesian neural network". *Materials Science and Engineering: A*, **336**(1): 22–29.

3 Artificial Neural Networks Based Real-time Modelling While Milling Aluminium 6061 Alloy

Shaswat Garg, Satwik Dudeja, and Navriti Gupta
Delhi Technological University

CONTENTS

3.1 INTRODUCTION

Milling is a machining process that progressively removes material from a work-piece, by the use of rotating multi-point cutting tools, to produce custom-designed components. For geometrically complex part designs, precise prediction of surface roughness and material removal rates ensure efficient time utilization and good product quality [1]. Aluminium 6061 alloy is one of the most commonly used aluminium alloys which finds purpose in several heavy industry applications like aircraft components, automobile parts, weapon casings, and high vacuum chambers. Ensuring low allowance values with utmost precision is desirable in these respective manufacturing industries. During milling, operators use their experience to find the optimal set of parameters to have a satisfactory product finish. Adjusting the milling parameters to ensure the optimum finish just on the basis of experience can compromise the productivity of the process. The ANN is a significant approach for the prediction of such milling parameters as it has the ability to decode complex relationships, similar to a neural system [2].

The ANN technique is successfully implemented in machining processes as an optimization technique, along with other machine learning techniques such as Genetic Algorithm, Particle Swarm Optimization, Ant Colony Optimization, etc. [3]. The ANNs usually suffer from overtraining and overfitting [4], but they can be mitigated using appropriate network architecture and techniques like regularization. They require greater computation resources. According to recent research [5], neural networks can extract relevant information in the presence of irrelevant data and can see through noise and distortion. The results of a previous paper [6] proved that the ANN performs best under conditions of high noise and low sample size. The ANN can be used to model complex non-linear relationship between dependent and independent variables [7]. Also, to develop the ANN, less formal statistical training is required. The ANNs are unaffected by missing data and learn by examples, making real-time modelling possible. Discrete outputs can also be predicted irrespective of minute errors in the inputs, with fast learning and good accuracy [8]. Even though some instances show unexplainable networks and reduced trust, such predictions help reduce research and experimental setup time and costs, as the model can be tweaked for a large array of materials and parameters.

3.2   LITERATURE REVIEW

Khorasani et al. [9] predicted accurately the dynamic roughness of surface during finishing and rough milling using ANNs. They took material type, cutting parameters, coolant fluid, white noise, and input parameters were taken as the X and Z components of milling machine vibrations. Accuracy of 99.7% and 99.8% was achieved for recall and testing processes.

Agarwal et al. [10] developed a hybrid cutting force model for end milling operation. The hybrid model was adopted to capture adequate process knowledge. They concluded that using the hybrid model, the cutting force could be predicted accurately compared to other machine learning algorithms, which predicted higher normal cutting forces. According to the authors, the results can be improved further using Reinforcement learning and Recurrent Neural Networks.

Serin et al. [11] developed an algorithm based on Deep Multi-layer Perceptron (DMLP) to predict specific cutting energy and roughness of surface for AL 7075 slot milling. Using Analysis of Variance (ANOVA) they examined the effect of input and output parameters. Results indicated that depth of cut and feed per tooth were the most influential parameters. They were able to achieve an accuracy of 91.5% and 90.7% for quality and energy efficiency, respectively, and therefore yield accurate results.

Bandapalli et al. [12] used optimization techniques to estimate surface roughness — ANN, Group Method Data Handling and Multiple Regression Analysis for high-speed micro end milling of Titanium alloy (Grade-5). The authors learnt that feed rate and depth of cut had the most influence on the surface roughness. They concluded that ANN trained on 70% of the data gave better predictions compared to GMDH and MRA. GMDH provided the least error of estimation.

Al-Abdullah et al. [13] used the ANN to develop force and temperature models for bone milling of artificial tissues with cancellous properties. Feed rate and spindle speed were taken as input variables. Full Factorial Design of Experiments was used to collect the experimental data. Using the experimental results, it was found that the mean temperature of milling bur increases with feed rate and drops with increasing spindle speed. But fresh milled bone temperature drops by increasing spindle speed and feed rate.

Malghan et al. [14] predicted surface finish, cutting force, and power utilization for the milling process of 6061-4.5%Cu-5%SiCp composite. Three process parameters — feed rate, depth of cut, and spindle speed — were taken. The ANN model created was able to accurately learn the experimental data.

Daniel et al. [15] used the ANN to optimize particle size and mass fraction of SiC as well as feed, depth of cut, and cutting speed in milling of Al5059/SiC/MoS2. To analyze the impact of control factors on the response variable, the Taguchi S/N ratio method was used. The results demonstrated that the ANN outperformed regression models for every response parameter.

Dhobale et al. [16] developed an ANN model based on an Multi Layer Perceptron classifier to classify the tool conditions of face milling. The MLP classifier was able to achieve an accuracy of 97.33%. The authors concluded that the best tool for condition monitoring was a combination of the ANN and statistical feature extraction.

Mundada et al. [17] used the Simulated Annealing Algorithm and the ANN to optimize the surface roughness. Feed rate tool rake angle, cutting speed and nose radius were taken as input machining parameters. Results from the simulated annealing optimization technique indicated that for good surface finish, lower feed rate, medium values of rake angle and nose radius, and high cutting speed is required.

Sanjeevi et al. [18] proposed a methodology to use the ANN for the prediction of the roughness of the Al-6061 surface in Computer Numerical Control milling. Speed, feed rate, and depth of cut were taken to be the input variables. The ANN model was able to predict the roughness of the Al surface with 98.35% accuracy.

Parmar et al. [19] configured and trained the ANN model for the prediction of performance evaluation parameters such as machining time, material removal rate, tool life, torque, cutting force, and power. For the input parameters, mechanical properties of the used material and process variables of end milling were used. The ANN model developed provided 98.657% for Material Removal Rate, 95.705% for power, 97.315% for machining time, 99.189% for cutting force, 99.197% for torque, and 99.894% for tool life.

Very few literature studies are available for parameter monitoring of milling for Aluminium 6061 alloy using the ANN approach. Therefore, in the given research, milling of Aluminium 6061 alloy is modelled using the ANNs. Speed, feed rate and depth of cut are taken as input parameters. In the literature [20–22], it has been shown that feed rate, cutting speed and depth of cut are the most important parameters in determining the surface roughness and material removal rate with feed rate and cutting speed having the most influence. We performed exploratory data analysis on the experimental data to study the impact of input parameters in Section 3.3. In Section 3.4, a brief introduction to the ANNs is given. And then in Section 3.5, we explain the ANN architecture and the hyperparameters that yielded the best results.

3.3 EXPLORATORY DATA ANALYSIS

In this work, the ANN analysis has been performed on an experimental dataset [24] (Tables 3.1 and 3.2).

Taguchi method was employed as it is capable of studying the impact of all design factors on experimental response with a minimum of experiments [23]. In this analysis, the research done by [24] is being analyzed using the ANN technique. The experimental results derived in original experimental research [23] are in synchronization with the ANN predicted results. In the original research, three study input factors — Speed (932–1042 rpm), Depth of cut (1–3 mm), and Feed rate (95–145 mm/min), over three levels — were used.

TABLE 3.1
Dataset

Run Order	Speed (rpm)	Feed Rate (mm/min)	Depth of Cut (mm)	MRR (mm³/min)	Ra (µs)
1	932	95	1	1140.00	1.52
2	932	95	1	1142.00	1.54
3	932	95	1	1143.00	1.51
4	932	120	2	3435.13	1.33
5	932	120	2	3432.99	1.29
6	932	120	2	3436.13	1.26
7	932	145	3	5220.00	1.47
8	932	145	3	5223.55	1.46
9	932	145	3	5221.00	1.44
10	1037	120	1	1359.96	1.33
11	1037	120	1	1357.00	1.25
12	1037	120	1	1359.01	1.28
13	1037	145	2	3422.00	1.29
14	1037	145	2	3425.00	1.33
15	1037	145	2	3428.00	1.30
16	1037	95	3	3005.29	1.33
17	1037	95	3	3007.53	1.33
18	1037	95	3	3005.71	1.33
19	1142	145	1	3359.83	1.29
20	1142	145	1	3358.29	1.33
21	1142	145	1	3359.83	1.29
22	1142	95	2	2251.01	1.10
23	1142	95	2	2254.01	1.09
24	1142	95	2	2251.01	1.10
25	1142	120	3	3467.00	1.33
26	1142	120	3	3469.50	1.33
27	1142	120	3	3465.00	1.28

TABLE 3.2
Neural Net Configuration

Factors	Parameters
Network type	Feed forward back propagation
Training function	TRAINLM
Adaptive learning function	LEARNGDM
Performance function	MSE
Number of layers	5
Number of neurons in hidden layers	3–5
Transfer function	TANSIG
Number of epochs	1000

Variance of response parameters Material Removal Rate and Surface Roughness, w.r.t. input parameters Feed Rate, Depth of Cut and Speed

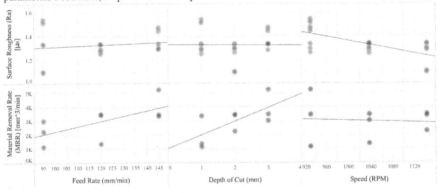

FIGURE 3.1 Exploratory data analysis — trend lines between the input and response parameters in the dataset representing variance between different milling parameters

Exploratory data analysis was performed to evaluate the relation between the input and output variables. Figure 3.1 signifies the non-existence of observable trends between the input and target parameters. Due to this non-linearity between parameters, the given problem couldn't be solved using regression techniques. Therefore, the ANNs were used owing to their ability to learn and model non-linear and complex relationships.

3.4 ARTIFICIAL NEURAL NETWORKS

Artificial Neural Networks (ANNs), also known as Neural Nets or Deep Neural Networks, are computing systems that are meant to simulate the working of a human brain. With the help of experience and data, the ANN improves itself using artificial neurons. The ANN consists of elementary units called neurons that take one or more inputs to produce an output [2].

At each node, the following computations are carried out.

$$Z^{[i]} = W^{[i]} * A^{[i-1]} + b^{[i]}$$

$$A^{[i]} = f\left(Z^{[i]}\right)$$

where

$W^{[i]}$ — Weights of the connection
$A^{[i-1]}$ — Output from the previous layer
$b^{[i]}$ — Bias of the connection
$f(x)$ — Non-linear activation function

A neural network comprises input, hidden, and output layers. A parallel group of neurons, without any interaction between them, makes up a layer. Neurons in the input layer are further connected to the layer of hidden units, which are then connected to neurons in the output layer.

To tune the weights and the bias to minimize the loss function, and increase the model accuracy, the gradient descent-based back propagation technique is used.

3.5 OUR MODEL

The *nntool* in MATLAB was used for creating the neural network for our desired optimization. The input and target datasets were created by segmentation of the original dataset into, firstly, train and test data and then into input and response variables.

The following configuration was used to train the network. Levenberg–Marquardt algorithm was chosen as the training function for model curve fitting, due to its applications in solving non-linear problems (Figures 3.2 and 3.3).

Stochastic gradient descent is the optimization algorithm used for adaptive learning as it minimizes the gradient and adjusts weights accordingly. Weights and biases are tuned in an iterative manner to obtain optimum values for the least error.

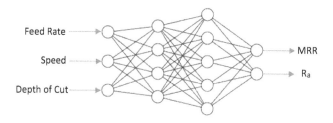

FIGURE 3.2 Neural network architecture — feed rate, speed, and depth of cut — passed through two layers of 4 and 5 neurons, respectively, resulting in material removal rate and surface roughness.

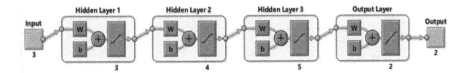

FIGURE 3.3 Neural network MATLAB schematic — detailed layout of the layers used in our ANN, created on MATLAB, with their respective activation functions and the number of neurons

The loss function, for performance evaluation, is chosen as Mean Square Error. This sum of squared distances between the target and predicted values is minimum for the most accurate prediction.

Hyperbolic tangent sigmoid transfer function calculates the output of the layer from the net inputs, in less time and with sufficient accuracy.

Hyperparameters, like model depth, layer size, learning rate, and weight initialization, were tuned iteratively for best results.

3.6 RESULTS

The neural network architecture created is able to predict end milling parameters with high accuracy on, both, training and testing data, making the model generalized and reliable. The achieved accuracy of the model, as shown in Figure 3.4, was 99.91% on the training dataset and 99.89% on the testing data. The figure is a representation of how well the regression aligns with the data points.

Table 3.3 shows the predicted and original experimental values of surface roughness and material removal rate. Error was calculated in percentages for each value, to observe the minimal cumulative error. Low error values signify a well-trained and generalized model. The predicted values show acceptable error and good accuracy.

The regression plots for the training, testing and validation datasets are shown in Figure 3.4. The graphs are a representation of the fitting of the model, where R is the square of the correlation between the predicted and response values. A value closer to 1 signifies a good fit for the model.

The plot from Figure 3.5 shows that the minimum value of the loss function was reached in the ninth epoch where Mean Squared Error (MSE) was obtained to be the lowest. This gave the best performance for our network. Figure 3.6 is a visualization of the gradient descent of the model for all epochs. The model converges to a perfect fit as the gradient decreases.

Figures 3.7 and 3.8 visualize the marginal differences between the experimental and predicted values of material removal rate and surface roughness. As suggested by the model accuracy, the predicted values align well with the experimental ones, with minimum error. Thus, the network is capable of predicting surface roughness and material removal rate very close to experimental values on new data as well.

TABLE 3.3

Experimental vs Predicted Values

	Experimental		Predicted		% Error	
S. No.	MRR (mm³/min)	Ra (µs)	MRR (mm³/min)	Ra (µs)	MRR (mm³/min)	Ra (µs)
1	1140.00	1.52	1141.67	1.49	−0.15	2.11
2	1142.00	1.54	1141.67	1.49	0.03	3.38
3	1143.00	1.51	1141.67	1.49	0.12	1.46
4	3435.13	1.33	3436.12	1.46	−0.03	−9.62
5	3432.99	1.29	3436.12	1.46	−0.09	−13.02
6	3436.13	1.26	3436.12	1.46	0.00	−15.71
7	5220.00	1.47	5221.00	1.40	−0.02	5.08
8	5223.55	1.46	5221.00	1.40	0.05	4.43
9	5221.00	1.44	5221.00	1.40	0.00	3.10
10	1359.96	1.33	1358.66	1.31	0.10	1.20
11	1357.00	1.25	1358.66	1.31	−0.12	−5.12
12	1359.01	1.28	1358.66	1.31	0.03	−2.66
13	3422.00	1.29	3425.00	1.23	−0.09	4.81
14	3425.00	1.33	3425.00	1.23	0.00	7.68
15	3428.00	1.30	3425.00	1.23	0.09	5.55
16	3005.29	1.33	3006.41	1.25	−0.04	5.93
17	3007.53	1.33	3006.41	1.25	0.04	5.93
18	3005.71	1.33	3006.41	1.25	−0.02	5.93
19	3359.83	1.29	3359.06	1.23	0.02	4.53
20	3358.29	1.33	3359.06	1.23	−0.02	7.40
21	3359.83	1.29	3359.06	1.23	0.02	4.53
22	2251.01	1.10	2252.01	1.29	−0.04	−17.38
23	2254.01	1.09	2252.01	1.29	0.09	−18.45
24	2251.01	1.10	2252.01	1.29	−0.04	−17.38
25	3467.00	1.33	3467.16	1.23	0.00	7.86
26	3469.50	1.33	3467.16	1.23	0.07	7.86
27	3465.00	1.28	3467.16	1.23	−0.06	4.26
Cumulative error					−0.06	−6.31

3.7 CONCLUSION

In this study, the optimization of multi-response milling parameters of Al-6061 alloy was carried out. Taguchi L27 orthogonal array with three factors namely — Feed rate, Speed, and Depth of cut — was used. Optimization was done by examining the variance of these inputs parameters on output parameters — material removal rate and surface roughness. We concluded that due to non-linearity between the

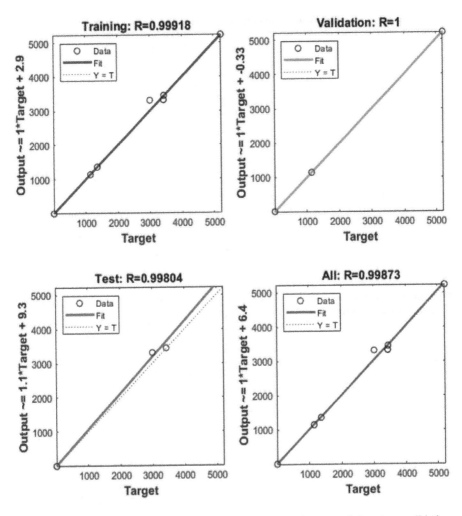

FIGURE 3.4 Regression plots — model fitting visualization on training, test, validation, · and overall data segments. High accuracy and good fit are observed.

parameters, regression techniques would yield poor results. Therefore, analytical models for material removal rate and surface roughness were developed using an ANN. Cumulative errors for each parameter were as low as 0.06% for material removal rate and 6.31% for surface roughness as the ANN model was able to predict with an accuracy of 99.91% on the training dataset and 99.89% on the test dataset. This signifies a well-fitted and generalized model.

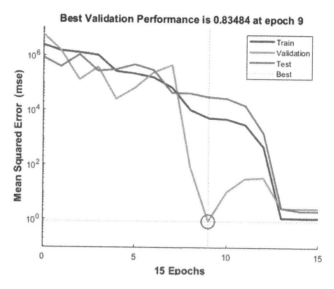

FIGURE 3.5   Validation performance of the ANN, as illustrated by MATLAB, emphasizing the point of lowest MSE

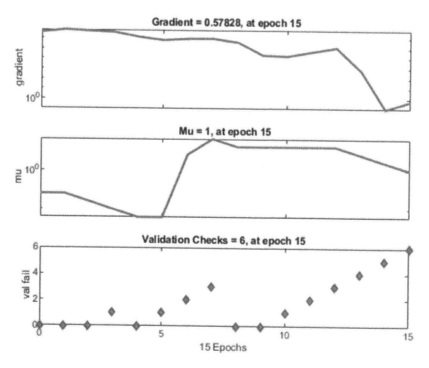

FIGURE 3.6   Gradient descent — MATLAB illustration of model convergence and decreasing gradient as training progresses

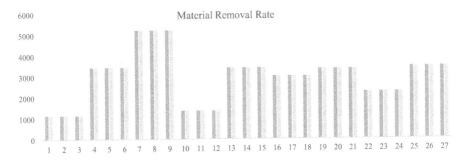

FIGURE 3.7 Experimental vs predicted values for material removal rate — 0.06% cumulative error inferred from model predictions

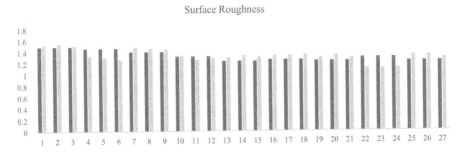

FIGURE 3.8 Experimental vs predicted values for surface roughness — 6.31% cumulative error inferred from model predictions

REFERENCES

1 Felhő, C., Karpuschewski, B., & Kundrák, J. (2015). Surface roughness modelling in face milling. *Procedia CIRP*, 31, 136–141.
2 Aggarwal, C. C. (2018). *Neural Networks and Deep Learning: A Textbook* (1st ed.). Springer, Cham.
3 Anand, A., & Suganthi, L. (2018). Hybrid GA-PSO optimization of artificial neural network for forecasting electricity demand. *Energies*, 11(4), 728.
4 Tu, J. V. (1996). Advantages and disadvantages of using artificial neural networks versus logistic regression for predicting medical outcomes. *Journal of Clinical Epidemiology*, 49(11), 1225–1231.
5 Sholom, M. Weiss, & Kapouleas, I. (1989). An empirical comparison of pattern recognition, neural nets, and machine learning classification methods. *Proceedings of the 11th International Joint Conference on Artificial Intelligence*, California, 1, 781–787.
6 Marquez, L., Hill, T., Worthley, R., & Remus, W. (1991). Neural network models as an alternative to regression. *Proceedings of the Twenty-Fourth Annual Hawaii International Conference on System Sciences,* Hawaii, 129–135.
7 Livingstone, D., Manallack, D., & Tetko, I. (1997). Data modelling with neural networks: Advantages and limitations. *Journal of Computer-Aided Molecular Design*, 11(2), 135–142.

8   Bejou, D., Wray, B., & Ingram, T. N. (1996). Determinants of relationship quality: An artificial neural network analysis. *Journal of Business Research*, 36(2), 137–143.

9   Zain A.M., Haron H., Sharif S. (2010) Prediction of surface roughness in the end milling machining using artificial neural network. *Expert System Applications* 37(2):1755–1768.

10   Agarwal, A., & Desai, K. A. (2020). Amalgamation of physics-based cutting force model and machine learning approach for end milling operation. *Procedia CIRP*, 93, 1405–1410.

11   Serin, G., Sener, B., Gudelek, M. U., Ozbayoglu, A. M., & Unver, H. O. (2020). Deep multi-layer perceptron based prediction of energy efficiency and surface quality for milling in the era of sustainability and big data. *Procedia Manufacturing*, 51, 1166–1177.

12   Bandapalli, C., Sutaria, B. M., Bhatt, D. V., & Singh, K. K. (2017). Experimental investigation and estimation of surface roughness using ANN, GMDH & MRA models in high-speed micro end milling of titanium alloy (Grade-5). *Materials Today: Proceedings*, 4(2), 1019–1028.

13   Al-Abdullah, K. I. A., Abdi, H., Lim, C. P., & Yassin, W. A. (2018). Force and temperature modelling of bone milling using artificial neural networks. *Measurement*, 116, 25–37.

14   Malghan, R. L., Shettigar, A. K., Rao, S. S., & D'Souza, R. J. (2018). Forward and reverse mapping for milling process using artificial neural networks. *Data in Brief*, 16, 114–121.

15   Daniel, S. A. A., Pugazhenthi, R., Kumar, R., & Vijayananth, S. (2019). Multi objective prediction and optimization of control parameters in the milling of aluminium hybrid metal matrix composites using ANN and Taguchi -grey relational analysis. *Defence Technology*, 15, 545–556.

16   Dhobale, N., Mulik, S., Jegdeeshwaran, R., & Ganer, K. (2020). Multipoint milling tool supervision using artificial neural network approach. *Materials Today: Proceedings*, 45, 1898–1903.

17   Mundada, V., & Narala, S. K. R. (2018). Optimization of milling operations using artificial neural networks (ANN) and simulated annealing algorithm (SAA). *Materials Today: Proceedings*, 5(2), 4971–4985.

18   Sanjeevi, R., Nagaraja, R., & Radha Krishnan, B. (2021). Vision-based surface roughness accuracy prediction in the CNC milling process (Al-6061) using ANN. *Materials Today: Proceedings*, 37, 245–247.

19   Parmar, J. G., Dave, K. G., Gohil, A. V., & Trivedi, H. S. (2021). Prediction of end milling process parameters using artificial neural network. *Materials Today: Proceedings*, 38, 3168–3176.

20   Wang, M. Y., & Chang, H. Y. (2004). Experimental study of surface roughness in slot end milling AL2014-T6. *International Journal of Machine Tools and Manufacture*, 44(1), 51–57.

21   Zhang, J. Z., Chen, J. C., & Kirby, E. D. (2007). Surface roughness optimization in an end-milling operation using the Taguchi design method. *Journal of Materials Processing Technology*, 184(1–3), 233–239.

22   Quintana, G., Ciurana, J. D., & Ribatallada, J. (2010). Surface roughness generation and material removal rate in ball end milling operations. *Materials and Manufacturing Processes*, 25(6), 386–398.

23   Ghani, J., Choudhury, I., & Hassan, H. (2004). Application of Taguchi method in the optimization of end milling parameters. *Journal of Materials Processing Technology*, 145(1), 84–92.

24   Pradhan M., Meena M., Sen S., Singh A. (2015). Multi-objective optimization in end milling of Al-6061 using Taguchi based G-PCA. *International Journal of Mechanical, Aerospace, Industrial, Mechatronic and Manufacturing Engineering*, 9(6), 6.

4 Smart Techniques of Microscopic Image Analysis and Real-Time Temperature Dispersal Measurement for Quality Weld Joints

Rajesh V. Patil and Abhishek M. Thote
Dr. Vishwanath Karad MIT World Peace University

CONTENTS

4.1 INTRODUCTION

In the manufacturing arena, the joining of components is the pillar of the whole world's necessity. The welded assembly impacts weld quality which rests on the joint limits [1]. In joining, weld bead geometry defines bead penetration, height, and width.

DOI: 10.1201/9781003154518-4

49

Generally, weld bead geometry quantifies by diverse measurement devices and systems [2]. The correct dimension of weld bead geometries indirectly forecasts the mechanical properties of the joined assembly. The weld bead geometry examination by radiographic testing plays important role in today's joining industries. Mostly, weld bead geometry revealed ample information associated with penetration depth and is considered as a major parameter for weld quality joint [3]. Today, everywhere for measuring this kind of task, various tools are readily available that are specifically operated by human intervention and their accuracy, precision based on the visual capability of the operator [4]. Then for final judgment of weld quality totally rely on the operator's skill set and many times found diversify the results through operator many times while estimating the results. In the era of digitization, already Industry 4.0 is initiating its footprint in every sector of industry [1]. In automotive components manufacturing, still, many processes are operator dependent and many times found problematic for final quality check analysis. One of the most demanding techniques in this area is the welding of components while maintaining their sound quality joint. In spite of reliable welding machines and equipment, still, weld components are not achieving the demanded weld quality joints [5]. To overcome the dependency on the operator in the proposed work, the author developed two smart techniques for defining the sound weld quality joint named Microscopic image analysis and Real-Time temperature dispersal measurement. The microscopic image analysis validates the promising results in comparison with manual techniques of defining weld bead geometry, whereas the Real-Time temperature dispersal measurement technique provides the online temperature during the welding at various locations of specimen for identifying the heating and cooling relations for sound weld quality joints. Finally, both the techniques found promising results during experimentation of various materials through welding and are really beneficial for better implementation of Industry 4.0. The author delivered the work mainly in two parts. The first part is the investigation of weld bead geometry by manual experimentation and microscopic image analysis techniques. And the second part is the Real-Time temperature dispersal measurement during welding using data logger unit at various locations.

4.2 ALLIED INVESTIGATION

Several authors contributed works on online weld superiority measurement by microscopic image analysis techniques and temperature measurement. Bestard et al. [1] reviewed the arc welding to gather various detection methods for approximation of bead geometry. Singh et al. [2] measured weld bead geometry by image texture analysis techniques on the strength of its pixels. An image examination technique was used to effectively quantify five diverse regions on imprinted cross-sections of welding.. Bestard et al. [3] developed an image processing technique to estimate weld bead depth on its complete length and obtained facts assuring to active model size. The sensory fusion methods proposed for approximation of bead weld depth and width by novel data processing technique. Tomas et al. [6] proposed an exclusive photographic camera correction method through the jet of computer arithmetic regulate mechanism planned for imaging technique composed allowing photographic camera location relation to examining exterior and its orientation. They found fault of calibration amount lesser than 1 pixel. Ghanty et al. [7] showed bead weld geometry by Artificial Neural Network (ANN) and studied the composite and individual models and found that the individual model is better for estimating the weld bead geometry. Patil et al. [8] presented temperature as the subtle pointer depth of penetration and quantified penetration depth satisfactorily by image texture analysis technique. Soares et al. [5] proposed bead weld geometric analysis system using the hidden markov model to detect weld bead edges and estimate various evaluation phases to detect geometric failures. Moradpour et al. [9] implemented a machine vision system to measure weld bead geometry for steel plates. Using image analysis techniques acquired better measurements as compared to the manual one. Chandrasekhar et al. [10] found the smart model compounding processing of the image by Adaptive network-based fuzzy inference system (ANFIS) to forecast bead width and penetration depth more precisely after Infrared (IR) thermal picture of weld pool arena. Finally, the ANFIS performance with lesser computation time was found better as compared to the ANN. Chokkalingham et al. [11] predicated penetration depth and bead weld from IR thermal pictures of pool weld by modelling of the ANN for online observing and regulating bead weld geometry. Wei et al. [12] developed a phase improvement technique based Real-Time ratio and assigned it to quantify the weld depth of the pool surface. At last, validation was performed based on simulation. Wang et al. [13] developed penetration weld specialist care methods by weld sound for features extraction and selections. The wavelet packet transforms methods were used to identify welding sound signals, and, finally, the ANN classified the various penetration states along with appreciable accuracy. Ghanty et al. [14] developed a fuzzy approach for the forecast of bead weld geometry. The fuzzy systems were found better than the ANN. Liu & He et al. [15,16] estimated penetration depth under different weld pools with the identification of the ANFIS model to relate the behind bead width and refer to an online forecast of the behind bead width in actual time. Jin & Sumesh et al. [17, 18] attempted comparison of arc sound by weld superiority and measured the absence of fusion and burn over defects. The raw information points taken from arc sound were transformed into amplitude signals and classified into three modules such as decent weld, weld by the absence of fusion, and burn over. Pathak & Shah et al. [19,20] proposed that texture examination maintained GLCMs and estimated gap among pixels along with angle excessive position on final results. Patil et al. [21] presented techniques of local binary pattern to finalise pixel and adding by GLCM to explore statistical texture features. Patil et al. [22,23] used ANN and Support Vector Machine (SVM) classifiers to detect weld imperfections. Wang et al. [24] proposed gradient discovery filter, the variance method and GLCM allocated to eliminate the irregular background. The spline fitting improvement technique eliminates fuzziness. Furthermore, slope difference distribution-based threshold selection scheme selected and assigned to part laser lines from background. Patil et al. [8] assessed the relationship between penetration depth and temperature distribution in laser welding and found promising results. Lankapalli et al. [25] developed prototypical connecting temperature circulation in the workpiece to the depth of penetration, weld speed, and width and measured temperature found varies sensitive indicator of penetration depth. Shannon et al. [26] investigated the keyhole steadiness by a rapid camera to regulate the weld joint quality. Hardt et al. [27] investigated the ultrasonic pulse resonance examination to regulate weld pool proportions. John et al. [28] investigated the acoustic discharge monitoring through laser welding and discovered for potential claims in Real-Time monitoring process. Miyamoto et al. [29] investigated light emission from plume observed by photosensors to regulate the laser weld joint quality. Watanabe et al. [30] examined the performance of the laser-made plasma by nursing the spectrum emission, acoustic release, and plasma producing potential to advance connections between signals and weld joint features.

4.3 EXPERIMENTAL INVESTIGATION OF WELD BEAD GEOMETRY

Gas Tungsten Arc Welding (GTAW) was carried out on 304L stainless steel sheet of 300 mm × 150 mm × 1.5 mm. The chemical and mechanical properties are shown in Table 4.1. Moreover, argon gas is used as a shielding medium to avoid atmospheric contamination. According to the investigation, voltage, current, and gas flow rate are independent input variables and major impacting variables on weld bead geometry as shown in Table 4.2, whereas the depth of penetration is found to be a dependent output variable. The 304L stainless steel sheet was cut into rectangular shape by Electrical Discharge Machining (EDM) of size 300 mm × 150 mm with thickness of 1.5 mm. Lastly, GTAW beads made by welding using different combinations of voltage 5–7 V, current 30–40 A, and glass flow rate of 4.5–5.5 liters/minute as shown in Table 4.3. This Design of Experiment (DOE) was designated by welding variables of voltage, current, and gas flow rate with three levels each and determined penetration depth and width by L9 orthogonal array as shown in Table 4.4. The response function of the weld joint, stated as Y, is the function of voltage, current, and Gas Flow Rate (GFR), i.e., $Y = f (V, I, GFR)$. The second-order polynomial equation represents the response surface for factors by

$$Y = b_0 \sum_{i=1}^{4} b_i x_i + \sum_{i=1}^{4} b_{ii} x_i 2 + \sum_{i=1, i<j}^{4} b_{ii} x_i j_j \qquad (4.1)$$

The second order response model is stated as follows:

$$Y_0 = b_0 + b_1 V + b_2 I + b_3 GFR + b_{11} V^2 + b_{22} I^2 + b_{33} b_{33} GFR^2 + b_{12} V \times I + b_{13} V \times GFR$$
$$+ b_{23} I \times GFR \qquad (4.2)$$

TABLE 4.1
304L Stainless Steel Chemical and Mechanical Properties

C	Si	Mn	P	S	Cr	N	Ni
0.03	0.75	2.00	0.045	0.03	19.00	0.10	8
Proof stress (0.2%): 170 Mpa			Tensile strength: 485 Mpa		Elongation: A5 (%) – 40	Hardness: HB 201 HRB 92	

TABLE 4.2

Process Ranges of 304L Stainless Steel

Sheet Thickness (mm)	Voltage (V)	Current (A)	Gas Flow Rate (lit/min)
1.5	5–7	30–40	4.5–5.5

TABLE 4.3

Process Variable Quantity and Levels

Variables	Sheet Thickness	Voltage	Current	Gas Flow Rate
1	1.5	5	30	4.5
2	1.5	6	35	5
3	1.5	7	40	5.5

TABLE 4.4

Design Matrix Along with Variables Quantity

Sample	1	2	3	4	5	6	7	8	9
V	5	5	5	6	6	6	7	7	7
C	30	35	40	30	35	40	30	35	40
GFR	4.5	5	5.5	5	5.5	4.5	5.5	4.5	5
ST	1.5	1.5	1.5	1.5	1.5	1.5	1.5	1.5	1.5

where b0 is the constant of regression equation whereas constants such as $b_1, b_2, b_3,$ $b_{11}, b_{22}, b_{33,}$ and b_{12}, b_{13}, b_{23} are linear, quadratic, and interactive terms used. Subsequently, we calculate the coefficients and mathematical models assigned to advance and specified in (4.3) and (4.4). All facts are assigned to produce regression calculations to estimate the Depth of Penentration (DOP) and Bead Width (BW) through equation (4.3) and (4.4).

$$BL = 937.6064 - 421.469*V + 44.1408*I + 0*GFR + 25.3234*V^2 + 0.2441*I^2 \tag{4.3}$$

$$+ 2.3681*GFR^2 - 2.9171*V*I + 46.1685*V*GFR - 8.55*I*GFR$$

$$DP = -28.5284 + 6.1996*V + 0.0719*I + 0*GFR - 0.2141*V^2 + 0.0065*I^2$$

$$+ 0.1846*GFR^2 + 0.05385*V*I - 0.36*V*GFR + 0.01241*I*GFR \tag{4.4}$$

The weld trials were polished continuously at that time lapping and achieved by disc polishing. Finally, etchings through aqua regia 3:1 HNO_3:HCL aimed at 30 seconds to 1 minute were done; and by an image analyzer, DOP and BW were calculated. We selected nine trials to weld by various process parameters and found their acceptable weld bead and penetration depth, as shown in Table 4.5.

TABLE 4.5

Metallographic Inspection of Weld Specimen

Weld Specimen 1

DoP: 2.446 mm U.T.S: 562.48 N/mm²

Weld Specimen 2

DoP: 2.044 mm U.T.S: 506.19 N/mm²

Weld Specimen 3

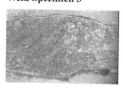

DoP: 2.708 mm U.T.S: 620.713 N/mm²

Weld Specimen 4

DoP: 2.335 mm U.T.S: 583.826 N/mm²

Weld Specimen 5

DoP: 1.66 mm U.T.S: 469.197 N/mm²

Weld Specimen 6

DoP: 2.379 mm U.T.S: 589.2 N/mm²

4.4 WELD BEAD GEOMETRY PROCESSING AND TEXTURE FEATURES EXTRACTION

The proposed technique validates the approach of feature extraction to identify features of DOP and BW of weld sheet that represent the best images. Gray-level co-occurrence matrix (GLCM) widespread textures feature extraction system to regulate the texture association among pixels by acting process giving to second-order statistics in image. It possesses an image specified as matrix by the quantity of rows and columns as per grey standards image. The elements of matrix hinge on the frequency of two stated pixels. Together pixel sets can differ dependent on their zone. These matrix elements comprise second-order statistical values liable on grey value of rows and columns. If intensity values are extensive, transient matrix moderately huge and generates long method load. Through GLCM feature matrix efficiently signify with minimum parameters using properties. GLCMs are built with frequencies along with the number of pixels with fixed place and grey-level bonding. It classifies circulation of grey level proof near images to build them explicitly by path, different quantities and local surroundings. The weld picture I is $[M] \times [N]$ and its grey level $[L]$, at that moment GLCM as span in dual pixels, θ accepted angle and extent of matrix $[P]$ is $[L] \times [L]$ and $[I] [x, y]$ is grey level of imaging (x, y), d is span between dual pixel. This training, choose four variables such as homogeneity, correlation, energy and contrast.

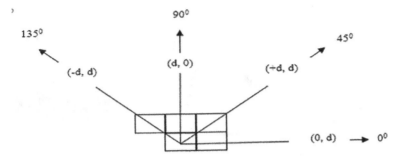

FIGURE 4.1 Pixel pair for grey level co-occurrence matrix.

To get other data to approximate imperfections type, $d=1$ and $\theta = \{0°, 45°, 90°, 135°\}$ selected to roughly calculate GLCMs of images, which standard to complete as shown in Figure 4.1. In the experiment, 12 grey-level images of 285×296 pixels were used. Primarily for digitization, recognized characteristics of images principle such as minor contrast among background and weld regions are used. Using preprocessing, eliminated noise enclosing in film and improved visibility through filters. In preprocessing, selected area near the seam of images as ROI for further processing. Next, the ROI assigns contrast modifications to improve the intensity difference of assigned input and to highlight weld regions. This enables weld identifications to appropriate location and representation. At last, segmentation governs weld image superiority and calculated values of penetration depth and bead weld are shown in Table 4.6.

$$P\left(i,j,d,\theta\right) = P\,I\left(x,y\right) = i, I\left(x+d\cos\theta, y+d\sin\theta\right) = j \qquad (4.5)$$

$$\text{Energy }\left(f_1\right) = \sum_{i=1}^{L}\sum_{j=1}^{L}\left[p(i,j)\right]^2 \qquad (4.6)$$

$$\text{Contrast }\left(f_2\right) = \sum_{i=1}^{L}\sum_{j=1}^{L}(i,j)^2\,p(i,j) \qquad (4.7)$$

$$\text{Correaltion }\left(f_3\right) = \sum_{i=1}^{L}\sum_{j=1}^{L}\frac{\left(i-u_x\right)\left(j-u_y\right)p(i,j)}{\sigma_x\sigma_y} \qquad (4.8)$$

$$\text{Homogeneity }\left(f_4\right) = \sum_{i=0}^{L}\sum_{j=0}^{L}\frac{P_{ij}}{1+(i+j)^2} \qquad (4.9)$$

Where u_x ; u_y; σ_x; σ_y are as follows

$$u_X\sum_{i=1}^{L}i\sum_{j=1}^{L}p\left(i,j\right) ; u_y\sum_{j=1}^{L}j\sum_{i=1}^{L}p\left(i,j\right) \qquad (4.10)$$

TABLE 4.6

Weld Bead Geometry Processing & Texture Feature Extraction by GLCM

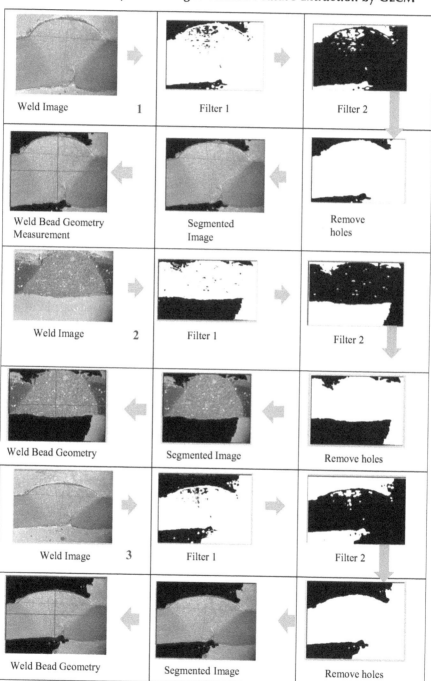

TABLE 4.6 (*Continued*)
Weld Bead Geometry Processing & Texture Feature Extraction by GLCM

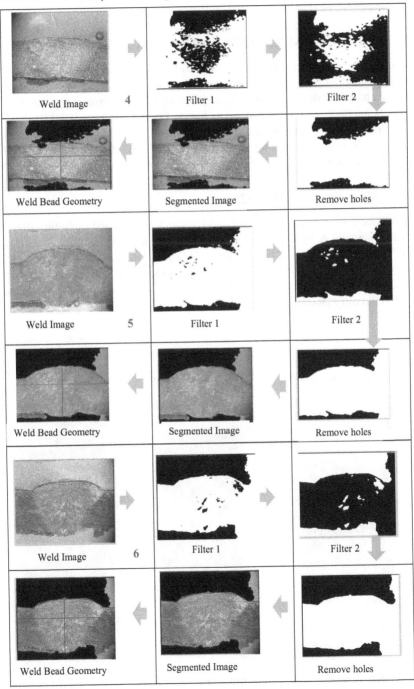

$$\sigma_X = \sum_{i=1}^{L}(i-u_x)^2 \sum_{j=1}^{L} p\,(i,j)\; ; \;\; \sigma_y = \sum_{j=1}^{L}(j-u_y)^2 \sum_{i=1}^{L} p\,(i,j) \qquad (4.11)$$

4.5 REAL-TIME TEMPERATURE DATA MEASUREMENT LOGGER

A temperature data measurement logger found consistent and precise facts gathering device under critical environmental conditions as shown in Figure 4.2. The author developed handheld device that initially requires input as temperature measure by thermocouple interface with temperature data logger. Once the process is initiated, access the real-time data and downloaded it directly to any device. Major list of components involved such as Microprocessor 89S52, Multiplexer 4051, RS232, ADC 320, LCD. The real-time temperature data measurement logger circuitry is shown in Figure 4.15.

4.5.1 MICROPROCESSOR (89S52)

The AT89S52 is an effective control and reliable CMOS-based eight-bit microcontroller using eight K bytes of computer program flash-based memory. The features of AT89S52 such as flash of eight K bytes, RAM of 256 bytes, thirty-two I/O lines, watchdog clock, dual information indicators, trio sixteen-bit timer/counters, interrupt architecture of 6 vector 2 level, a serial port of complete duplex, oscillator on chip and circuitry clock as shown in Figure 4.3.

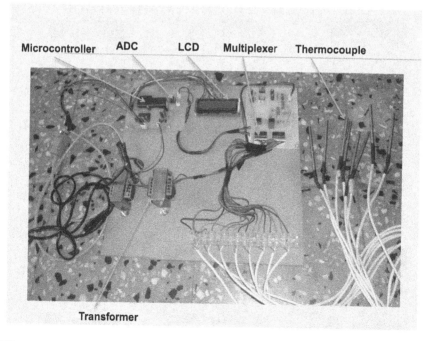

FIGURE 4.2   Real-time temperature data measurement logger.

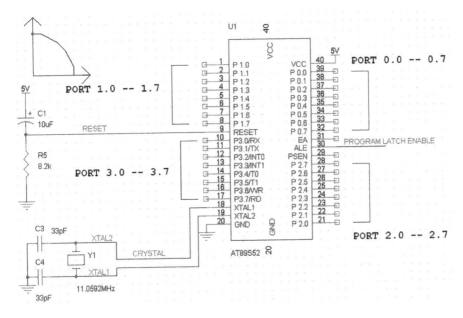

FIGURE 4.3   Microcontroller 89S52 circuitary.

4.5.2   OPERATIONAL AMPLIFIER

The author used two amplifier stages consisting of two operational amplifiers (op-amp) LM 358. In the first op-amp input is given to three pins of op-amp (non-inverting input). Two resistors of 10k pot and 4.7 kohm form a voltage partition circuit. This circuit is used to increase the input impedance (resistance) of the overall circuit as shown in Figures 4.4 and 4.5. More input impedance is better for process and helps to reduce noise in the input signal. The next section consists of the two diodes (4148). These diodes are linked to protect the input of op-amp over voltage, once input voltage of first op-amp increases, the one of diodes goes in forward bias and conducts extra current to ground. The first op amp has a gain of $1 + \dfrac{r_f}{r_1}$ where, $r_f = 100\,\text{k}$, $r_1 = 2$ therefore, $2 + \dfrac{100\,\text{k}}{2\,\text{k}} = 50$ is improvement of initial op-amp. Likewise, gain of the

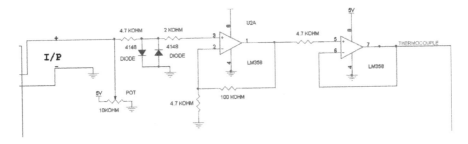

FIGURE 4.4   Operational amplifier.

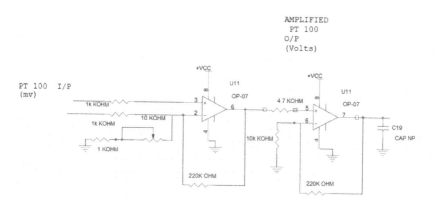

FIGURE 4.5 Operational amplifier with ADC3202 circuitary.

second op-amp is apply as unity gain. It is basically used to reduce the output imped-ance of circuit and also this op amp will invert the incoming signal and output of the second op-amp is then given to ADC 3202.

4.5.3 THERMOCOUPLE INPUT AND OUTPUT

There are two inputs to a thermocouple that are to be associated with the input of signal conditioning circuit as shown in Figure 4.6. For this reason, we have chosen two multiplexers 4051. The first multiplexer is to select the first input of the first thermocouple and the second multiplexer is used to select the second input of the first thermocouple. In the same way, we are joining the first input of the first to

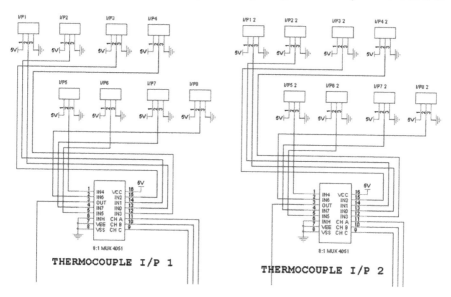

FIGURE 4.6 Thermocouple input 1 and 2 circuitry.

eight thermocouples to the second multiplexer 4051. In this way, we can sample all the eight thermocouples via multiplexers. As explained earlier we are using the two multiplexers to choose from first to eight inputs of thermocouple. To do this, we are shorting the channel select lines of both the Multiplexer together and connecting them to the input/output pins of the microcontroller (Pin No. 2.5, 2.6, and 2.7) as shown in Figure 4.7. By choosing the binary combination we can choose the corresponding Channel Number 000 for the selection of thermocouple one, 001 for the selection of thermocouple two, up to selection of eight thermocouples. Finally, the output of two multiplexers is given to the input of signal conditioning circuit which is used to amplify the temperature signal. This amplified signal is further given to the 12-bit analog to digital converter 3202 as shown in Figure 4.8.

4.5.4 ANALOG TO DIGITAL CONVERTER CIRCUIT (3202)

We have used 12 bits analog to digital converter works on SPI bus in our unit for better resolution as shown in Figure 4.9. Chip select is linked to the I/O pin of microcontroller to select the ADC converter and the DIN pin as start of conversion. The clock is used to convert the analog data to digital and the DOUT pin is given to the input/output pin of microcontroller. Finally, the digital data is available on the DOUT pin.

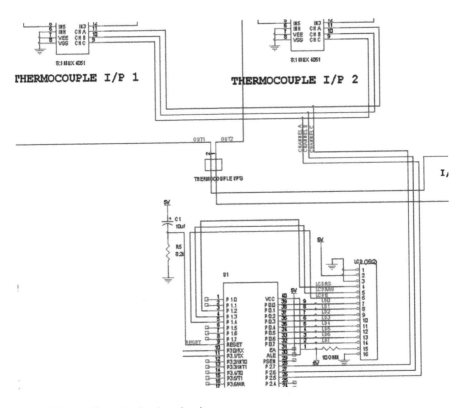

FIGURE 4.7   Channel selection circuitry.

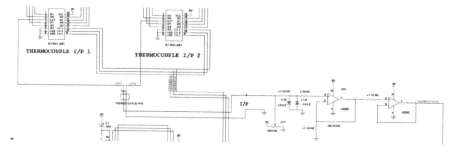

FIGURE 4.8　Thermocouple output circuitry.

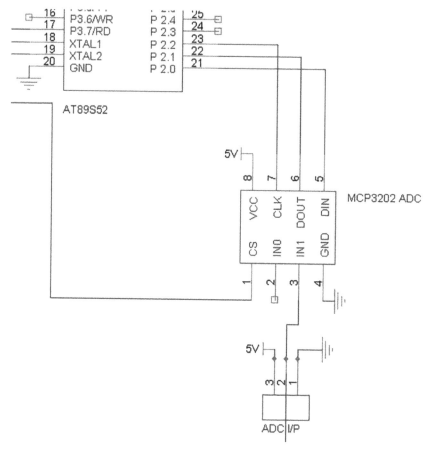

FIGURE 4.9　Circuit diagram of ADC 3202.

4.5.5 LCD Section

Primary Vcc and GND are one and two number of LCD pins used to energy the LCD with three milliampere current feeding. Furthermore, Vcc and GND is fifteen and sixteen number of LCD pins are used to energy rear light of LCD

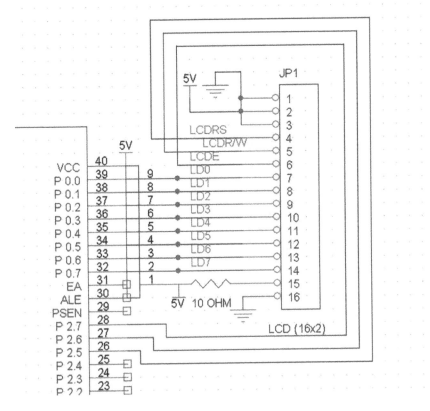

FIGURE 4.10 LCD circuitry.

with hundred milliampere current as shown in Figure 4.10. Finally, total current consumption found 103 milliampere. To lessen current condition by linking a 5-ohm resistance in sequence through rear light VCC pin. This resistance current consumption is a division of 100 ma/10 ohm = 10 ma. As a result, the new current feeding is the sum of ten milliampere and three milliampere beyond thirteen milliampere as shown in Figure 4.10. The LCD has eight data and three control lines. Eight information lines of LCD pin number seven to fourteen linked to zero port of microcontroller 89S52 (P0.0 – P0.7). The control lines are as shown in Figure 4.11. These three lines are linked to two ports of 89S52 microcontroller (P2.5, P2.6, P2.7, respectively). The LCD RS is used for picking information or cipher list and LCDR/W is used to mark on LCD. LCDE is used for allowing or restricting the LCD as shown in Figure 4.11.

4.5.6 RS 232 Interface with 89S52

RS 232 is an initiator IC to change microcontroller TTL judgement. It has two pairs of TTL and RS232 judgement. The first and second pair pin number is 7–10 and 11–14 of RS 232 as shown in Figure 4.12. The system is capable to run on any of pair and also by using two serial ports used both the pairs simultaneously. By connecting four capacitors to RS232 get conversion of TTL judgement.

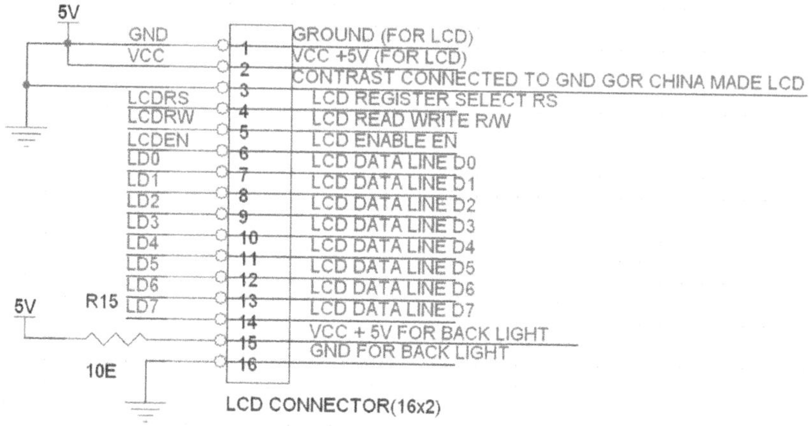

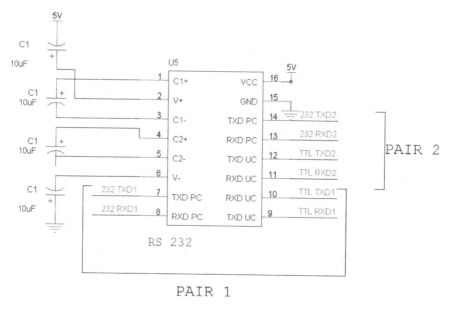

FIGURE 4.11　LCD connector circuitry.

FIGURE 4.12　Circuit diagram of RS 232 interface with 89S52.

4.5.7　TWIN VOLTAGE CONVERTER

The MAX 220–249 has dual inner care pumps changes +5 to ±10 volt for RS-232 operation as shown in Figure 4.13. The initial and second convertor practices electrical condenser C1 from positive five volts to positive ten-volt input on C3 at volt positive output and capacitor C2 to invert positive ten volts to negative ten volts on C4 at volt negative output. We used RS232 through connect two pairs of sequential devices, one device that works on serial. RS-232 chip is used to interface microcontroller to pc.

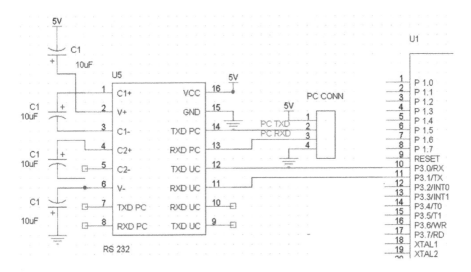

FIGURE 4.13 Circuit diagram dual charge-pump voltage converter.

4.5.8 BRIDGE RECTIFIER

The capacitor and bridge rectifier input filter developed free DC voltage used as input of IC 7805. As least terminate voltage is two volts for IC 7805, the voltage at initial fatal must as a minimum of seven volts. C1 is filter electrical condenser and C2 and C3 linked crosswise the controller to progress the temporary reply of regulator as shown in Figure 4.14. Assuming that two volts terminate voltage and the least DV voltage crosswise capacitor C1 must be up to seven volts (Figure 4.15).

4.6 REAL-TIME TEMPERATURE DISTRIBUTION MEASUREMENT

Welding process contains heat movement over joining to reach the needed joint. Reliant upon heating and cooling series, divergent classes of microstructure initiate in weld bead structure and heat pretentious area, and this summits to changing

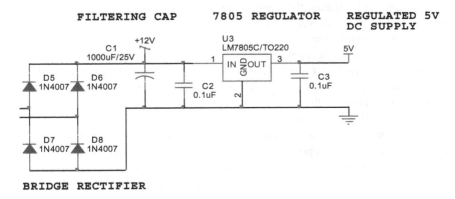

FIGURE 4.14 Circuit diagram of bridge rectifier and I/P filter.

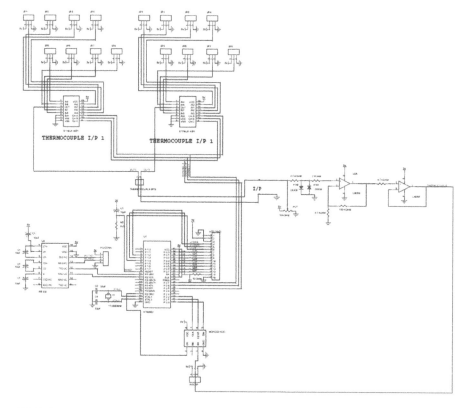

FIGURE 4.15 Real-time temperature data measurement logger circuitry.

mechanical assets of varied weldment regions. In addition to the result of heat movement in joining, there are added spectacle elaborate such as residual stresses, distortion, chemical and physical variations to achieve a weldment of needed requirement to accomplish adequately in providing to hold the outcomes of heat over joining. This may be reached by stating the temperature movement over joining; hence, to work out the cooling pace in several commands with comparative to joint axis, the author introduced real-time temperatures circulation measurement logger unit. Mostly, it is a consistent and true information gathering device in any eco-friendly surroundings as shown in Figure 4.16. Eight K contact type of thermocouple used to quantify the operational temperature of workpiece bottom at diverse places over cyphering by visual basic. Schematic diagram of sensor position as shown in Figure 4.17. The core criteria concerning about mountings are to concealment entire area, i.e., span and height of sample for real-time measurement bottommost temperature. Once the process started with set input process parameters by clicking the start button in the given system as shown in Figure 4.18. The online measurement of temperature captured by thermocouple and till continue until welding process is not initiated to stop otherwise immediately sensors stop sensing the temperature and presented temperatures of appropriate location as shown in Table 4.7.

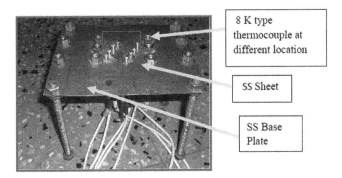

FIGURE 4.16   K type thermocouple mounted on plate at different location.

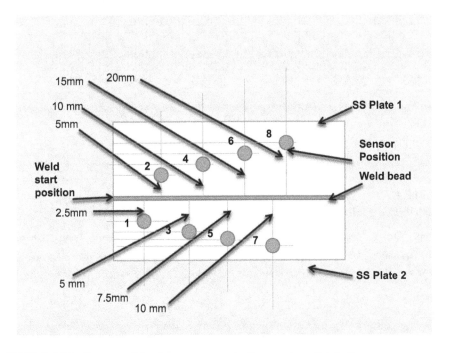

FIGURE 4.17   Sensor position for measurement of temperature distributions.

4.7   RESULT AND DISCUSSION

In modern engineering, weld joint quality still cannot be definite due to the absence of efficient and operational welding imperfections monitoring techniques. To overcome this problem, online weld joint examination by radiographic testing is significantly needed for welding industries. The weld joint quality mainly on penetration depth and defect will majorly influence weld penetration depth. Though estimating the penetration depth, the identification of defect is majorly demanded in industry. This work proposed conventional along with the proposed novel technique of image analysis for measurement

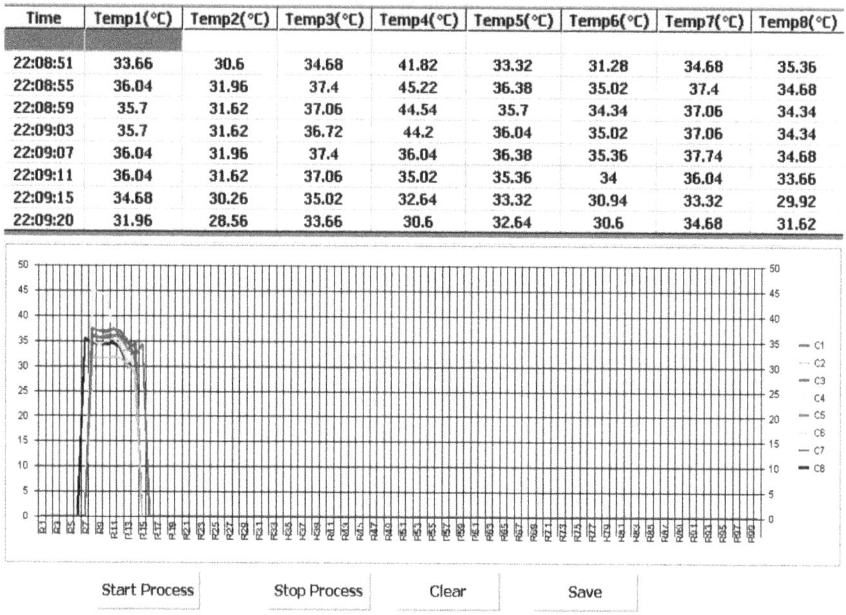

Time	Temp1(°C)	Temp2(°C)	Temp3(°C)	Temp4(°C)	Temp5(°C)	Temp6(°C)	Temp7(°C)	Temp8(°C)
22:08:51	33.66	30.6	34.68	41.82	33.32	31.28	34.68	35.36
22:08:55	36.04	31.96	37.4	45.22	36.38	35.02	37.4	34.68
22:08:59	35.7	31.62	37.06	44.54	35.7	34.34	37.06	34.34
22:09:03	35.7	31.62	36.72	44.2	36.04	35.02	37.06	34.34
22:09:07	36.04	31.96	37.4	36.04	36.38	35.36	37.74	34.68
22:09:11	36.04	31.62	37.06	35.02	35.36	34	36.04	33.66
22:09:15	34.68	30.26	35.02	32.64	33.32	30.94	33.32	29.92
22:09:20	31.96	28.56	33.66	30.6	32.64	30.6	34.68	31.62

Start Process   Stop Process   Clear   Save

FIGURE 4.18   GUI of real-time temperature dispersal measurement.

TABLE 4.7
Distributed Online Temperature Values

Temp. (°C)	Temp1	Temp2	Temp3	Temp4	Temp5	Temp6	Temp7	Temp8
Time (seconds)	Sensor1	Sensor2	Sensor3	Sensor4	Sensor5	Sensor6	Sensor7	Sensor8
1	200.6	191.76	121.38	102.68	87.66	85.66	82.34	78.67
5	253.64	191.42	173.74	120.34	145.28	102.34	97.92	63.92
9	243.44	212.16	186.32	140.3	117.6	93.16	87.72	57.8
13	226.1	224.74	184.28	135.26	113.22	82.96	74.12	62.22
17	244.8	198.88	185.3	108.12	98.45	89.42	77.52	60.18
21	267.58	230.91	223.04	184.28	118.66	106.76	94.92	73.92
22	231.54	225.42	216.24	194.82	165.34	128.18	118.32	62.22

of penetration depth and successfully explored the results of weld bead geometry. The nine-weld sample of a thick plate of 1.5 mm done experimentally by GTAW. The several penetration depths at each weld sample by different method parameters mainly as current, voltage and shielding gas found most influencing penetration depth during actual experimentation. Moreover, during experimentation of second specimen, when the current rises up to 35 amperes as compared to 30 amperes of the first specimen with constant voltage and increase gas flow rate, immediately found increase level of penetration depth in weld joint. Furthermore, for specimen three along with constant voltage and increase current and gas flow rate the penetration depth found lesser than weld specimen two and first. Whereas, the increased voltage with increase current and gas flow rate observed moderate penetration depth in specimen four, five and six as compared to earlier. Finally, the observation made due to low voltage level along with the increased combination of current and flow rate of gas for welding of 1.5 mm thickness sheet is not melt properly or excessive melt. For the next trial with increased voltage level as compared to earlier along with variable current and gas flow rate the scattered depth of penetration in specimen seven, eight and nine found. Finally, this technique revealed some observations such as when voltage and current rises with increase sheet thickness, the penetration depth and bead length rise too. Furthermore, the shielding gas as an argon plays a significant role in influencing penetration depth and bead length. Moreover, the lesser welding speed generates more penetration depth and bead length. Finally, the penetration depth to length ratio rises when voltage and current in lesser level. Subsequently, the weld bead geometry measurement by conventional techniques was validated by extracting texture features of weld bead geometry using GLCM and observed more promising results as compared to the actual experimentation technique. The proposed texture features, such as homogeneity, energy, correlation and contrast releveled promising results of penetration depth. The offered image analysis techniques selected for features extraction and segmentation found precise for measurement of penetration depth and bead length. At last, both techniques found with closer tolerance as shown in Figure 4.19. The outcomes validate features extraction by grey level co-occurrence matrix discovered significantly better than other traditional methods and also fixes critical position evidence promisingly. Several authors projected mathematical models to understand temperature contours in the 304L SS sheet and observed temperature circulation is multipart pointer for weld pool profiles. The determined and through an experiment weld pool error percentage of profiles found 16%–18%, whereas the projected temperature distribution measurement discovered temperature is a delicate pointer of depth of penetration and found error percentage measured up to 2%–4%. The projected work discovered temperature shape falls suddenly neighbouring weld line and accordingly decreases to some extent within the zone isolated from weld portion.

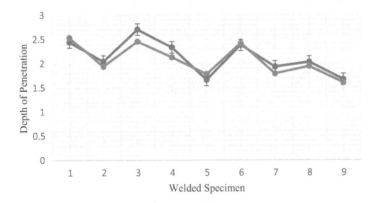

FIGURE 4.19 Measurement of penetration depth through experimentation and GLCM technique.

The thermal conductivity of solid materials upsurges the cooling amount with increased sheet size and increased welding velocity upsurges the cooling proportion too. Finally, the cooling proportion of material dropping with significance to distance from centre weld portion as temperature dispersed is dropping since the grain growth amount sturdily rests on temperature dispersed.

4.8   CONCLUSION

We have found the following observations:

- Grey level co-occurrence matric revealed promising textures feature of weld bead geometry and was found closer to the experimental results.
- Experimental results confirmed the proposed grey level co-occurrence matrix technique by extracting weld seam shape and also determine critical location information.
- Measurement of penetration depth through experimentation and grey level co-occurrence matrix in image processing technique found satisfactorily.
- Experimental results of online temperature measurement found a steady indicator of depth of penetration and that the association is sensitive to assign sensor places.

REFERENCES

1. G. A. Bestard, S. C. A. Alfaro, "Measurement and estimation of the weld bead geometry in arc welding processes: the last 50 years of development", *Journal of the Brazilian Society of Mechanical Sciences and Engineering*, vol. 40, (2018), 1–19.
2. A. K. Singh, V. Dey, R. N. Rai, T. Debnath, "Weld bead geometry dimensions measurement based on pixel intensity by image analysis techniques", *Journal of the Institution of engineers (India); Series C*, vol. 100 (2019), 379–384.
3. G. A. Bestard, R. C. Sampaio, J. A. R. Vargas, S. C. A. Alfaro, "Sensor fusion to estimate the depth and width of the weld bead in real time in GMAW processes", *Sensors*, vol. 18, no. 962, (2018), 1–26.
4. J. E. Pinto-Lopera, J. M. S. T. Motta, "Real-time measurement of width and height of weld beads in GMAW processes", *Sensors*, vol. 16, (2016), 1–14.
5. L. Soares, A. Weis, B. Guterres, R. Rodrigues, S. Botelho, "Computer vision system for weld bead analysis," In *Proceedings of the 13th International Joint Conference on Computer Vision, Imaging and Computer Graphics Theory and Applications*, Portugal, vol. 4, (2018), 402–409.
6. T. F. Comas, C. Diao, J. Ding, S. Williams, Y. Zhao, "A passive imaging system for geometry measurement for the plasma arc welding process," *IEEE Transactions on Industrial Electronics*, vol. 64, no. 9, (2017), 7201–7209.
7. P. Ghanty, S. Paul, D. P. Mukherjee, M. Vasudevan, N. R. Pal, A. K. Bhaduri, "Modelling weld bead geometry using neural networks for GTAW of an Austenitic stainless steel," *Science and Technology of Welding and Joining*, vol. 12, no. 7, (2017), 649–658.
8. R. V. Patil, Y. P. Reddy, "Correlation Assessment of Weld Bead Geometry and Temperature Circulation by Online Measurement in Nd: YAG Laser Welding", In *Advances in Engineering Materials. Lecture Notes in Mechanical Engineering.* Springer, Singapore. https://doi.org/10.1007/978-981-33-6029-7_3

9. M. A. Moradpour, S. H. Hashemi, K. Khalili, "Machine vision implementation for off-line measurement of weld bead geometry in API X65 pipeline steel," *University POLITEHNICA of Bucharest Scientific Bulletin Series D*, vol. 76, no. 4, (2014), 138–148.

10. N. Chandrasekhar, M. Vasudevan, A. K. Bhaduri, T. Jayakumar, "Intelligent modeling for estimating weld bead width and depth of penetration from infra-red thermal images of the weld pool, *Journal of Intelligent Manufacturing*, vol. 26, (2013), 59–71.

11. S. Chokkalingham, N. Chandrasekhar, M. Vasudevan, "Predicting the depth of penetration and weld bead width from the infra-red thermal image of the weld pool using artificial neural network modeling," *Journal of Intelligent Manufacturing*, vol. 23, (2012), 1995–2001.

12. Y. Q. Wei, N. S. Liu, X. Hu, X. Ai, "Phase-correction algorithm of deformed grating images in the depth measurement of weld pool surface in gas tungsten arc welding," *Optical. Engineering*, vol. 50, no. 5, (2011), 57209-1–57209-6.

13. J. F. Wang, H. D. Yu, Y. Z. Qian, R. Z. Yang, S. B. Chen, "Feature extraction in welding penetration monitoring with arc sound signals," *Journal of Engineering Manufacture, Proceedings of the Institution of Mechanical Engineers Part B*, vol. 225, (2011), 1683–1691.

14. P. Ghanty, S. Paul, A. Roy, D. P. Mukherjee, N. R. Pal, M. Vasudevan, H. Kumar, A. K. Bhadur, "Fuzzy rule-based approach for predicting weld bead geometry in gas tungsten arc welding," *Science and Technology of Welding and Joining*, vol. 13, no. 2, (2008), 167–175.

15. B.Y. K. Liu, W. J. Zhang, Y. M. Zhang, "Estimation of weld joint penetration under varying GTA pools," *Welding Journal*, vol. 92, (2013), 313s–321s.

16. Y. He, Y. Xu, Y. Chen, H. Chen, "Weld seam profile detection and feature point extraction for multi-pass route planning based on visual attention model", *Robotics and Computer Integrated Manufacturing*, vol. 37, (2016), 251–260.

17. B. Z. Jin, H. Li, Q. Wang, H. Gao, "Online measurement of the GMAW process using composite sensor technology," *Welding Journal*, vol. 96, (2017), 133–142.

18. A. Sumesh, K. Rameshkumar, K. Mohandas, R. Shyam Babu, "Use of machine learning algorithms for weld quality monitoring using acoustic signature", *Procedia Computer Science*, vol. 50, (2015), 316–322.

19. B. Pathak, D. Barooah, "Texture analysis based on the grey level co-occurrence matrix considering possible orientations," *International Journal of Advanced Research in Electrical, Electronics and Instrumentation Engineering*, vol. 2, no.9, (2013), 7–12.

20. H. N. M. Shah, Z. Kamis, M. Sulaiman, M. Z. A. Rashid, M. S. M. Aras, A. Ahmad, "Characteristics of butt-welding imperfections joint using co-occurrence matrix," *Indian Journal of Geo Marine Sciences*, vol. 48, no. 7, (2019), 1164–1169.

21. R. V. Patil, Y. P. Reddy, "Weld imperfection classification by texture features extraction & local binary pattern," *Smart Innovation, System and Technologies*, vol. 206, no. 1, (2020), 367–378.

22. R. V. Patil, Y. P. Reddy, "Multi class weld defect detection and classification by support vector machine and artificial neural network," *Smart Innovation, System and Technologies*, vol. 206, no. 1, (2020), 429–438.

23. R. V. Patil, Y. P. Reddy, "An autonomous technique for multi class weld imperfections detection and classification by support vector machine," *Journal Nondestruction Evaluation*, vol. 40, (2021), 1–33.

24. Z. Wang, C. Zhang, Z. Pan, Z. Wang, L. Liu, X. Qi, S. Mao, J. Pan, "Image segmentation approaches for weld pool monitoring during robotic Arc welding," *Applied Science*, vol. 8, no. 2445, (2018), 1–16.

25. K. N. Lankalapalli, J. F. Tu, K. H. Leong, M. Gartner "A model for estimating penetration depth of laser welding processes," *Journal of Applied Physics*, vol. 29, (1996), 1831–1841.

26. G. J. Shannon, W. M. Steen, "Investigation of keyhole and melt pool dynamics during laser butt welding of sheet steel using a high-speed camera," *Proceeding ICALEO'* Florida, (1992), 130–138.

27. D. E. Hardt, Katz J. M., "Ultrasonic measurement of weld penetration," *Welding Journal*, (1984), 218S–273S.

28. C. M. John, *Welding Journal*, (1985).

29. I. Miyomoto, K. Mori, "Properties of keyhole plasma in Co_2 laser welding", *Proceeding ICALEO*, California, (1995).

30. M. Watanabe, H. Okado, "Features of various in process monitoring and their applications to laser welding," *Proceeding ICALEO*, Florida, (1992), pp. 553–562.

5 Industrial Informatics Cache Memory Design for Single Bit Architecture for IoT Approaches

Reeya Agrawal and Neetu Faujdar
GLA University, Mathura

CONTENTS

DOI: 10.1201/9781003154518-5

5.1 INTRODUCTION

In the mid-90s, the decision by Intel to include six transistors static random access memory cell (STSRAMC) in its manufacturers caused damage to worldwide independent STSRAMC suppliers. The largest STSRAMC (PC Cache) demand disappeared overnight, leaving only a few niche applications. Higher pricing and density constraints greatly limited the STSRAMC value proposal as a high-efficiency memory (lower access time, reduced standby power consumption). Since STSRAMC is equipped with four to six cell transistors, Dynamic Random-Access Memory Cells (DRAMCs) and the Flash memories cannot match (both have one transistor per cell); smaller transistors are equipped to reduce board density and lower costs per cell [1]. STSRAMC is thus an inefficient option for conventional storage applications – which represent 98% of the industry. After Intel began incorporating STSRAMCs, most STSRAMC vendors either shut down or diversified their product portfolios beyond STSRAMCs. STSRAMC uses high performance, often in manufacturing, automobile and defence areas, shifts to particular applications [2]. Apart from being more economical, it was also a superior approach from a technical point of view – embedded STSRAMCs have more excellent access time than external STSRAMCs because access is the main element for cache memories (Figures 5.1 and 5.2).

As processors get more robust, they need to boost cache memory accordingly. However, increasing embedded cache memory for each new process node simultaneously becomes a rising challenge. This means that the number of transistors per centimeter square is vast for smaller process nodes [5].

5.1.1 THE RETURN OF STSRAMS TO MAINSTREAM EMBEDDED DESIGN

The irony of the return to STSRAMCs is that it's being driven by a reversal of the clear trend that aimed to replace it. When Intel opted to incorporate STSRAMC, this was a prudent route to follow. Incorporated STSRAMCs have better access time than external STSRAMCs as access time is the essential component in the cache memory

FIGURE 5.1 Technologies associated with IoT. (Reproduced from Li et al. [3] under the terms of the Creative Attribution Commons License 4.0 (CC-By 4.0). https://creativecommons.org/licenses/by/4.0/.)

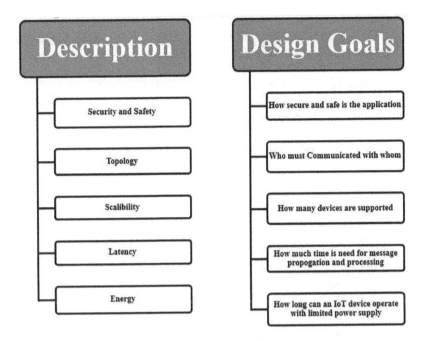

FIGURE 5.2 Design consideration for industrial IoT applications. (Reproduced from Gehrmann et al. [4], with permission from Springer Nature. Copyright (2021).)

but is also technologically more cost-effective [6]. As central processing units (CPUs) get more robust, they need to enhance cache memory accordingly. That indicates that the number of transistors per centimetre square is huge with fewer process nodes [7].

The STSRAMC region is more vulnerable to defects due to process variations because of the decrease in bit cells and higher transistor density. These defects reduce the processor chip's total performance [8].

5.1.2 Consumption of Power Increases

STSRAMC transistors will be sized smaller than the logical transistors if the STSRAMC bit cells are the exact sizes as the bit logic cells. The scale of the transistors increases the leakage current, and hence the standby electricity demand rises. This problem can be addressed in two ways. One will have separate process technology nodes in a chip processor or device for STSRAMC and logic areas. This will lead to a case where the STSRAMC is an essential part of a processor. The reason the processor chip should be shrunk will be defeated in such a situation. Another way will be the processor or controller to isolate the STSRAMC. Any technical advances are now accelerating this option [9].

5.1.3 Wearable Electronics STSRAMCs

Today's world contains a broad spectrum of microcontroller units (MCUs). A big surge in portable computing is the technology we are seeing now. Size and strength are essential considerations for wearables such as smartwatches and fitness bands. Due to the restricted board size, the MCU must be very compact and work on the smooth power supplied by portable batteries. The on-chip cache is constrained to meet the above specifications. In this case, the on-chip store is short, and an external supply is required [10]. STSRAMCs will be the most suitable choice for acting as an external cache for all memory options available. This comes out of comparison with DRAMC and lowers access time as DRAMC and Flash because of their lower stationary power usage. STSRAMCs would need to adapt to fit into the small wearable boards. Current STSRAMC parallel problems include:

- too many pins necessary for MCU communications
- too big for printed circuit board (PCB) fitting.

5.1.4 STSRAMCs AND INTERNET OF THINGS

For recent decades, the STSRAMC space has been split into two distinct commodity families – swift and low power, each with its own set of characteristics, applications, and costs. The systems used by STSRAMCs need to be high-speed or medium, but not both. However, demand for high-performance devices with low electricity usage for complex operations when using portable electricity is growing. A new wave of medical equipment, manual instruments, consumer electronics products, networking systems, and industrial controls drives this market across IoT [11]. IoT development is conducted in two different ways – intelligent wearables and automation. STSRAMCs with a minimal footprint and low power consumption would be better serviced for wearables as described earlier. In parallel, the effect on industrial, economic, big-scale, and the automation of individual homes into large manufacturers, and whole cities can be felt across the Internet of Things. In IoT implementations, STSRAMCs can maintain high-speed power while reducing energy consumption in a bit of packet. Microcontrollers from many important players, through specific modes like Deep Power-Down and Deep-Sleep, have already adapted to the evolving needs of these transversal systems. The peripherals and memory modules can also save power during these modes [12].

With the expansion of the VLSI industry, there is an increasing need for mobile devices and battery-operated embedded systems. Approximately 60%–70% of a chip's area is taken up by cache memory, which is critical for data execution. Microprocessor speed decreases as chip usage rises [13]. Because one million transistors increase and degrade the efficiency of a single chip failure rate, the industry is attempting to develop a fast and efficient memory circuit to help with VLSI system development. In this article, the focus is on the sensory amplifier. Cache memories currently use more than half of the transistors in high-performance microprocessors, and this proportion is expected to rise in the future [14].

Consequently, the development of low-power, high-performance computers was given significant focus. The device can use STSRAMC memory cells that are the correct size for the system's requirements because they are integrated within the STSRAMC. Efficiency gains occur when speed and power are increased. SA is a critical component that responds to high frequency in all STSRAMC memory blocks. The setting of SA [15] determines the access time and power consumption of the memory. As an energy-operated circuit, SA speeds up a signal transmission from a memory cell's perimeter logic circuit and converts any number of Boolean logic levels to digital logic levels [16]. Their output greatly influences memory access time and overall memory capacity degradation. Using complementary metal-oxide-semiconductor (CMOS) memories, as with other integrated circuits (ICs), may improve speed, power, and heat dissipation. These objectives are opposed in terms of SA memory architecture [17]. As memory capacity increases, the bit-line parasite space also expands in most cases. Increasingly power-hungry memory has led to a rise in this bit line [18]. Agricultural, medical industrial, and internet-of-things uses of semiconductors have increased in the rising trend of a VLSI industry. Power consumption also rises as the IC's functional properties improve with time [19]. Today's modern technology necessitates the use of products with minimal power dissipation. As a result of the minimal number of plugs surrounding portable handles, they require a powerful battery backup system that consumes less energy when inactive [20].

Simple SA's are cross-coupled CMOS inverter types. Both the input and the output lines are active at the same time. Delay and power both dissipate a lot of energy. Because portable handle devices have fewer power plugs in the vicinity, they require a large battery backup that uses less energy when not in use; the memory cell and all of the STSRAMC blocks are essential in this work, even if STSRAMC SA does not attract widespread attention in modern technology [21]. STSRAMC and DRAMC material are read using sense amplifiers principally. According to their theory, an appropriate noise spectrum and high-quality information are what they mean by a memory cell's substance. They have a high noise threshold. Many circuits require immediate sense amplifiers to achieve low latency, with memory bit-line reading being the most prevalent use [22,23].

5.2 LITERATURE SURVEY

Zhao et al. developed carbon nanotube field transistors in a ternary STSRAMC sensory amplifier in a novel proposal. The CNFET chirality controls the threshold voltage to grasp ternary logic. Simulation on HSPICE at 0.9V compares the results with a conventional ternary DRAMC and ternary STSRAMC [24].

Pahuja et al. described three distinct power reduction schemes in the STSRAMC and Charge-Recycling, Power Gating, and low-energy architecture incorporated in this article. This documentation contains 45 nm technology, showing that the average power decreased by one-tenth in amplifier design and decreased reading and write cycle latency of 64-bit SRAMC Array Architecture [25].

Kyung et al. described system-on-chip (SOC) models that have been noted for providing a set of multi-port memory IP blocks supporting multiple simultaneous operations in the same memory bank to increase performance. Conventional 2-read/write 8T dual-port STSRAMC (2RW) has read and type troubles when both words are simultaneously activated in a single row. 1-read, 1-write 8T dual-port cells (1R1W) mitigate reading disruption by preventing load shared with internal storage nodes when the read word line is activated [26].

YoungBac et al. VLSI circuits, mainly STSRAMCs used to form the SOC cache, are increasingly concerned about leakage power consumption in deep-submicron technology. This research proposes an 8T SRAM with low leakage power based on Carbon Nanotube Field-Effect Transistors [27].

Stefan et al. ICs are more prone to transistor ageing with chronic downgrades in C_{MOS} technology due to biassed temperature instability. We compare the BTI effect in three modes, including low power (LP), middle power/output (MP), and high power, using a variety of voltages and supply temperatures (HP). The three prototypes' SD is estimated for various working loads using 45 nm technology [28].

Bingyan et al. CMOS technology improve while transistor variations and incompatibilities increase, leading to the larger offset voltage. Broad offset voltage, higher dynamic power utilization through a reading process, and degradation of the correct decision rate of sensing and running speed can all improve speed. Because of transistor threshold voltage inaccuracy, the offset voltage is the essential measure for STSRAMC sense amplifiers (SAs). The author advocated using an approach known as digitizing multiple body bias offset cancellation. The threshold voltage mismatch of SA transistors in this system is corrected digitally and continuously by altering the body-biased voltage [29].

Mottaqiallah et al. reported that a lot of work is published in STSRAMC on influences from BTI, but many papers concentrate only on collecting a memory cell. SRAMC also includes peripheral circuits such as address decoders, sense enhancements, and so on. This paper discussed the cumulative impact of BTI on the sensory amplifier of various technology nodes and changes in voltage temperature. For a range of tasks, the assessment measure is tested. This paper provides a quantification of BTI's better influence on all technology scaling parameters in comparison to past work [30].

ByungKy et al. described that due to increased procedure variances and a reduction in supply tension, the read yield was discovered to be deteriorating. The author proposes a LOC-SA (latch offset sensory amplifier) that cancels the latch offset function, leading to considerable voltage growth time decreases and sensing speed increases [31].

Hanwool et al. described the increase in efficiency and minimization of power consumption using the same pull-up PMOS transistor to detect and pre-load the bit line. The guard employs a bit-line leak compensator with a minimum operating voltage [32].

5.3 MOTIVATION AND OVERVIEW

The modern Digital system requires high-speed memories to store and retrieve a large amount of data. The 90% region of a chip is occupied by memory by 2017 by the 2002 ITRS (International Technology Roadmap for Semiconductor). The operating speed increases; the chip size also increases, so the power consumption by the circuit becomes very important [33]. Increasingly, the speed of the VLSI chip is constrained by the signal latency of long interconnection lines. When using Current Differential Sense Amplifier (CDSA) rather than Voltage Differential Sense Amplifier (VDSA) signal transport methods, significant speed and power changes are feasible [34]. The memory cell size can also be minimized with the current mode sensing. Since most memory-related activities are read operations, the memory's net power dissipation is significantly reduced. SA's dissipates a significant amount of short circuit power, a considerable amount of dynamic control [35].

5.4 PROBLEM STATEMENT

One of the critical problems when developing a VLSI device is power dissipation. Dynamic power was the single biggest problem up to a specific time; but, as the scale of the technology function shrinks, static power as emotional power has become an important issue. However, suppose transistors are allowed to float. In that case, a device may have to wait a long time to consistently recover the missing state and suffer severely degraded performance for a device that needs a quick response even though in an inactive state; maintaining a state is therefore essential. Once again, the sleepy keeper process has excellent pace requirements but more static and dynamic capacity than the sleepy stack is needed.

5.5 THE NEED FOR LOW POWER VLSI DESIGN

Power consumption in VLSI is still a big challenge as feature size shrinks and chip density and operation frequency increase [36]. It causes overheating, which decreases the chip lifetime and degrades the efficiency of the portable systems. The need for optimizing power consumption in a chip is intensified because of mobile networking devices and computer systems. As moving towards integrating VLSI circuits, the demand for low power grows day by day. Many aspects influence the power usage in the circuits [37,38].

- C_{BL} increases as the number of memory cells per bit-line increases, while R_{BL} increases as the bit-line length increases.
- Current records are lowered when more memory is incorporated on a single chip for heavy capacity. This results in a lower voltage swing on the bit-line and a rise in C_{BL}.
- Low supply voltage results in a lower margin of noise.

5.6 CACHE MEMORY DESIGN FOR SINGLE BIT STSRAM SA ARCHITECTURE

On STSRAMC transistor sizing, these two specifications place contrasting requirements [39] (Figure 5.3).

5.6.1 CWD WORKING AND SCHEMATIC

The write-enabled signal (WE) enables CWD to pull the bit-line down from the pre-charge stage. CWD uses five P_{MOS} (P_{M1}, P_{M2}, P_{M3}, P_{M4}, P_{M5}) and five N_{MOS} (N_{M1}, N_{M2}, N_{M3}, N_{M4}, and N_{M5}). If WE let the input data make one transistor PM_1 or NM_1, a strong 0 is added as BTL and BTL_{BAR} are discharged from the pre-charge to the ground stage [40] (Figure 5.4).

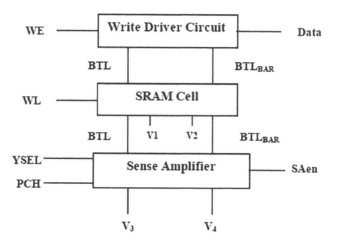

FIGURE 5.3   Single bit STSRAMC SA architecture functional block diagram.

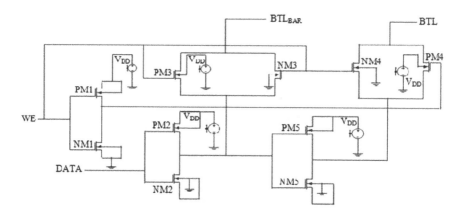

FIGURE 5.4   CWD schematic. (Reproduced from Geethumol et al. [41] under the terms of the Creative Attribution Commons License 4.0 (CC-By 4.0). https://creativecommons.org/licenses/by/4.0/.)

5.6.2 STSRAMC WORKING AND SCHEMATIC

For a variety of reasons, the design considerations of STSRAMC are relevant. First, the architecture of the STSRAMC is essential for the safe and robust functioning of the STSRAMC [42]. Secondly, the STSRAMC designers are inspired to increase the packing density thanks to their continuous effort to improve the storage capacity of chips. The STSRAMC, therefore, needs to be as small and as stable, quick, powerful, and yield constraints as possible. The word line defines modes of operation. When all transistors are removed, and cells are separated [43]. The word line pulls high (WL=high) for reading and writes functions that allow access to access transistors (N_{M8} and N_{M9}) to be enabled (Figure 5.5).

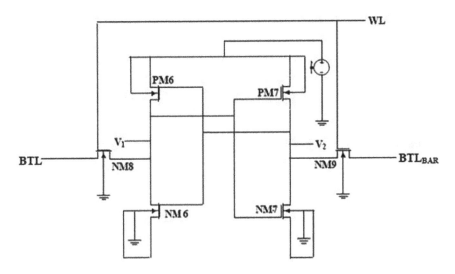

FIGURE 5.5 STSRAMC schematic. (Reproduced from Arora, et al. [44], under the terms of the Creative Attribution Commons License 4.0 (CC-By 4.0). https://creativecommons.org/licenses/by/4.0/.)

5.6.3 SENSE AMPLIFIERS

SA is a critical component of in-memory architecture. A new circuit class has emerged due to the wide variety of SAs found in semiconductor memories and their impact on the final design requirements. STSRAMCs don't require data to refresh circuits after sensing, so long as the operation is non-destructive [45]. It is of two types:

(i) Differential Sense Amplifier (DSA)
(ii) Latch Sense Amplifier (LSA)

5.6.3.1 DSA

Metal oxide semiconductor (MOS) sense amplifier circuits incorporate all of the components required for differential sensing. Using an amplifier, famous noise may be filtered out, and the actual difference between the two indicators is magnified. Due to large power dispersion and an inherent high offset, the main difference amplifier is not in memories because of the slow operation rate [46].

5.6.3.1.1 VDSA Working and Schematic

A voltage differential is created using BTL and BTLBAR pairs when the word line is pulled high. The sense amplifier is removed high (SA_{EN}), which causes the cross-coupled inverter to enter into a positive feedback loop to convert its differentials to maximum rail output, triggered when the appropriate differential depends on technology and circuit [47]. The sense amplifier output node connecting with the bit-line is zero while the other output SA_1 stays elevated with a lower voltage, e.g., SA_2. N_{MOS} (N_{M10} and N_{M11}) go into saturation when the sense amplifier is activated. The V_{DD}

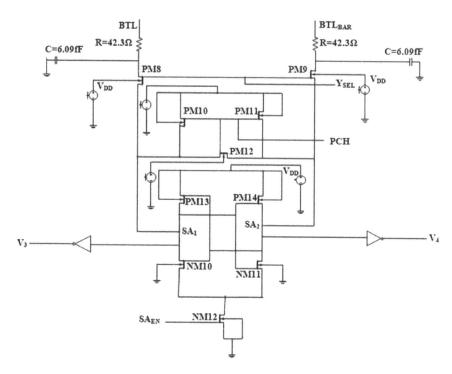

FIGURE 5.6 VDSA schematic. (Reproduced from Agrawal and Tomar [49], with permission from Elsevier. Copyright (2021).)

input voltage of the entire NM_{11} device is higher than the V_{gs} voltage of the NM_{10} device. There is a continuous positive feedback loop until the voltage SA_2 is low enough for device NM_{12} to enter the linear zone and turn on the other inverter's PM_{13} to push the output very far [48] (Figure 5.6).

5.6.3.1.2 CDSA Working and Schematic

This can minimize bit-line power pre-charge. The current mode sense amplifier functions in two steps: pre-charge and evaluation [50]. The bit lines are pre-loaded by a pre-charge circuit which attaches to the bit lines during the pre-loading stage. The SA_1 and SA_2 sense amplifier output nodes are pre-loaded by P_{MOS} devices P_{M12} and P_{M13}. The P_{M12} and P_{M17} devices are ON during pre-loading, equalizing the sensing circuit inputs and outputs. Y_{SEL} is pulled low ($Y_{SEL} = $ low) and ($SA_{EN} = $ high) during the evaluation phase [51]. A high benefit positive feedback amplifier forms the cross-connected inverters made of P_{M14}, P_{M15}, N_{M10}, and N_{M11}. Because of the positive feedback, either N_{M10} or N_{M11} are impeded to the N_{M10} or N_{M11} source terminal, resulting in N_{M10} and N_{M11} beginning to source a portion of the difference. The power nodes are not connected to high-capacity bit lines, and they can react quickly, contrary to the sense amplifier. On bit lines, the CDSA will swing lower voltage [52] (Figure 5.7).

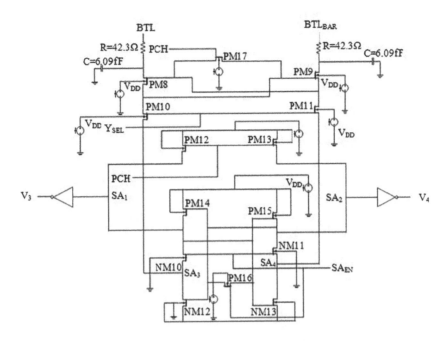

FIGURE 5.7 Current differential sense amplifier schematic. (Reproduced from Agrawal and Tomar [49], with permission from Elsevier. Copyright (2021).)

5.6.3.1.3 CTDSA Working and Schematic

CTDSA works by redistributing high-capacity bit lines to low-capacity amplifier output nodes [53,54]. Because of the following equation, the voltage produced across the first element and its capabilities will equalize to a series of interactions between two capacitive elements in a charging device the voltage product across the second element and its voltage potential:

$$V_{SMALL}C_{SMALL} = Q = V_{LARGE}C_{LARGE}$$

Therefore, the voltage increase is achieved because a small voltage change over the sizeable capacitive element causes a more considerable voltage change across the minor capacitive component [55] (Figure 5.8).

5.6.3.2 LSA

Pre-loading and equalizing the LSA in the high-gain metastable area are the first steps in the sensing process. Because an LSA does not separate its inputs and outputs, insulation transistors are required to prevent a 0-bit line from being completely unloaded, which consumes more power and time [57].

5.6.3.2.1 VLSA Working and Schematic

Pass transistors NM_{12}, PM_8, and PM_9, are turned on when the WL=High, but they are turned off when the sense amplifier signal is applied [58]. The random bit on the

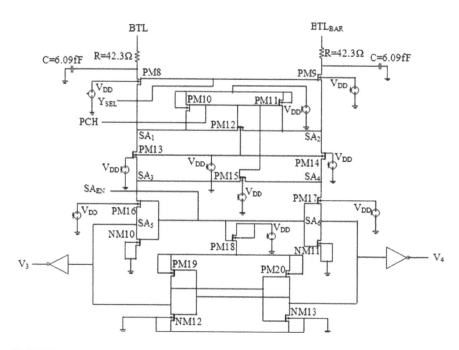

FIGURE 5.8 CTDSA schematic. (Reproduced from Agrawal and Goyal [56], with permission from Springer Nature. Copyright (2021).)

internal nodes of the sense amplifier has a suitable voltage difference as the differential on the bit lines grows. When the SA_{EN} sensing amplifier signal is asserted, the PM_{10}, NM_{10}, PM_{11}, and NM_{11} cross-linked inverters increase the differential voltage to its maximum swing output [59] (Figure 5.9).

5.6.3.2.2   CLSA Working and Schematic

SA is a critical circuit in cache memory design. In the reading process, one bit-line is released while the other bit-line is kept at a voltage that supplies power to the processor [61]. SA_{EN} is pulled high if both SA_1 and SA_2 begin discharge at high outputs. This results in a higher N_{M12} power than N_{M13} due to its higher V_{gs}. This makes it possible to discharge the V_3 output faster than the V_4. When the sense amplifier signal is low enough to power ON P_{MOS} device P_{M16}, the powerful positive feedback loop is triggered, which causes SA_2 to be recharged and its output isolated from its inputs [62] (Figure 5.10).

5.7   METHODOLOGY

The fundamental operational approach for leakage power reduction methods is covered in this section, such as Power Reduction Sleep Transistor Technique, Power Reduction Dual Sleep Technique, Power Reduction Forced Stack Technique, and

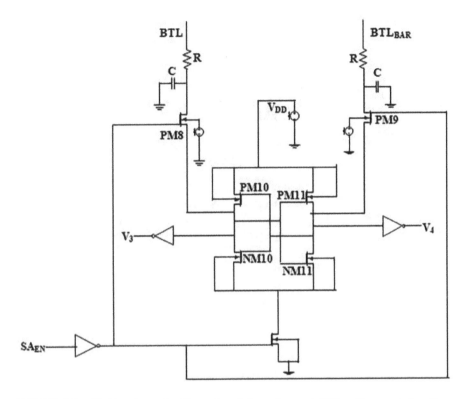

FIGURE 5.9 VLSA schematic. (Reproduced from Agrawal [60], with permission from Springer Nature. Copyright (2021).)

Power Reduction Sleep Stack Technique, which have been used to evaluate various parameters in the STSRAMC circuit [63,64]:

(i) State saving
(ii) State destructive

5.7.1 POWER REDUCTION SLEEP TRANSISTOR TECHNIQUE

The sleep transistor technique is the most widely used to reduce power consumption. Between V_{DD} and the pull-up network in a circuit, P_{MOS} is used in the sleep transistor approach I between the pull-down network and GND in-circuit, N_{MOS} is used [65] (Figures 5.11 and 5.12).

5.7.2 POWER REDUCTION DUAL SLEEP TECHNIQUE

The area requirements for this approach are maximized by using four transistors: two P_{MOS} and two N_{MOS}. Two extra pull-up and pull-down transistors in sleep mode in either an OFF or ON state have implemented the power reduction dual sleep technology [66].

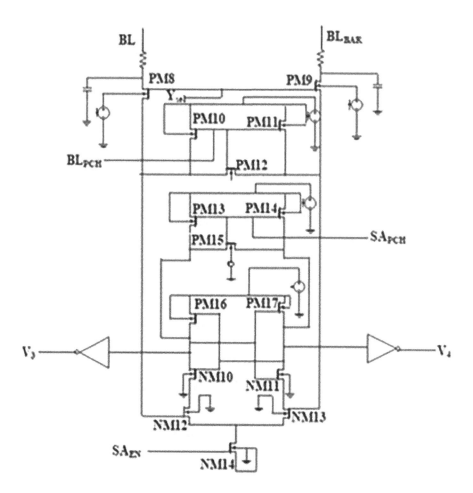

FIGURE 5.10 CLSA schematic. (Reproduced from Agrawal [60], with permission from Springer Nature. Copyright (2021).)

5.7.3 Power Reduction Sleepy Stack Technique

Another way to reduce power consumption is to use the stack method, which reduces the size of an existing transistor into two half-sized transistors. The generated inversion distance between the two transistors minimizes the leakage current by switching off concurrently [67] (Figures 5.13 and 5.14).

5.7.4 Power Reduction Forced Stack Technique

In this technique, both mos have the same input. In this technique, when PM_0 is in the active region, NM_0 is in the cut-off part [68–70]. Due to this, the circuit doesn't have a power supply, which helps to consume less power.

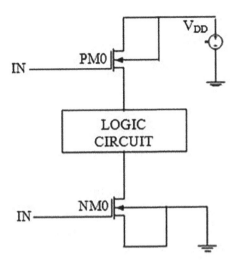

FIGURE 5.11 Power reduction sleep transistor technique schematic. (Reproduced from Agrawal and Tomar [49], with permission from Elsevier. Copyright (2021).)

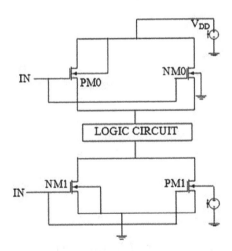

FIGURE 5.12 Power reduction dual sleep technique schematic. (Reproduced from Agrawal and Tomar. [49], with permission from Elsevier. Copyright (2021).)

5.8 RESULT AND DISCUSSION

This chapter discusses the methodology and results. As the feature size of technology decreases, the threshold voltage of MOS decreases because of the scale down the threshold voltage MOS transistor is turned on at a lower voltage. Hence,

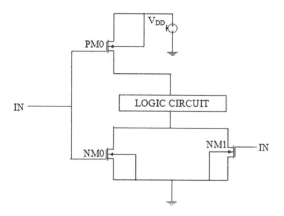

FIGURE 5.13 Power reduction sleepy stack technique schematic. (Reproduced from Agrawal and Tomar [49], with permission from Elsevier. Copyright (2021).)

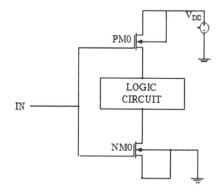

FIGURE 5.14 Power reduction forced stack technique schematic. (Reproduced from Agrawal and Tomar [49], with permission from Elsevier. Copyright (2021).)

the delay of the circuit decreases, and the power dissipation as the supply voltage decreases.

5.8.1 Simulation of Single Bit STSRAMC VDSA Architecture

In the schematic, internal node voltages out and outb are initialized with the logic 0 and 1. The pre-charge circuitry uses the low PCH signal to charge both bit lines. SA is activated when SA_{EN} = high, which is a digital signal (Figure 5.15).

CWD output waveform can be described in four cases (Figures 5.16–5.18):

Case 1: WE are low, and Data is low BTL = high and BTL_{BAR} = high,
Case 2: WE are high, Data is low, BTL = low, and BTL_{BAR} = high.
Case 3: Data is high and WE are low, BTL = BTL_{BAR} = high/2,
Case: 4 Data is high, WE are high, BTL = high, and BTL_{BAR} = low.

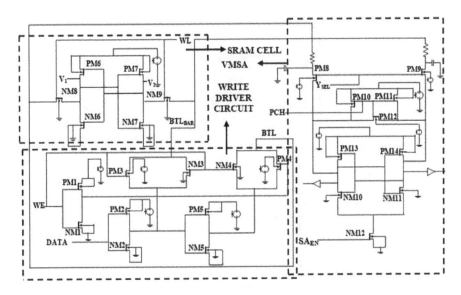

FIGURE 5.15   Single bit STSRAMC VDSA architecture schematic.

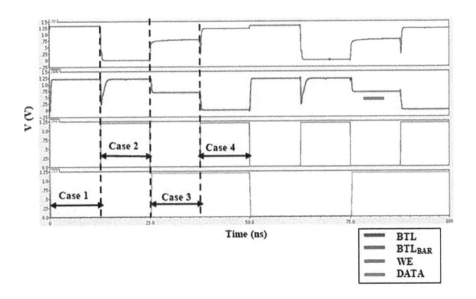

FIGURE 5.16   CWD output waveform.

5.8.2   Simulation of Single Bit **STSRAMC CDSA** Architecture

Signal activated the sense amplifier when SA_{EN} is high. A Precharge signal (PCH) is used to pre-charge the bit lines to equalize the potential on both bit lines. In the schematic, the internal node voltages V_1 and V_2 are initialized with logic 0 and 1 (Figures 5.19–5.22).

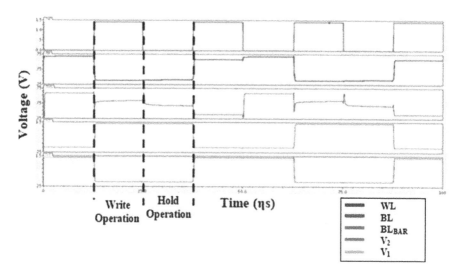

FIGURE 5.17   STSRAMC output waveform.

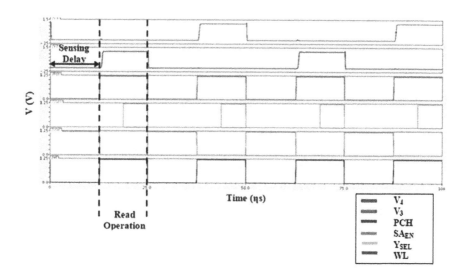

FIGURE 5.18   Single bit STSRAMC VDSA architecture output waveform.

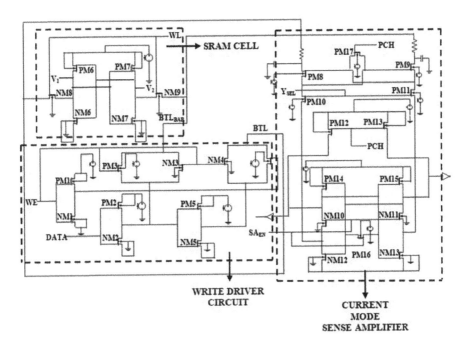

FIGURE 5.19 Single bit STSRAMC CDSA architecture schematic.

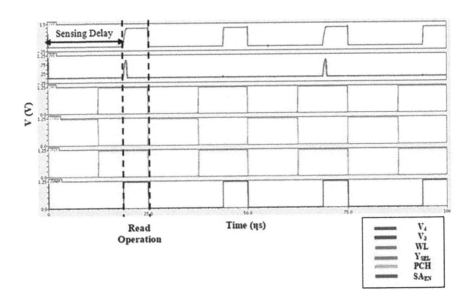

FIGURE 5.20 Single bit STSRAMC CDSA architecture output waveform.

5.8.3   SIMULATION OF SINGLE BIT **STSRAMC CTDSA** ARCHITECTURE

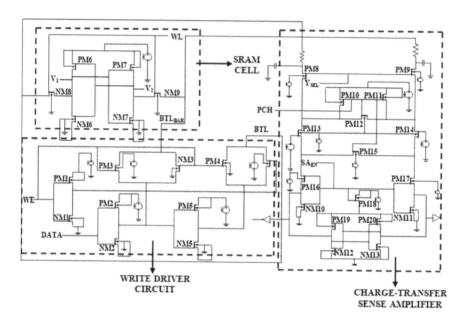

FIGURE 5.21   Single bit STSRAMC CTDSA architecture schematic.

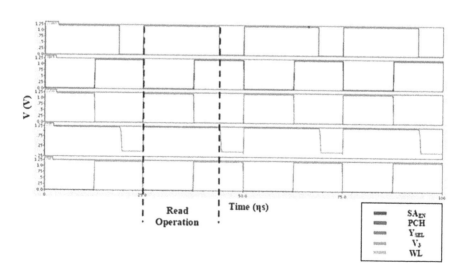

FIGURE 5.22   Single bit STSRAMC CTDSA architecture output waveform.

5.8.4 SIMULATION OF SINGLE BIT STSRAMC VLTSA ARCHITECTURE

The input bit lines establish a voltage differential on the circuit's internal nodes, which the circuit architecture relies on directly (Figures 5.23–5.29 and Tables 5.1–5.5).

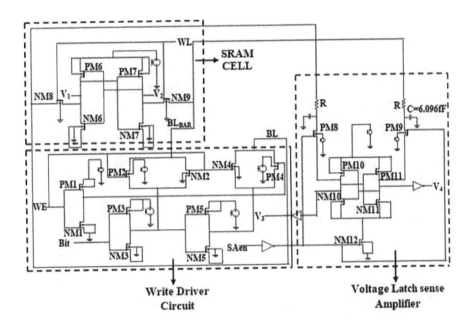

FIGURE 5.23 Single bit STSRAMC VLTSA architecture schematic.

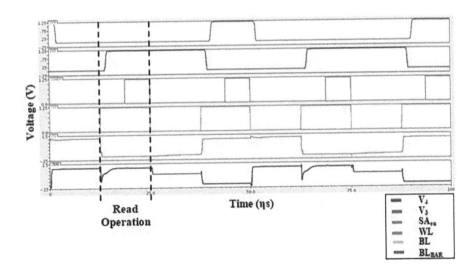

FIGURE 5.24 Single bit STSRAMC VLTSA architecture output waveform.

5.8.5   Simulation of Single Bit STSRAMC CLTSA Architecture

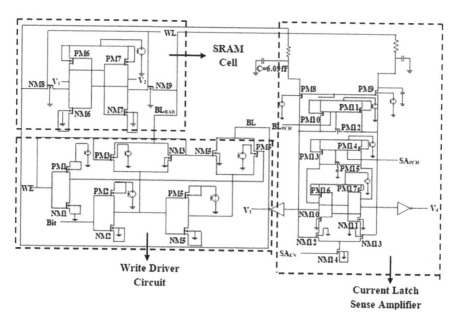

FIGURE 5.25   Single bit STSRAMC CLTSA architecture schematic.

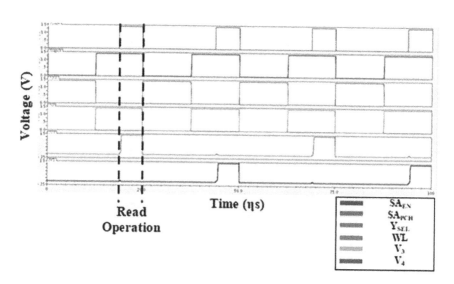

FIGURE 5.26   Single bit STSRAMC CLTSA architecture output waveform.

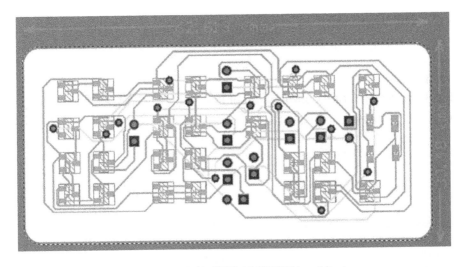

FIGURE 5.27 Chip design of single bit STSRAMC VDSA architecture.

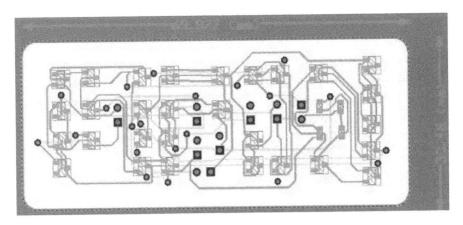

FIGURE 5.28 Chip design of single bit STSRAMC CDSA architecture.

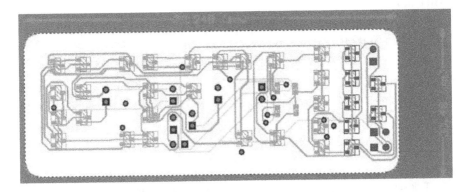

FIGURE 5.29 Chip design of single bit STSRAMC CTDSA architecture.

5.9 COMPARISON TABLE

TABLE 5.1
Single Bit Architecture Consumption of Power at $R = 42.3$ Ω, $V_{DD} = 1.2$ V

S. No	Parameters Architecture	NoT	DiS (ηs)	CoP (μW)
1	SBSVDSA	30	13.51	13.16
2	SBSCDSA	33	18.81	16.44
3	SBSCTDSA	37	18.95	44.63
4	SBSVLSA	29	13.50	36.57
5	SBSCLSA	35	18.68	26.78

CoP, consumption of power; NoT, number of transistors; DiS, delay in sensing; SBSVDSA, single bit STSTAMC VDSA architecture; SBSCDSA single bit STSRAMC CDSA architecture; SBSCTDSA, single bit STSRAMC CTDSA architecture; SBSVLSA, single bit STSRAMC VLSA architecture; SBSCDSA, single bit STSRAMC CLSA architecture.

TABLE 5.2
Single Bit Architecture Consumption of Power at $V_{DD} = 1.2$ V, $R = 42.3$ KΩ

S. No	Parameters Architecture	NoT	DiS (ηs)	CoP (μW)
1	SBSVDSA	30	13.51	11.34
2	SBSCDSA	33	18.81	18.81
3	SBSCTDSA	37	18.95	33.63
4	SBSVLTSA	29	13.50	14.32
5	SBSCLTSA	35	18.68	73.92

TABLE 5.3
Single Bit Architecture Consumption of Power When PRT Applying on VDSA, at $C = 6.09$ fF, and $R = 42.3$ KΩ

S. No	Techniques Over VDSA in Architecture	Single Bit STSRAMC VDSA Architecture		
		NoT	DiS (ηs)	CoP (μW)
1	PRSST	32	13.51	11.29
2	PRFST	32	13.70	11.29
3	PRSST	33	13.50	11.29
4	PRDST	34	13.66	11.03

PRSST, power reduction sleep transistor technique; PRFST, power reduction forced stack technique; PDSST, power reduction sleep stack technique; PRDST, power reduction dual sleep technique.

TABLE 5.4

Single Bit Architecture Consumption of Power on Applying PRT Over STSRAMC at $C = 6.09$ fF, and $R = 42.3$ KΩ

S. No	Techniques over STSRAMC in Architecture	Single Bit STSRAMC VDSA Architecture		
		NoT	DiS (ηs)	CoP (μW)
1	PRSST	32	13.12	9.18
2	PRFST	32	13.64	9.10
3	PRSST	33	13.36	10.38
4	PRDST	34	13.51	10.13

TABLE 5.5

Single Bit Architecture Consumption of Power on Applying PRT Over STSRAMC and VDSA at $C = 6.09$ fF and $R = 42.3$ KΩ

S. No	Techniques Over STSRAMC and VDSA in Architecture	Single Bit STSRAMC VDSA Architecture		
		NoT	DiS (ηs)	CoP (μW)
1	Sleep transistor	34	12.75	9.27
2	Forced stack	34	13.14	9.20
3	Sleepy stack	36	12.75	8.46
4	Dual sleep	38	13.34	9.74
5	STSRAMC (forced stack) + VDSA (dual sleep)	36	12.14	8.078

5.10 CONCLUSION AND FUTURE SCOPE

In cache memory architecture, CWD, STSRAMC, and different types of sense amplifiers such as VDSA, CDSA, CTDSA, VLSA, and CLSA have been described in this chapter, as well as all architectures with different SA's implemented over cadence tool and power dissipation of all architectures have been calculated. In this chapter, cache memory architecture (CMA) with varying types of SA such as VDSA, CDSA, CTDSA, VLSA, and CLSA has been implemented and compared on different values of resistance (R) with other parameters such as consumption of power (CoP), delay in sensing (DiS) and a number of transistors (NoT). Results depicted that CMA having VDSA consumes the lowest power consumption (11.34 μW). Furthermore, techniques of power reduction (TPR) such as power reduction sleepy sleep transistor technique (PRSTT), power reduction sleepy forced stack technique (PRFST), power reduction sleepy stack technique (PRSST), and power reduction dual sleep technique (PRDST) are applied over different blocks of CMA to optimize power consumption. The conclusion arises that STSRAMC with forced stack technique and VDSA with dual sleep technique in CMA consumes the least power. It is also observed that VDSA has the lowest area, 30.48×62.613 mm^2, compared to other SAs. In the future scope, this work can be done in the form of an array. A conclusion arise that CDSA with PRT consumes low power, but VDSA consumes the most insufficient power among all SA. So, in STSRAMC Array Architecture, researchers can use these amplifiers, and the power dissipation through the circuit can be further reduced by using other TPR. Researchers also implemented STSRAMC with forced stack technique in array in CMA.

5.11 ABBREVIATIONS

STSRAMC   Six Transistor Static Random-Access Memory Cell
VLTSA   Voltage Latch Type Sense Amplifier
CLTSA   Current Latch Type Sense Amplifier
VDSA   Voltage Differential Sense Amplifier
CDSA   Current Differential Sense Amplifier
CTDSA   Charge Transfer Differential Sense Amplifier
TPR   Techniques of Power Reduction
CMDSBA   Cache Memory Design for Single Bit Architecture
DSA   Differential Sense Amplifier
LSA   Latch Sense Amplifier
PRSTT   Power Reduction Sleepy Sleep Transistor Technique
PRFST   Power Reduction Sleepy Forced Stack Technique
PRSST   Power Reduction Sleepy Stack Technique
PRDST   Power Reduction Dual Sleep Technique
DiS   Delay in Sensing
CoP   Consumption of Power
NoT   Number of Transistors
CMA   Cache Memory Architecture
VLSI   Very Large Integrated Circuit
ICs   Integrated Circuits
CMOS   Complementary Metal Oxide Semiconductor
DRAMCs   Dynamic Random Access Memory Cells
CPUs   Central Processing Units
MCUs   Microcontroller Units
PCB   Printed Circuit Board

REFERENCES

1. Eslami, N., B. Ebrahimi, E. Shakouri, et al. "A Single-Ended Low Leakage and Low Voltage 10T SRAM Cell with High Yield." *Analog Integrated Circuits and Signal Processing* 105.2 (2020): 263–274.
2. Bazzi, H., A. Harb, H. Aziza, et al. "RRAM-Based Non-Volatile SRAM Cell Architectures for Ultra-Low-Power Applications." *Analog Integrated Circuits and Signal Processing* 106.2 (2020): 351–361.
3. Da Xu, L., W. He, S. Li. "Internet of Things in Industries: A Survey." *IEEE Transactions on Industrial Informatics* 10.4 (2014): 2233–2243.

4. Flügel, C., V. Gehrmann. "Scientific Workshop 4: Intelligent Objects for the Internet of Things: Internet of Things-Application of Sensor Networks in Logistics." *Communications in Computer and Information Science* 32 (2009): 16–26.
5. Pal, S., S. Bose, A. Islam. "Design of SRAM Cell for Low Power Portable Healthcare Applications." *Microsystems Technologies* 28 (2020): 833–844. Doi: 10.1007/s00542-020-04809-6
6. Wang, W., U. Guin, A. Singh. "Aging-Resilient SRAM-Based True Random Number Generator for Lightweight Devices." *Journal of Electronic Testing* 36 (2020): 301–311.
7. Khan, M. A., K. A. Abuhasel. "Advanced Metameric Dimension Framework for Heterogeneous Industrial Internet of Things." *Computational Intelligence* 37.3 (2020): 1367–1387.
8. Abuhasel, K. A., M. A. Khan. "A Secure Industrial Internet of Things (IIoT) Framework for Resource Management in Smart Manufacturing." *IEEE Access* 8 (2020): 117354–117364.
9. Simopoulos, T., et al. "Simultaneous Accessing of Multiple SRAM Subregions Forming Configurable and Automatically Generated Memory Fields." *International Journal of Circuit Theory and Applications* 49.7 (2021): 2238–2254.
10. Dounavi, H., Y. Sfikas, Y. Tsiatouhas. "Periodic Aging Monitoring in SRAM Sense Amplifiers." *2018 IEEE 24th International Symposium on On-Line Testing and Robust System Design (IOLTS)*, Platja d'Aro, 2018, pp. 12–16.
11. Pathak, A., D. Sachan, H. Peta, M. Goswami. "A Modified SRAM Based Low Power Memory Design." *2016 29th International Conference on VLSI Design and 2016 15th International Conference Embedded Systems (VLSID)*, Kolkata, 2016, pp. 122–127.
12. He, Y., J. Zhang, X. Wu, X. Si, S. Zhen, B. Zhang. "A Half-Select Disturb-Free 11T SRAM Cell with Built-In Write/Read-Assist Scheme for Ultralow-Voltage Operations." *IEEE Transactions on Very Large-Scale Integration (VLSI) Systems* 27.10 (2019): 2344–2353.
13. Fragasse, R., et al. "Analysis of SRAM Enhancements through Sense Amplifier Capacitive Offset Correction and Replica Self-Timing." *IEEE Transactions on Circuits and Systems I: Regular Papers* 66.6 (2019): 2037–2050.
14. Gupta, S., K. Gupta, B. H. Calhoun, N. Pandey. "Low-Power Near-Threshold 10T SRAM Bit Cells with Enhanced Data-Independent Read Port Leakage for Array Augmentation in 32-nm CMOS." *IEEE Transactions on Circuits and Systems I: Regular Papers* 66.3 (2019): 978–988.
15. Sridhara, K., G. S. Biradar, R. Yanamshetti. "Subthreshold Leakage Power Reduction in VLSI Circuits: A Survey." *2016 International Conference on Communication and Signal Processing (ICCSP)*, Melmaruvathur, 2016, pp. 1120–1124.
16. Jeong, H., T. W. Oh, S. C. Song, S.-O. Jung. "Sense-Amplifier-Based Flip-Flop with Transition Completion Detection for Low-Voltage Operation." *IEEE Transactions on Very Large-Scale Integration (VLSI) Systems* 26.4 (2018): 609–620.
17. Pandey, S., S. Yadav, K. Nigam, D. Sharma, P. N. Kondekar. "Realization of Junctionless TFET-Based Power Efficient 6T SRAM Memory Cell for the Internet of Things Applications." *Proceedings of First International Conference on Smart System, Innovations and Computing.* Springer, Singapore, 2018, pp. 515–523.
18. Tao, Y., W. Hu. "Design of Sense Amplifier in the High-Speed SRAM." *2015 International Conference on Cyber-Enabled Distributed Computing and Knowledge Discovery*, Xi'an, 2015, pp. 384–387.
19. Kondapally Madhava Rao, D., M. Tiwari. "Local Bitline 8t Differential Sram Architecture Based on 22 Nm Finfet for Low Power Operation." *Annals of the Romanian Society for Cell Biology* 25.4 (2021): 3404–3418.
20. Lv, J., et al. "A Read-Disturb-Free and Write-Ability Enhanced 9T SRAM with Data-Aware Write Operation." *International Journal of Electronics* 109.1 (2021): 23–37.

21. Tamilarasan, A. K., D. S. Edward, A. S. T. Sarasam. "KLECTOR: Design of Low Power Static Random-Access Memory Architecture with reduced Leakage Current." (2021). https://doi.org/10.21203/rs.3.rs-232660/v1.

22. Mishra, J. K., H. Srivastava, P. K. Misra, M. Goswami, "A 40nm Low Power High Stable SRAM Cell Using Separate Read Port and Sleep Transistor Methodology." *2018 IEEE International Symposium on Smart Electronic Systems (iSES) (Formerly iNiS)*, Hyderabad, 2018, pp. 1–5.

23. Arora, D., A. K. Gundu, M. S. Hashmi. "A High-Speed, Low Voltage Latch Type Sense Amplifier for Non-Volatile Memory." *2016 20th International Symposium on VLSI Design and Test (VDAT)*, Guwahati, 2016, pp. 1–5.

24. Liu, Z., T. Pan, S. Jia, Y. Wang, "Design of a Novel Ternary SRAM Sense Amplifier Using CNFET." *12th International Conference on ASIC (ASICON)*, Guiyang, 2017, pp. 207–210.

25. Vashist, G., H. Pahuja, B. Singh, "Design and Comparative Analysis of Low Power 64-Bit SRAM and Its Peripherals using Low-Power Reduction Technique." *5th International Conference on Wireless Networks and Embedded Systems (WECON)*, Rajpura, 2017, pp. 1–6.

26. Zhang, Y., Z. Wang, C. Zhu, L. Zhang, A. Ji, L. Mao. "28nm Latch Type Sense Amplifier Coupling Effect Analysis." *2016 International Symposium on Integrated Circuits (ISIC)*, Singapore, 2016, pp. 1–4.

27. Kim, Y.B., Q. Tong, K. Choi, "Novel 8-T CNFET SRAM Cell Design for the Future Ultra-low Power Microelectronics." *IEEE International SOC Design Conference (ISOCC)*, Jeju, 2016, pp. 243–244.

28. Cosemans, S., F. Catthoor. "Comparative BTI Analysis for Various Sense Amplifier Designs." *IEEE 19th International Symposium on Design and Diagnostics of Electronic Circuits & Systems (DDECS)*, Kosice, 2016, pp. 1–6.

29. Liu, B., J. Cai, J. Yuan, Y. Hei. "A Low Voltage SRAM Sense Amplifier with Offset Cancelling Using Digitized Multiple Body Biasing." *IEEE Transactions on Circuits and Systems II* 64 (2016): 442–446.

30. Taouil, M., S. Hamdioui. "Integral Impact of BTI and Voltage Temperature Variation on SRAM Sense Amplifier." *IEEE 33rd VLSI Test Symposium (VTS)*, Napa, CA, 2015, pp. 1–6.

31. Jong, B., T. Na, J. Kim. "Latch-Offset Cancellation Sense Amplifier for Deep Submicron STT-RAM." *IEEE Transaction on Circuits and System-I: Regular Paper* 62.7 (2015): 1776–1784.

32. Jeong, H., T. Kim, K. Kang. "Switching PMOS Sense Amplifier for High-Density Low-Voltage Single-Ended SRAM." *IEEE Transaction on Circuits and Systems-I: Regular Paper* 62.6 (2015): 1555–1563.

33. Gajjar, J. P., Zala, A. S., S. K. Aggarwal. "Design and Analysis of 32-Bit SRAM Architecture in 90nm CMOS Technology." *International Research Journal of Engineering and Technology* 3.4 (2016): 2729–2733.

34. Vanama, K., R. Gunnuthula, G. Prasad. "Design of Low Power Stable SRAM Cell." *2014 International Conference on Circuit Power and Computing Technologies (ICCPCT)*, Nagercoil, 2014, pp. 1263–1267.

35. Saun, S., H. Kumar. "Design and Performance Analysis of 6T SRAM Cell on Different CMOS Technologies with Stability Characterization." *IOP Conference Series: Materials Science and Engineering* 561 (2019) 012093.

36. Bhaskar, A. "Design and Analysis of Low Power SRAM Cells." *2017 Innovations in Power and Advanced Computing Technologies (i-PACT)*, Vellore, 2017, pp. 1–5.

37. Tao, Y.-P., W. Hu. "Design of Sense Amplifier in the High-Speed SRAM." *International Conference on Cyber-Enabled Distributed Computing and Knowledge Discovery*, Xi'an, 2015, pp. 384–387.

38. Sinha, M., S. Hsu, A. Alvandpour, W. Burleson, R. Krishnamurthy, S. Borhr. "High-Performance and Low-Voltage Sense-Amplifier Techniques for Sub-90nm SRAM." *Proceedings of the IEEE International [Systems-on-Chip] SOC Conference*, Portland, OR, 2003.

39. Dutt, R., M. Abhijeet. "High-Speed Current Mode Sense Amplifier for SRAM Applications." *IOSR Journal of Engineering* 2 (2012): 1124–1127.

40. Wang, Y., F. Zhao, M. Liu, Z. Han. "A New Full Current-Mode Sense Amplifier with Compensation Circuit." 2011 9th IEEE International Conference on ASIC, Xiamen, 2011, pp. 645–648.

41. Geethumol, T., K. Sreekala, P. J. I. Dhanusha. "Power and Area Efficient 10T SRAM with Improved Read Stability." *ICTACT, Journal on Microelectronics* 3.1 (2017): 337–344.

42. Heller, L., D. Spampinato, Y. Yao. "High-Sensitivity Charge-Transfer Sense Amplifier." *IEEE International Conference on Solid-State Circuits. Digest of Technical Papers*, 1975. https://doi.org/10.1109/JSSC.1976.1050808.

43. Na, T., S. Woo, J. Kim, H. Jeong, S. Jung. "Comparative Study of Various Latch-Type Sense Amplifiers." *IEEE Transactions on Very Large-Scale Integration (VLSI) Systems* 22.2 (2014): 425–429.

44. Arora, D., A. K. Gundu, M. S. Hashmi. "A High-Speed Low Voltage Latch Type Sense Amplifier for Non-volatile Memory," 2016 20th International Symposium on VLSI Design and Test (VDAT), Guwahati, 2016, pp. 1–5.

45. Schinkel, D., E. Mensink, E. Klumperink, E. van Tuijl, B. Nauta. "A Double-Tail Latch-Type Voltage Sense Amplifier with 18ps Setup+Hold Time." *2007 IEEE International Solid-State Circuits Conference. Digest of Technical Papers*, San Francisco, CA, 2007, pp. 314–605.

46. Tripathi, V. M., S. Mishra, J. Saikia, A. Dandapat. "A Low-Voltage 13T Latch-Type Sense Amplifier with Regenerative Feedback for Ultra Speed Memory Access." *2017 30th International Conference on VLSI Design and 2017 16th International Conference on Embedded Systems (VLSID)*, Hyderabad, 2017, pp. 341–346.

47. Hemaprabha, A., K. Vivek. "Comparative Analysis of Sense Amplifiers for Memories." *2015 International Conference on Innovations in Information, Embedded and Communication Systems (ICIIECS)*, Coimbatore, 2015, pp. 1–6.

48. Jefremow, M., et al., "Time-Differential Sense Amplifier for Sub-80mV Bit Line Voltage Embedded STT-MRAM in 40nm CMOS." *2013 IEEE International Solid-State Circuits Conference Digest of Technical Papers*, San Francisco, CA, 2013, pp. 216–217.

49. Agrawal, R., V. Tomar. "Analysis of Cache (SRAM) Memory for Core i™ 7 Processor." *2018 9th International Conference on Computing, Communication and Networking Technologies (ICCCNT)*, Bengaluru, 2018, pp. 1–8.

50. Ahmad, S., B. Iqbal, N. Alam, M. Hasan. "Low Leakage Fully Half-Select-Free Robust SRAM Cells with BTI Reliability Analysis." *IEEE Transactions on Device and Materials Reliability* 18.3 (2018): 337–349.

51. Reddy, B. N. K., K. Sarangam, T. Veeraiah, R. Cheruku. "SRAM Cell with Better Read and Write Stability with Minimum Area." *TENCON 2019-2019 IEEE Region 10 Conference (TENCON)*, Kochi, 2019, pp. 2164–2167.

52. Surkar, A., V. Agarwal. "Delay and Power Analysis of Current and Voltage Sense Amplifiers for SRAM at 180nm Technology." 2019 3rd International Conference on Electronics, Communication, and Aerospace Technology (ICECA), Coimbatore, 2019, pp. 1371–1376.

53. Pasuluri, B., et al. "Design of CMOS 6T and 8T SRAM for Memory Applications." *Proceedings of Second International Conference on Smart Energy and Communication*, Springer, Singapore, 2021.

54. Sheu, M. H., et al. "Stable Local Bit-Line 6 T SRAM Architecture Design for Low-Voltage Operation and Access Enhancement." *Electronics* 10.6 (2021): 685.

55. Dinesh Kumar, J. R., et al. "Performance Investigation of Various SRAM Cells for IoT Based Wearable Biomedical Devices." *Inventive Communication and Computational Technologies*, Springer, Singapore, 2021, 573–588.

56. Agrawal, R., V. Goyal. "Analysis of MTCMOS Cache Memory Architecture for Processor." In Proceedings of International Conference on Communication and Artificial Intelligence, Springer, Singapore, 2021, pp. 81–91.

57. Shiba, K., et al. "A 3D-Stacked SRAM Using Inductive Coupling Technology for AI Inference Accelerator in 40-nm CMOS." *Proceedings of the 26th Asia and South Pacific Design Automation Conference*, 2021. https://doi.org/10.1145/3394885.3431642

58. Agrawal, R., V. K. Tomar. "Analysis of Low Power Reduction Techniques on Cache (SRAM) Memory." *2018 9th International Conference on Computing, Communication, and Networking Technologies (ICCCNT)*, IEEE, Bengaluru, 2018.

59. Agrawal, R. "Cache Memory Architecture for Core Processor." *Proceedings of International Conference on Advanced Computing Applications*, Springer, Singapore, 2022.

60. Agrawal, R. "Comparative Study of Latch Type and Differential Type Sense Amplifier Circuits Using Power Reduction Techniques." *International Conference on Microelectronic Devices, Circuits and Systems*. Springer, Singapore, 2021 pp. 269–280.

61. Agrawal, R. "Analysis of Cache Memory Architecture Design Using Low-Power Reduction Techniques for Microprocessors." *Recent Advances in Manufacturing, Automation, Design, and Energy Technologies*, Springer, Singapore, 2022, pp. 495–503.

62. Agrawal, R. "Low-Power SRAM Memory Architecture for IoT Systems." *Recent Advances in Manufacturing, Automation, Design, and Energy Technologies*, Springer, Singapore, 2022, pp. 505–512.

63. Agrawal, R., N. Faujdar, A. Saxena. "Low Power Single-Bit Cache Memory Architecture." *IOP Conference Series: Materials Science and Engineering* 1116.1 (2021): 012136.

64. Agrawal, R., V. K. Tomar. "Implementation and Analysis of Low Power Reduction Techniques in Sense Amplifier." *2018 Second International Conference on Electronics, Communication and Aerospace Technology (ICECA)*, IEEE, Coimbatore, 2018.

65. Carvalho, D. R., A. Seznec. "Understanding Cache Compression." *ACM Transactions on Architecture and Code Optimization (TACO)* 18.3 (2021): 1–27.

66. Applegate, M. C., D. Aronov. "Flexible Use of Memory by Food-Caching Birds in a Laboratory Behavioural Paradigm." *bioRxiv* (2021).

67. Ghose, M., and H. K. Kapoor. "WeiSub: Weighted Subset-based Cache Replacement Policy for Last Level Caches." *2021 12th International Conference on Computing Communication and Networking Technologies (ICCCNT)*, IEEE, Kharagpur, 2021.

68. Zou, Y., et al. "ARES: Persistently Secure Non-Volatile Memory with Processor-Transparent and Hardware-Friendly Integrity Verification and Metadata Recovery." *ACM Transactions on Embedded Computing Systems* 1.1 (2021): 1–32.

69. Kommareddy, V. R., et al. "DeACT: Architecture-Aware Virtual Memory Support for Fabric Attached Memory Systems." *2021 IEEE International Symposium on High-Performance Computer Architecture (HPCA)*, Seoul, IEEE, 2021.

70. Kang, Z., et al. "Coloring Embedder: Towards Multi-Set Membership Queries in Web Cache Sharing." *IEEE Transactions on Knowledge and Data Engineering*, 2021. https://doi.org/10.1109/TKDE.2021.3062182.

6 The Bending Behavior of Carbon Fiber Reinforced Polymer Composite for Car Roof Panel Using ANSYS 21

Mohd Faizan
MMMUT

Swati Gangwar
NSUT

CONTENTS

DOI: 10.1201/9781003154518-6

103

6.1 INTRODUCTION

Composites are materials that are composed of two different substances: matrix and reinforcement. Two phases together work on a macroscopic scale and improve the characteristics of composites. Composites are heterogeneous mixtures of two dissimilar substances with different compositions, properties, and morphology [1]. The characteristics of composites differ from their single components depending on where they were produced. Because of their better characteristics, such as reduced weight, improved surface finished, corrosion resistance, high tensile strength and higher fatigue strength, they are widely used in various applications[2]. The main aim is to concentrate on the benefits of various biomedical applications in relation to different manufacturing techniques of the polymer matrix-based composite materials. Polymer matrix-based composites are widely used in several biomedical fields, mainly in the synthesis of artificial body parts, dental applications, tissue engineering, and regenerative medicine. When the matrix is synthetic polymer or natural biopolymer and the reinforcement substances are taken from natural fibers, polymer composites offer good mechanical properties and can be used in various biomedical fields [3].

The fibers of biobased origin are mostly naturally occurring fibers derived from plant origins. This kind of polymer matrix-based composites is bioefficient and environmentally friendly, biodegradable, recyclable lightweight and comparatively cheap. Wood fibers are divided into two types: crystal cellulose fibers, which are generally less common, and hardwood and soft wood fibers [4]. Fibers that are not obtained from wood are made up of lignin and cellulose, which have good mechanical and physical properties and are used in various industries. Composites containing natural fibers help in the recovery of living body tissues or the transformation of undeveloped parts of the living body, and they were used in the past. The combination of several components that can enhance some required characteristics and outperform the individual single component [5].

Polymer matrix-based composites consist of two phases, at least one of which is polymer [6]. The combination of these several components results in basic physical characteristics that differ from the individual substance alone [7]. The primary objective that affects making of such kind of substances in vast areas such as construction [8], aerospaces [9] and automotive [10] is the manipulation of their thermal and mechanical properties. Consequently, the importance of highly developed polymer composite materials exceeds on a large scale, such as the thermal and mechanical aspects, allowing different ways to develop a large variety of material processing methods and basic physical properties.

When considering FEM-based concepts, the deformation of an object is approximated using discretized methodology and is mainly utilized in deformation modeling, where the stress-strain relationship for the deformation is controlled by material parameters and constructive model [11]. The finite element method (FEM) describes the maximum deformation for off-road tires caused by contact forces generated by granular terrain while using the coupling method. Discrete element method (DEM) was used to gather information about the discontinuation in properties of the granule sand [12]. The DEM-FEM input parameters form the critical predefined conditions for obtaining real simulation output, particularly in the case of granules [13].

The complex structure is subdivided into smaller parts called as elements, and then the whole analysis required is carried out using proper simulation software. The obtained generated results are then approximated for the whole existing structure, and then the the result is validated.

6.2 MATERIALS

The materials taken for investigation consisted of carbon fiber as a reinforcement and PVC foam, resin polyester and resin epoxy as matrices for simulation of required composite. The combination of carbon fiber and resin epoxy shows high damping property and can be used to minimize the vibration. Carbon fiber offers more strength to the composite.

6.2.1 MATERIALS SPECIFICATIONS

6.2.1.1 Reinforcement

The reinforcement substance, carbon fiber, has a density and Poisson's ratio of $1800\,kg/m^3$ and 0.2, respectively [14].

6.2.1.2 Matrices

(i) **Resin Epoxy**

Resin epoxy is defined as a material that is used for several applications. It has a high damping property when combined with carbon fiber. The density was $1160\,kg/m^3$ and the Poisson's ratio was 0.35 [14].

(ii) **Resin Polyester**

Resin polyester is defined as synthetic resins which is manufactured by the reaction of polyhydric alcohols and dibasic organic acids. The density was $1200\,kg/m^3$ and the Poisson's ratio was 0.316 [14].

(iii) **PVC Foam**

PVC foam is defined as an inter-crossed network of polymers. The density was $60\,kg/m^3$ and the Poisson's ratio was 0.3, respectively [14].

6.3 METHODOLOGY

6.3.1 VARIOUS STEPS INVOLVED IN DESIGNING AND ANALYSIS OF CARBON FIBER REINFORCED POLYMER COMPOSITE

* First, open the ANSYS software and reach to the Workbench platform of the ANSYS software.
* Select the proper analysis system in which analysis needs to be performed. We have selected the Static Structural Analysis for our simulation purpose.
* Click the engineering data option and select the required materials. If material is not listed in the library, then there is option of adding the new material along with their properties.
* After adding the required materials to the engineering data, go to the geometry option and open the design modeler. In this, draw the geometry

required for analysis. Because my analysis is based on a composite, we have made the composite composed of five layers using the add material and add frozen technique. In the case of add material layer, we have selected the reinforcement part, and in the case of add frozen part, we have selected matrix material.

- Moving on to the meshing option, we have meshed the generated composite sample using linear elements to split the structure into various smaller different elements.
- Applied the bending boundary conditions which were required for our analysis purpose.
- Finally, results were generated after the application of boundary conditions and the images of various generated results were saved.

We have performed the three-point bending test using the boundary conditions on the composite sample. The failure model used was based on von mises yield criterion/ equivalent stress yield criterion. This failure model was used to know about the exact deformation and equivalent stress at failure condition so that we can safely use the composite sample for application purpose.

The sample sizes were considered in one -third ratio obtained in dimensions of mobile photovoltaic car roof which has length as 0.48 m, width as 0.33 m and thickness as 0.005 m [15].

6.3.2 COMPOSITE SAMPLE

Sample is composed of alternate five layers of matrix and reinforcement, which can be seen in Figure 6.1. The other two samples were simulated by just changing the

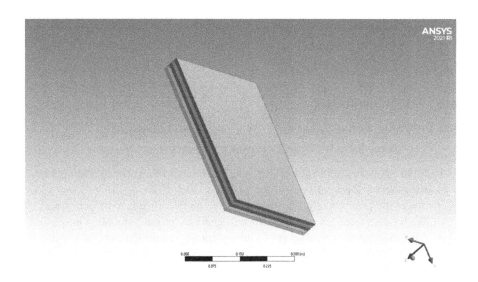

FIGURE 6.1 Composite sample.

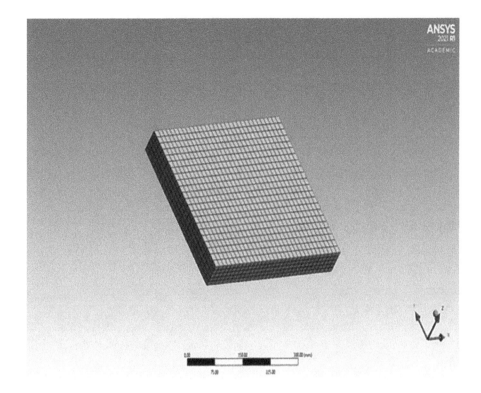

FIGURE 6.2   Meshed composite sample.

matrix materials as resin polyester for second and PVC foam for third sample respectively (Figure 6.1).

6.3.3 MESHING

Linear meshing resulted in 3520 number of elements and 2,6005 number of nodes, as shown in Figure 6.2.

6.3.4 BOUNDARY CONDITIONS

One end is fixed, and the opposite end is given displacement as zero. One of the faces connecting these two ends is subjected to compressive load of 400 N in Z-direction, as shown in Figure 6.3.

6.4   RESULTS AND DISCUSSION

Because we have applied all of the required boundary conditions, the first priority is to know about the result. ANSYS 21 software simulated the composite

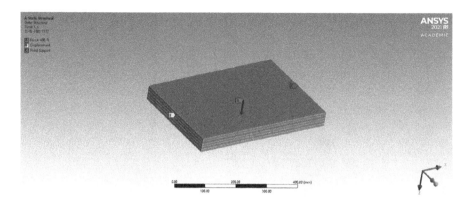

FIGURE 6.3   Boundary conditions.

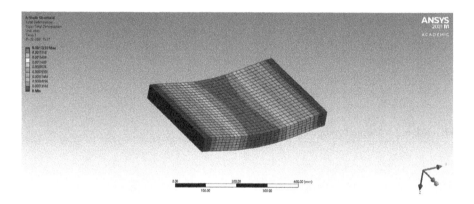

FIGURE 6.4   Bending total deformation for Resin Epoxy Sample.

sample for required results. In result part, we have tried to calculate the total and directional deformation, and also equivalent and normal stresses. Different values of deformation and stress were obtained for the three composite samples. After obtaining the values, we were able to identify the best composite sample out of the three. Fig ures 6.4–6.15 show the result obtained after simulation for the three composite sample.

6.4.1   COMPOSITE SAMPLE HAVING CARBON FIBER AND RESIN EPOXY

The maximum total deformation was 1.7233e-006 m and maximum directional deformation was 1.7222e-006 m, as shown in Figures 6.4 and 6.5.

The maximum equivalent stress was 5.0772e+005 Pa and maximum normal stress was 5.2392e+005 Pa and it has been shown in Figures 6.6 and 6.7.

FIGURE 6.5 Bending directional deformation for Resin Epoxy Sample.

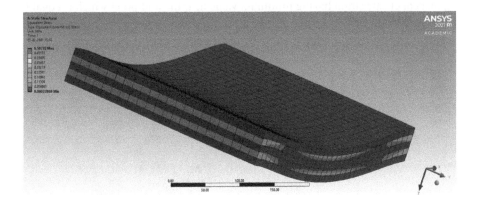

FIGURE 6.6 Bending equivalent stress for Resin Epoxy Sample.

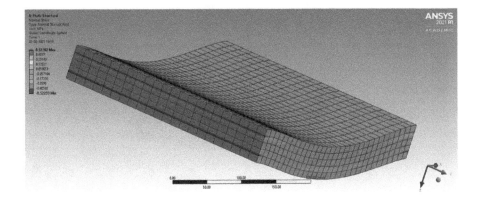

FIGURE 6.7 Bending normal stress for Resin Epoxy Sample.

6.4.2 Composite Sample Having Carbon Fiber and Resin Polyester

The maximum total deformation was 1.9096e-006 m and maximum directional deformation was 1.9086e-006 m, as shown in Figures 6.8 and 6.9.

The maximum equivalent stress was 5.54e+005 Pa and maximum normal stress was 5.7138e+005 Pa, as shown in Figures 6.10 and 6.11.

6.4.3 Composite Sample Having Carbon Fiber and PVC Foam

The maximum total deformation was 2.7458e-007 m and maximum directional deformation was 2.7451e-007 m, as shown in Figures 6.12 and 6.13.

The maximum equivalent stress was 1.6476e+005 Pa and maximum normal stress was 2.0646e+005 Pa, as shown in Figures 6.14 and 6.15.

Krishnamurthy et al. found that after applying a load of 800 N on the leaf spring made up of composite, the maximum value of deformation occurs at mid-point with value 0.20123 mm. Minimum value of deformation occurs on ends denoting equivalent elastic strain having minimum value near the mid-point which is equal to 3.2392e-008 unit [16].

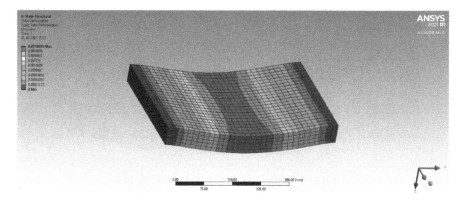

FIGURE 6.8   Bending total deformation for Resin Polyester Sample.

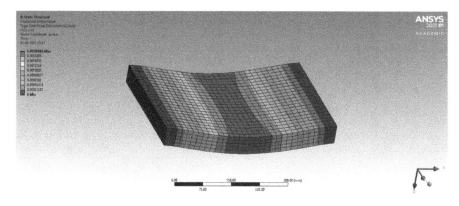

FIGURE 6.9   Bending directional deformation for Resin Polyester Sample.

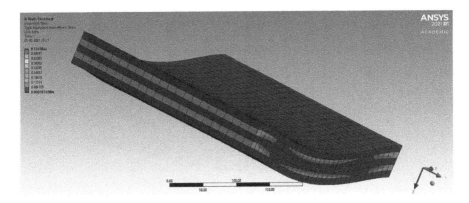

FIGURE 6.10   Bending equivalent stress for Resin Polyester Sample.

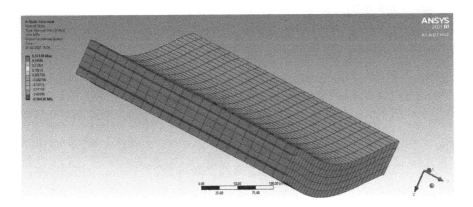

FIGURE 6.11   Bending normal stress for Resin Polyester Sample.

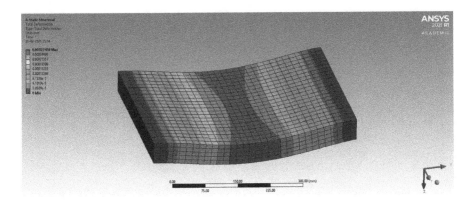

FIGURE 6.12   Bending total deformation for PVC Foam Sample.

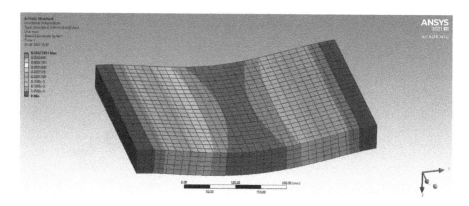

FIGURE 6.13   Bending directional deformation for PVC Foam Sample.

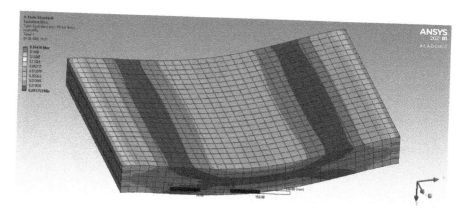

FIGURE 6.14   Bending equivalent stress for PVC Foam Sample.

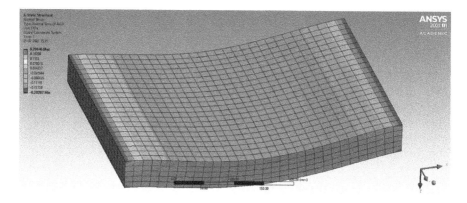

FIGURE 6.15   Bending normal stress for PVC Foam Sample.

6.5 CONCLUSIONS

After performing bending test on three composite samples and obtaining the deformation and stresses values, we can conclude the following.

1. Composite sample having carbon fiber and resin epoxy gave total deformation of 1.7233e-006 m which is smaller when compared with other two composite samples.
2. Composite sample having carbon fiber and PVC Foam gave least maximum value of equivalent stress of 1.6476e+005 Pa and least maximum value of normal stress of 2.0646e+005 Pa when compared with other two composite samples.

So, composite sample having carbon fiber and resin epoxy provided high life cycle because of its smaller total deformation and maximum stress bearing capacity.

REFERENCES

1. I.I. Marhoon, Mechanical properties of composite materials reinforced with short random glass fibers and ceramics particles, *Int. J. Sci. Technol. Res.* 7 (2018) 50–53.
2. R.R. Nagavally, Composite materials-history, types, fabrication techniques, advantages, and applications, *Int. J. Mech. Prod. Eng.* 5 (2017) 82–87.
3. F. Hussain, M. Hojjati, M. Okamoto, R.E. Gorga, Polymer-matrix nano-composites, processing, manufacturing, and application: an overview, *J. Compos. Mater.* 40 (2006) 1551–1575.
4. S. Thirumalini, M. Rajesh, Reinforcement effect on mechanical properties of bio-fiber composite, *Int. J. Civil Eng. Technol.* 8 (2017) 160–166.
5. S. Bavan, M.K.G. Channabasappa, Potential use of natural fiber composite materials in India, *J. Reinf. Plast. Comp.* 29 (2010) 3600–3613.
6. J. Ahmad, *Machining of Polymer Composites*, Springer, Boston, MA, 2009, pp. 1–315, https://doi.org/10.1007/978-0-387-68619-6.
7. K.P. Ashik, R.S. Sharma, A review on mechanical properties of natural fiber reinforced hybrid polymer composites, *J. Miner. Mater. Char. Eng.* 3 (2015) 420–426, https://doi.org/10.4236/jmmce.2015.35044.
8. L.C. Hollaway, M.K. Chryssanthopoulos, S.S.J. Moy (Eds.), *Advanced Polymer Composites for Structural Applications in Construction*, Woodhead Publishing Limited, Sawston, 2004.
9. P.E. Irving, C. Soutis (Eds.), *Polymer Composites in the Aerospace Industry*, Elsevier, 2014, https://doi.org/10.1016/C2013-0-16303-9.
10. K. Friedrich, A.A. Almajid, Manufacturing aspects of advanced polymer composites for automotive applications, *Appl. Compos. Mater.* 20 (2013) 107–128, https://doi.org/10.1007/s10443-012-9258-7.
11. A. Abdulali, I.R. Atadjanov, S. Lee, S. Jeon. Realistic haptic rendering of hyper-elastic material via measurement-based FEM model identification and real-time simulation, *Comput. Graph.* 89 (2020) 38–49, https://doi.org/10.1016/j.cag.2020.04.004.
12. H. Zeng, W. Xu, M. Zang et al. Calibration and validation of DEM-FEM model parameters using upscaled particles based on physical experiments and simulations, *Adv. Powder Technol.*, https://doi.org/10.1016/j.apt.2020.06.044.
13. B.M. Ghodki, M. Patel, R. Namdeo, et al. Calibration of discrete element model parameters: soybeans. *Comput. Particle Mech.* 6 (1) (2019) 3–10.

14. Engineering data properties imported from the in-built software ANSYS 21, version R1.
15. C. Pisantia. Design and energetic evaluation of a mobile photovoltaic roof for cars, *Energy Procedia* 81 (2015) 182–192.
16. K. Krishnamurthy, P. Ravichandran, A. Shahid Naufal, R. Pradeep, K.M. Sai HarishAdithiya. Modeling and structural analysis of leaf spring using composite materials, *Mater. Today: Proc.* 33 (2020) 4228–4232.

7 Sustainable Spare Parts Inventory and Cost Control Management Using AHP-Based Multi-Criterion Framework

Perspective on Petroleum & Fertilizer Industries

Sandeep Sharda and Sanjeev Mishra
Rajasthan Technical University

CONTENTS

DOI: 10.1201/9781003154518-7

7.1 INTRODUCTION

Even today, spare parts inventory control is normally done using the traditional approach of the thumb rule with the almost same degree of consideration by most of the petroleum and fertilizer industries. Normally, procurement of spare parts is first carried out during the project stage along with the equipment as recommended by the manufacturer and does not include a dedicated review by stakeholders. Spare parts inventory magnifies over time as a result of uneven risk consideration by the user department and a lack of team review. Because such industries have an average annual spare parts inventory ranging from 40,000 to 100,000 and associated cost from 100 to 300 million USD, there is a huge scope for controlling sustainable stock levels with the use of tailor-made integrated multi-stock classification. Molenaers et al. (2012) reported in a case study for criticality classification research for spare parts of a petrochemical complex that the physical levels of inventory are more than 100 thousand SKUs with an associated total stock value of about USD 120 million. As shown in Figure 7.1, individual departments are using selective aspects to control spare parts inventory. It leads to a better insight of single dimensions such as frequency of movement of spares and unit price, but it cannot optimize to a sustainable stock level. Multi-criterion classification for spare parts inventory with critical evaluation has become an essential feature for service departments of such industries to lead in terms of economic sustainability. According to a study conducted by Wild (2002), instead of high stock availability, an optimum stock level of spare parts may be ensured.

 Based on Figure 7.1, individual department is keen to control spare parts inventory for their criteria for the same spare parts inventory. The user department tries to safeguard spare parts inventory and may classify equipment based on vital, essential and

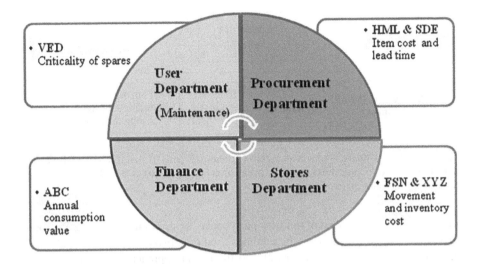

FIGURE 7.1 Various Control Aspect methods used in different departments (framework part). (Individual selective control methods preferably used by different departments by industries i.e.VED, HML, FSN, XYZ and ABC.)

desirable (VED) selective control category irrespective of other criteria. Similarly, the procurement department focuses only on the pricing of spare items and to obtain discounts irrespective of movement and requirement of spare parts over lead time cycle, which is indicated as selective category high, medium and low (HML). Stores department emphasizes spare parts to be stocked based on their movement such as fast, slow and non-moving (FSN), rather than price and impact on plant production. The finance department focuses on the annual consumption value of all spares with the criteria of always better control (ABC) philosophy, which is based on the planned budget by user and procurement department. The disparity in specific considerations for the same spare parts leads to uneven spares inventory levels, procurement cycles and budget variations, all of which have an impact on the total spare parts inventory cost in the warehouse.

An approach of sustainable criteria of cost economics is considered to reduce the total spare parts inventory while ensuring their availability during business-centred maintenance practices. Reducing obsolesces and scraps gathered due to stock of non-moving spare parts at the factory warehouse is also considered. Hence, to overcome the above flaws of the conventional practice of thumb rule and individual selective control aspect, a framework is proposed using an integrated multi-criterion selective micro-level group classifications of spare parts and associated them with an applicable stocking policy. An overall stocking policy considering different scenarios applicable to the industry practice is also developed as a part of the framework.

7.2 REVIEW OF RELEVANT LITERATURE

Three approaches have been undertaken in the review process of literature in order to obtain an overall perspective of a combination of theoretical research base ahead and

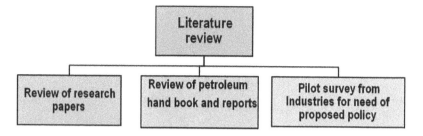

FIGURE 7.2 Literature review approaches (framework part). (Literature review is carried out based on three approaches i.e. review of research papers, review of petroleum handbooks, report, etc. and pilot survey from industries.)

to assess the practical need of industry perspective, as shown in Figure 7.2. Research papers were reviewed to know the methods used over two decades. The study indicates the practice started with bathtub to the recent approach of selective control aspect. A general guideline for total spare parts inventory is also reviewed through the petroleum handbook and related reports. A pilot survey is also conducted through the survey by industry experts to assess the applicability of the multi-criterion classification approach for sustainable needs.

7.2.1 REVIEW OF RESEARCH PAPERS

The focus of research studies from 1985 to 1990 was mainly on repair work and using maintenance bathtub practice to control spares. For example, a scheduled maintenance approach was described by Matta (1985) for armed force equipment on an individual basis or in batched during nonworking time.

Subsequently, research studies were carried out with a reliability approach from 1991 to 1995 to curtail scheduled and uniform maintenance practices and to follow a policy based on the criticality of functional service of equipment. For example, the spare parts stocking policy proposed by Sheikh et al. (1991) considering the parameter of the criticality of equipment, cost of the item and lead time. Criticality was based on the consequences of the failure of equipment. This is categorized into three levels: production loss, system failure and only equipment stoppage. During this period, industries were also using manual bin systems for information, which was later switched over to computerized systems for efficient record keeping. A computer-based inventory spare parts control was proposed by Nagen et al. (1994) indicating better system efficiency over bin system and it provides an auto-trigger for the replenishment. Another study conducted by Vereecke & Verstra et al. (1994) described a linear algorithm, by simulating it using a Poisson distribution for different demand patterns of items by categorizing them based on requirements from stores as lumpy, slow and fast movers. This was conducted for a large chemical plant, located in Belgium. Better control was observed by using a single distribution and comparing the classified group reorder point as demand for 34,000 spare parts items.

Demand forecasting was an added dimension during the period 2006–2009, which was integrated with reliability. Also, a phase of the selective control aspect of inventory was started. Kocaga & Sen (2007) conducted research by categorizing 64 representative parts based on order demand into four categories as critical with immediate and with defined lead time and similarly for non-critical category respectively. The approach of distinguishing lead time reflected 14% of saving in hand inventory and associated cost for a manufacturing unit of capital equipment keeping the same service level in the supply chain (SC). Another research was proposed by Eric & Rommert (2008) by classifying spare parts inventory-based criticality and on different reorder level points with reference to the average consumption pattern for an oil refinery. The results indicate better spare parts inventory control and saving potential in holding cost of about 6.5%. The research was also carried out by Donath et al. (2002) as an initiative of selective control approach by combining two selective categories as fast, slow and non-moving (FSN) along with high, medium and low-value (XYZ) items. The items under the category NX need close monitoring prior to procurement and are kept with sustainable need avoiding longer stay in stores leading to as an obsolete/salvaged. Another research was conducted by Braglia (2004) using the methodology of analytical hierarchy process for multi-attributes of reliability centred maintenance (RCM) to control the spare parts management specially to focus on shortage and leading to stoppage of production units and on the contrary some of the spare parts available in excess which may have stayed for a longer time in stores. A case study conducted for a paper industry revealed the reduction in inventory based on this research.

Research studies conducted from 2010 onward were more or less focused on the selective aspect of inventory control along with reliability and forecasting.

The multi-criterion model approach was illustrated by Bosnjakovic (2010) wherein spare parts were ranked by value usages, criticality and demand pattern and classified based on similar attributes for efficient control and cost reduction. A model of an online condition monitoring system was proposed by Li & Ryan (2011) in predicting the deterioration process of the functioning part for rotating equipment, which was useful research to indicate the demand distribution of parts with time.

A multi-criterion model was proposed by Molenaers et al. (2012) using an analytical hierarchy process with criticality as a governing goal. Criteria considered under this were: probability of item failure, replenishment time, number of potential suppliers and availability of technical specification with output alternatives as VED. The basis of criticality levels classifies spare parts into four categories. The study was conducted for a petrochemical plant and is useful for the rationalization of spare parts inventory. A study conducted by Fu et al. (2012) for controlling the raw materials inventory used in the production using a combination of ABC and EOQ for a company manufacturing hinges and lockers based in Thailand. Another study conducted by Mitra et al. (2013) combined ABC and HML selective control techniques for items producing electric multiple units (EMUs) for a coach manufacturing industry to optimize inventory based on combinations. A combination of VED and FSN control techniques was used by Sanjeev & Ciby (2014) to indicate the scope of better control of spare parts inventory for the chemical industry. Another study was conducted by Roda et al. (2014) in which spare parts were classified based on current needs for a copper mining industry.

A study was carried out by Sagar et al. (2015) for controlling manufacturing parts of a tractor industry with a focus on reducing the inventory waste during processing by using a combination of selective control techniques ABC and VED. An analysis was carried out by Mitra et al. (2015) for a railway coach manufacturing industry, wherein items were categorized into six major categories to differentiate annual requirements to identify and control non-moving items. A study was conducted by Mehrotra & Basukala (2015) for annual medicine consumption using a combination of ABC & VED for a drug store of a hospital to ensure the availability of critical medicine for intensive care unit all the time and reduce the inventory of other items. Another study conducted by Moharana (2015) for classifying spare parts inventory using a multi-criterion approach based on a fuzzy-rule web-based model Fuzzy rule-based multi-criteria inventory control (FRMIC) considering the criteria of consumption value, unit price, replenishment lead time and commonality. The model synergizes with enterprise resource planning (ERP) based on materials management modules (MMM) and generates an optimum stoking level of spare parts required.

A model was proposed by Devarajan & Jayamohan (2016) by combining FSN & XYZ control techniques to analyze and control non-moving and high-value items for a chemical factory. The use of different selective inventory control techniques was explained by Praveen et al. (2016) based on their characteristics & consumption cycle in the pharmacy sector. A conceptual study was conducted by Sharda & Gorana (2016) using a combination of selective control techniques VED and FSN based on petroleum industries. The research was found useful for better and micro-level control of spare parts and future research work. A case study was presented by Keran & Hadad (2016) using ABC classification for a maintenance garage. It was conducted using applicable 57 spare parts and the findings were useful for addressing shortages in some of the items and excess inventory for others. The different approach to spare parts inventory management was illustrated by Salwinder et al. (2016) for effective control from a different perspective and provides a useful indicator for managing spare parts inventory. A conceptual framework, based on the life cycle cost of equipment, was proposed based on the use of spare parts till their economic life by Duran et al. (2016). It reveals the preposition of cash flow and the net present value of spare parts concerning equipment total cost.

An analysis was carried out by Yogesh et al. (2017) using combinations of ABC and HML control techniques for the sponge iron industry. The analysis indicates minimizing the high-value inventory items by critical evaluation of annual consumption. A combination of ABC & VED selective inventory techniques was proposed by Sandeep et al. (2017) for controlling the drug inventory during the lead time and SC network by a pharmacy store to cater to small medical vendors.

A discrete simulation technique was proposed by Zhang et al. (2018) for controlling manufacturing inventory items. This study was conducted for the additive manufacturing industry using demand characteristics for producing different types of additives. Combination of selective techniques VED & ABC analysis was proposed by Jonas & Ming (2018) through a thesis work to control the spare parts inventory and associated holding cost by strategic planning of maintenance action of different systems in the Swedish paper and pulp industry. Teixeira et al. (2018) described a policy for the categorization of spare parts in different groups taking both aspects of maintenance and logistics and classifying them into three levels based on criticality and for managing the lead-time inventory. The study was supported with a pilot case for a multinational manufacturing company.

A multi-item inventory model of the combination of selective inventory control (SIC) and exchange curve(EC) based on the EOQ basic model was suggested by Shenoy & Mal (2019) for a small business perspective of India. The model was developed by combining the characteristics of selective inventory control and the exchange curve. The purpose of the model was to provide a better ordering policy for all items and also involve managers in decision-making. The model was developed for providing a solution that is robust and practical for micro, small and medium enterprises (MSMEs) in India. The study was validated with real cases of inventory items used in the automotive sector by combining ABC, FSN with import and local inventory items categorization and integrating with the exchange curve technique. Different classification based on selective inventory techniques for effective spare parts control was carried out based on different criteria according to the need of a firm by Chandra & Desai (2019). It also includes a literature survey based on selective techniques combination as single-criteria, bi-criteria & multi-criteria for inventory classification. Further, it was revealed that bi-criteria are being utilized mainly in the medical field for considering the criticality of medicines using ABC and VED. Similarly, it was indicated that multi-criteria research studies on inventory control were conducted using Analytical Hierarchy Process (AHP), Fuzzy Analytical Hierarchy Process (FAHP) along ABC analysis conducted mainly for the automotive sector. Another study by Malviya at el. (2020) was conducted for an automobile dealer for 306 spare parts items by integrated classification using selective categories of ABC, XYZ and FSN. It provides a direction for controlling delayed selling items and an indication of the red mark for not to order further. Research was conducted by Gurumurthy et.al. (2020) for a health sector considering the best quality treatment and low-operating cost using lean thinking. A methodology of MUSIC with a selective aspect of ABC, VED and SDE was considered for consumption value, criticality and lead time was used to classify medical supplies for a Cath lab. The outcome of this research was useful for controlling better inventory management and availability of them in time with improved quality treatment. A case study was carried out by Sengottuvelu (2021) using a multi-unit selective combining the technique of ABC, FSN and SDE for the inventory of 720 traded parts for an auto-connected system company warehouse. The study reveals 94 items are non-moving and about 50% are easily available from them and hence the stock is to be strictly controlled.

A Pareto chart shown in Figure 7.3 indicates the distinguished focus of the research studies carried out for various sectors belonging to the spare parts inventory. It indicates that maximum research papers belong to the manufacturing sector i.e. twenty-six (28), sixteen (16) for the service sector, fourteen (14) for defence, ten (10) for petroleum & fertilizer, four (04) on power sectors, four (4) on literature review and three (3) as general papers, respectively.

Research studies carried out in the manufacturing sector include paper, capital equipment, machines manufacturing, aircraft, steel, mining, electrical transmission and automobile. Similarly, service sector research studies include construction machines, durable goods, copiers, computer systems, medical, electronics and

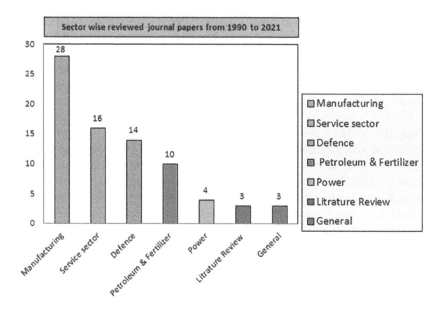

FIGURE 7.3   Sector-wise published papers for spares inventory control (1990–2020). (Pareto chart showing a summary of sector-wise published research papers i.e. manufacturing service sector, defence, petroleum & fertilizer, power sectors, literature review and general papers respectively.)

electrical transformers and IT. Review papers studied under the defence sector include naval, shipping, airlines, aviation and radar system. Review papers studied under the petroleum and fertilizer sector cover similar manufacturing industries. Research review papers in the power sector include thermal and wind. The literature review papers cover the collection of different research studies carried out. Similarly, the general paper covers the details of different perspectives used in research papers.

7.2.2   REVIEW OF PETROLEUM HANDBOOK AND REPORTS

The total cost of spare parts inventory should be 2%–3% of the total project cost of the petroleum industry as indicated in the handbook by Jones & David (2006). The total cost of the petroleum project industry on a global basis is USD 10 billion based on a bulletin report of petrochemical update (2018). Based on the same spare parts inventory total cost at a sustainable level could be in the range of USD 200–300 million. In addition, total spare parts inventory items are in the range of 40,000 to 100,000 as per the KPMG report by Koen (2014) in mega continuous manufacturing industries. A report by Cognizant insight (2012) indicates that the increase in revenue can be up by 20% by reducing the total inventory cost. Spare parts inventory management needs different stocking policies based on their distinguish requirement. This could not follow the similar policy as govern for raw materials and finished goods as indicated by Muller & Max (2003) in their book "Essentials of Inventory Management".

7.2.3 INDUSTRY NEED FOR MULTI-CRITERION APPROACH; A PILOT SURVEY

A survey was conducted to reveal the use of individual selective control techniques as current practice and the need for multi-criterion inventory control (MCIC) classification approach which may improve with distinguish need for stocking and lead to sustainability. In this regard, a pilot survey was conducted through an online questionnaire from fertilizer and petroleum industries in India and Gulf. A total of 70 valid responses were received from 38 industries were received. These responses are plotted on a bar scale to know the current practice and need for MCIC classification.

Figure 7.4 indicates the use of different selective techniques for spare parts inventory control by industries. It reveals that out of 140 total sample responses (combined sample maintenance and stores) indicates that 48 are not using any selective technique. 33 indicate FSN, 26 indicate ABC, 25 indicate VED and very few use HML based on the combined responses received, respectively.

Figure 7.5 indicates the use of a multi-criterion selective approach for spare parts inventory control by industries using combinations of selective techniques. It reveals that out of 140 total sample responses (combined sample maintenance and stores) indicates that only 35 responses indicate the use of a multi-criterion selective approach. A total of 72 responses indicate that organizations either do not in the practice of use or else do not know. Rest indicates the use of the individual selective technique.

The above data facts indicate that organizations are still in use of the conventional practice of the thumb rule. Very few of them are concerned with controlling spare parts inventory based on using individual selective inventory control aspects specially FSN in such industries. These organizations are less concerned about taking into consideration of HML selective aspect based on the responded data as shown in Figure 7.4. Similarly, data facts shown in Figure 7.5 indicate that emphasis on using a multi-criterion selective approach is very less. It shows that there is a need for a systematic framework with stocking policy and procedure using a multi-criterion

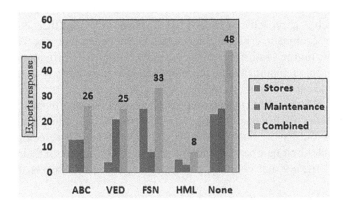

FIGURE 7.4 Frequency of use of selective control analysis by industries (framework part). (Industry experts' survey response for the use of different selective techniques by industries i.e ABC, VED, FSN and HML.)

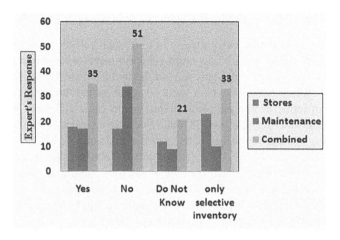

FIGURE 7.5 Use of multi-criterion selective approach by industries (framework part). (Industry experts' survey response for use of the multi-criterion selective approach for spare parts inventory control by industries.)

selective control technique. Also to reflect it as a better approach of controlling spare parts inventory as a cohesive chain of all departments leading to sustainability.

7.3   PROBLEM STATEMENT AND BASIS OF PROPOSED FRAME WORK

Extensive literature review indicates that spare parts inventory was primarily controlled by thumb rule practice and later by using the concept of reliability, forecasting and logistical characteristics, and in recent decades different selective perspectives of individual departments. The above approach results in the high, uneven stocking of spare parts inventory and enhancing inventory cost. Subsequently, from 2011 onward started using the multi-criterion approach in the research papers with combining two or three selective approaches such as VED, FSN and SDE and their corresponding parameters of equipment criticality, demand forecasting and logistics. This approach provided a beginning of uniform perspective as team goal of different departments for better control of manufacturing inventory and also spare parts inventory for pharmaceutical and service sectors.

There is still a need for tailor-made research work for continuous and voluminous production units especially fertilizer and petroleum industries due to the variety of equipment and having distinguished functional service. These equipment are in multiple double-digit numbers and need a precise review based on their service and equipment criticality and combining other selective control aspects for economic sustainability.

1. To nullify an uneven consideration of risk considered for spare parts inventory to safeguard against unpredicted probable failure of equipment and system. This also leads sometimes to the overflow of the purchase requisition.

2. The process of buying the spare parts as first fill is carried out along with equipment during the project stage as a normal practice. This practice includes the procurement of spare parts on a lumpsum basis between 4% and 5% of individual equipment and based on the recommendation of the original equipment manufacturer (OEM)/supplier. This leads to many spares more as required and few of them not covered remain as left out. It needs a prioritization-based integrated category of multi-criterion approach with spare parts review team (SPRT) of stakeholders. This also needs to guide/ share the proposed policy and procedure with lump-sum turnkey (LSTK) consultants and OEMs.

3. Need for integrating multi-classification by considering the user, procurement, stores and finance departments for all spare parts inventory.

4. Need to have a structured stocking policy for each multi-classification leading to sustainable inventory stocks and cost.

5. Need to prioritize the selective control techniques for developing an appropriate decision tree of spare parts inventory multi-criteria classification.

6. Reducing the spare parts which do not use frequently and stay very long in stores becoming obsolete. This also leads to another aspect of sustainability by reducing the deterioration of the local environment of the warehouse.

7.4 METHODOLOGY OF RESEARCH WORK AND PROCESS

In this chapter, a new model called multi-criterion inventory control (MCIC) is developed to classify spare parts inventory using the analytical hierarchy process technique along with indicating a stocking policy, respectively. It is based on economic consideration of sustainability using inductive-based qualitative research. The complete research process is carried out in three stages as depicted in Figure 7.6. In the first stage, a framework of the MCIC model is proposed with integrated selective classification and perspective stocking policy. In the second stage, hypotheses are developed to demonstrate the significance of each integrated classification of spare parts inventory and their relevant stocking policy. These hypotheses are tested statistically using SPSS 20 for the responses received from industries experts' obtained through a survey questionnaire. In the last stage, validation of the proposed framework is carried out with real cases taken from two industries.

7.4.1 RANKING OF SELECTIVE INVENTORY CONTROL METHODS USING AHP TECHNIQUE

AHP technique is used to rank and prioritize the three selective inventory control alternatives analogous output, shown in Figure 7.7. It is carried out to frame the logic decision tree diagram for multi-criteria classification.

7.4.1.1 Assumptions for Framework

(a) The framework is based on the normal operating condition of the plant and equipment. Also considering normal deterioration levels of individual equipment and excluding the requirement of spare parts during shutdown intervals.

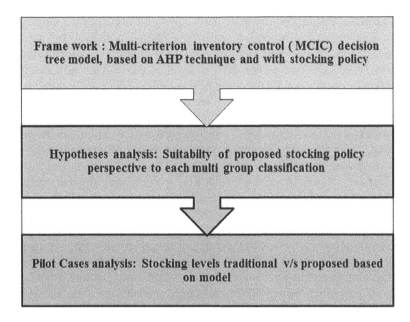

FIGURE 7.6   Stages of research process (framework part). (Framework of research work is carried out in three stages i.e. framework, hypotheses analysis, and pilot cases analysis.)

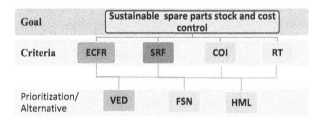

FIGURE 7.7   Hierarchy AHP tree for sustainable spare parts stock and cost control (framework part). (AHP process for prioritization of alternatives based on criteria for sustainable spare parts stock control.)

(b)   A constant Lead-time period is assumed which is 1 week for local items, 1 month for outside but within-country and 3–6 months for items to be procured from outside of the country except for an emergency. Lead time described as above in three categories is based on SDE Scare, difficult and easy category of selective control aspect. This aspect is not taken in the MCIC model, however, will be considered for sustainable stock of spare part inventory.

7.4.2   AHP PROCESS FOR DEVELOPING MCIC MODEL

A basic method given by Braglia et al. (2004) for the use of the multi-criteria classification provides the basis for the development of such classification. Subsequently, a few other models are described in the research papers for classifying spare parts based on using different criteria and different MCDM techniques. The AHP process is a powerful and flexible technique to integrate qualitative aspects and for assigning weights to different criteria. Hence, it is taken for the proposed model MCIC to integrate and develop the decision tree.

Figure 7.7 indicates a hierarchal tree of the AHP process. It is decomposed into three levels namely goal, criteria and alternative. Criteria are equipment criticality and failure rate (ECFR), spare parts replacement frequency (SRF), cost of the item (COI) & replenishment time (RT) and governed under the ruling goal of sustainable spare parts stock and cost control. Selective techniques alternatives VED, FSN and HML are integrated into the decision tree for the classification of spare parts inventory based on the weight analysis. In the AHP process, the criteria considered are based on experts' opinions, fulfilling the research gap with the tailor-made requirement. The brief importance of each criterion for spare parts classification is described as follows.

7.4.2.1 Equipment Criticality and Failure Rate

Equipment criticality is classified in the above industries based on the consequences of equipment failure, which is categorized based on the VED selective control aspect. Failure of equipment affects the stoppage of production, and therefore it is a vital category. Failure of equipment that affects stoppage of the local system is categorized as essential and similarly, mode of failure which stop only the equipment is categorized as desirable. Also, the functional service of equipment governs the rate of failure of equipment e.g., an acid service pump failure frequency will be more than water services pump failure frequency. Hence, ECFR will govern more as compared to VED as an output alternative.

7.4.2.2 Spares Replacement Frequency

The spare part replacement frequency is also governed by the factor ECFR. Spare parts replacement frequency are categorized based on selective inventory control FSN. Based on the opinion survey through industry experts', the criteria of FSN are considered based on the movement of spare parts from stores. Movement of spare parts is less than a year is treated as fast, from a year to 3 years are treated as slow and more than 5 years are treated as a non-moving category of spare parts. SRF will govern more as compared to FSN as an output alternative.

7.4.2.3 Cost of Item (COI)

In the integrated spare parts classification, the unit price also plays an important role and this needs a decision at strategic and tactical levels before procurement. The criteria for COI derived from experts' opinion are as follows. The spare parts with a unit price of more than USD 5000 are treated as high-value items, between USD 1500 and 5000 are treated as medium value and below USD 1500 are treated as low-value items. COI governs the output criteria more as compared to HML selective inventory control.

7.4.2.4 Replenishment Time (RT)

Spare parts stocking policy is also playing an important role with respect to replenishment lead-time. Severe production downtime situations may arise due to supply irregularities of spare parts and are not available sometimes during maintenance. The criteria for replenishment time are categorized based on SDE selective aspect and defined based on industry experts' survey. The spare parts are categorized as a scare for procurement lead time is within 3–6 months, items treated as difficult which takes procurement lead time within 1 month and considered under an easy category which takes lead time within a week. Hence, RT governs the output criteria more as compared to FSN selective inventory control. However, SDE is considered for stocking policy, as defined in Table 7.5.

7.4.2.5 Companywide Interchangeability/Commonality (CWI)

When identical spare parts are used in similar nature of equipment belonging to the different production plants of the same business unit is called companywide interchangeability. The total number of installed interchangeable parts in different equipment on a companywide basis is another measure to define sustainable stock levels. All equipment does not fail simultaneously and hence stock level could be rationalized for such interchangeable spare parts. This criterion is not considered in the AHP process since this is a separate exercise to be carried out by the spare parts review team (SPRT) and is considered under the stocking category S3and S4 as defined in Table 7.5.

7.4.3 Pairwise Comparison of Criteria

Pair-wise ranks are assigned against each criterion as indicated in Table 7.1, which is based on the average percentage weights obtained by industry experts through the structured questionnaire. These ranks are derived based on the average percentage for the criteria in the AHP process. The solution is given by the computation of the priority vector of the matrices and normalized eigenvector of the matrix. Table 7.1 shows the AHP judgment matrix checking for consistency and calculation of the weight of different criteria. Consistency index (C.I.) is observed as 0.03948. Random consistency indices (R.I.) is taken as 0.9 as a standard value for criterion 4. The consistency ratio (C.R.) is 0.0438 which is calculated from the value of C.I. and R.I. The CR calculated value is less than 0.1. Hence, the criteria's comparison is having reliable for the goal of sustainable spare parts stock and cost control.

7.4.4 Pairwise Comparison of Output Alternatives Based on Criteria

Pairwise comparison of selective inventory alternative is carried out for each criterion, by generating the pairwise matrix and keep because of impact consideration. The final score is calculated for each alternative output and different criteria, as shown in Table 7.2. Also, a final ranking of selective inventory alternatives is calculated based on the weight of criteria shown in Table 7.3. The final score shown in Table 7.3 is 0.556, 0.335 and 0.138 for VED, FSN and HML respectively. This analysis of prioritization of selective inventory criteria provides a direction for developing an integrated decision tree model of the multicriterion approach.

TABLE 7.1

Pairwise Comparisons of Criteria for Sustainable Spare Parts Stock and Cost Control

Criteria	Equip Failure & Criticality Rating (EFCR)	Spares Replacement Frequency (SRF)	Cost of Item (COI)	Replenishment Time (RT)	nth root of Product	Priority Vector (PV)
Equip failure & criticality rating	1	0.2	3	2	1.046635	0.220376634
Spares replacement frequency	8	1	3	5	2.942831	0.619634441
Cost of item	0.33333	0.333333	1	3	0.759836	0.159988925
Replenishment time	0.5	0.20000	0.33333	1	0.427287	0.089968384
Sum	4	1.733333333	7.333333	11.000000	4.749302	1.00
Sum*PV	0.881506	1.0740330	1.1732521	0.9896522	9.925891	
λmax	4.1184439					
CI	0.0394813					
CR	0.0438681					

Table indicates relative weight of factors (criteria) i.e. EFCR, SRF, COI and RT considered for sustainable spare parts and cost control.

TABLE 7.2

Final Score of Alternatives Based on Individual Criteria

Criteria	EFCR	SRF	COI	RT	Score
Alternatives	0.2238	0.6196344	0.159989	0.088996	1.092385
VED	0.785391188	0.785391188	0.059412602	0.0549	0.67679
FSN	0.14881507	0.14881507	0.652226618	0.289744	0.255645765
HML	0.065793742	0.065793742	0.288360781	0.655355	0.159948966
Sum	1	1	1		1

Table shows the final score values for alternatives VED, FSN and HML.

7.5 DECISION TREE MULTI-CRITERION INVENTORY CONTROL (MCIC) MODEL

The decision tree multi-criterion inventory control (MCIC) model is developed by integrating selective inventory control techniques VED, FSN and HML as shown in Figure 7.8. The decision tree is based on the ranking, as shown in Table 7.3, and is

TABLE 7.3

Ranking Among the Alternatives Based on Weightage

	Final Rank	
Alternative/Output	Rank	Weightage
VED	1	0.556802325
FSN	2	0.355894811
HML	3	0.138523526

Priortization of alternatives i.e. VED, FSN and HML respectively based on weightage.

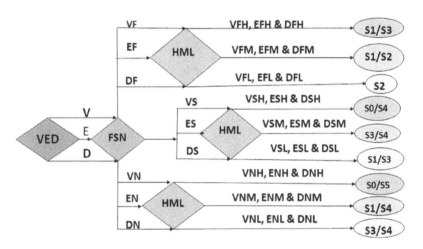

FIGURE 7.8 Multi-criterion inventory control (MCIC) Model (framework part). (Multi criterion inventory control (MCIC) model with relevant stocking category for stocking policy.)

derived from the AHP technique. A stocking policy is also developed as a part of the framework, as shown in Table 7.5. A suitable stocking category is also assigned to each multi-classification group, as indicated in Figure 7.8. Suitability of the stocking category for each classification group is derived based on the responses received from industry experts and statistically tested through derived hypotheses in the Section 4.3. The classification groups are verified for the proposed stocking policy with pilot cases based on the obtained data as shown in Tables 7.10 and 7.11 respectively.

7.5.1 DESCRIPTION OF SUSTAINABLE STOCKING CATEGORY AND POLICY GUIDELINE

Stocking categories are described as S0 to S5 as shown in Table 7.4. These are defined along with guidelines of stocking policy as essential and sustainable stock respectively. The essential stock is ist level and belongs to the requirement during maintenance of equipment. The sustainable stock is second and final level inclusive

TABLE 7.4

Stocking Category and Policy Guideline for Framework Model MCIC

	Stocking Policy	
Stocking Category	Essential Stock (Based on ECFR, SRF and Companywide Interchangeabilty (CWI) etc.	Sustainable Stock (Based on COI, RT and Service Level)
S0	No stock of spare parts, but detail is included in the system for future order	One-Imported items after review by SP team
S1	Only one stock quantity for any number of installed quantity	Two-for imported items after review by SP team
S2	Stock level more than one based on installed quantity	Add two or more quantities based on lead time, service level and frequency of use
S3	Stock level based on companywide interchangeability of item reviewed by SPT	Add two or more quantity based on lead time, service level and frequency of use
S4	Spare parts items categorize as not issued for 6 years or long follow S0 stocking category and needs review by SP team	One-Imported and/or to be procured outside local city, after review by SP team
S5	Capital and insurance spare: kept them in bonded ware house since, high value with unpaid custom duty till not used for equipment	Same and kept with preservation and with required steel structure

It is two level stocking policy for spare parts inventory i.e. essential stock and sustainable stock.

of essential stock and requirement consideration for replenishment time, service level and cost of items.

7.6 SUITABILITY OF STOCKING CATEGORY FOR GROUP CLASSIFICATION IN THE MCIC MODEL

Nine hypotheses are derived to statistically testing for suitability of assigned stocking policy to each group of multi-classification of spare parts inventory as shown in Table 7.6. A statistical test is conducted for each hypothesis from the obtained valid data from industry experts' using SPSS 20. A framework for sample size determination and response summary is followed in this section.

7.6.1 SAMPLE SIZE DETERMINATION

There are eighty-one (81) industries as per the directory of fertilizer of India and Gulf petroleum.

The following equation 7.1 is used for sample size determination applicable for finite population size with standard deviation from mean. This is taken from the "Research methodology by Kothari & Garg (2019)".

$$n = \frac{Z^2 N \sigma_p^2}{(N-1)ME^2 + Z^2 \sigma_p^2} \tag{7.1}$$

where

n = Number of Sample Size to be found

Z-Score = 1.96 (Standard deviate from mean population)

N = 81 (Finite Number of Population)

σ^2_p = 0.479583 (Standard Deviation of Population)

ME^2 = 0.05 (Marginal Error)

Therefore, sample size will be:

$$n = \frac{(1.96)^2 \; 81 \; (0.479583)^2}{(81-1)(0.05)^2 + (1.96)^2 (0.479583)^2}$$

$$n = \frac{75.122}{1.09}$$

$$n = 69.919$$

Therefore, the sample size is seventy for each maintenance and stores personnel. The total samples will be 140.

7.6.2 Response Summary

Out of 162 questionnaires sent as total population, 70 valid responses are received from (maintenance and stores personnel) as shown in columns A, B and C respectively of Table 7.5. The number of industries is taken from the online directory Petroleum industries in Gulf; (2016) and directory Fertilizers industries in India; (2017) respectively for the population. The survey was carried out from August 2018 till the end of December 2019 to get responses from the industry experts.

7.6.3 Hypotheses Design and Testing

Nine hypotheses are designed for analyzing the suitability of the proposed stocking policy for each group multi-classification, as shown in Table 7.6.

7.6.4 Reliability and Normality Test for the Group of Hypotheses

The Cronbach's alpha reliability test is carried out using SPSS 20 to ascertain the questionnaire consistency perspective to the hypotheses. The value obtained is 0.963 which is more than the required value, i.e. 0.6, as shown in Table 7.7. Hence, it is confirming the effectiveness of the questionnaire and hypotheses H_{01} to H_{09}.

Normality tests are carried out to ascertain the normality of response data. The P-value indicated in Table 7.8 for each hypothesis is less than .05. Hence, the data set based on experts' responses are found skewed, i.e. not normally distributed. Therefore, a non-parametric one-sample test is adopted for the data set and hypotheses testing.

TABLE 7.5
Summary of Questionnaire Sent & Responses Received from Industries

Country	Fertilizer Industries	Petroleum Industries	Grand Total Industries	Expected total responses	Response received (different levels) (A)	Response received summary		
						Response received from No. of Industries (B)	Percentage response Received (C)	Percentage industrywise Response received (D)
India	30	16	46	92	39	18	40%	39%
Gulf	4	31	35	70	34	20	48%	57%
Total	34	47	81	162	73 (70 valid)	38	45%	47%

Conducted from August 2018 to December 2019.
Valid 70 survey response obtained from industry experts' from thirty eight fertilizers and petroleum industries across India and Gulf.

TABLE 7.6

Hypotheses for Conducting Suitability of Stocking Category and Multi Classification Inventory Control Groups of MCIC Model

Hypothesis No	Hypothesis Description
H_{01}	Stocking policy S1/S4 is not suitable for better control for items under category VFH, EFH & DFH
H_{a1}	Stocking policy S1/S4 is suitable for better control for items under category of VFH, EFH & DFH
H_{02}	Stocking policy S0/ S4 is not suitable for better control for items under category VSH, ESH & DSH
H_{a2}	Stocking policy S0/S4 is suitable for items under category VSH, ESH & DSH and provides better control
H_{03}	Stocking policy S0/S5 is not suitable for better control for items under category VNH, ENH & DNH
H_{a3}	Stocking policy S0/S5 is suitable for better control for items under category VNH, ENH & DNH
H_{04}	Stocking policy S1/S2 is not suitable for better control for items under category VFM, EFM & DFM
H_{a4}	Stocking policy S1/S2 is suitable for better control for items under category VFM, EFM & DFM
H_{05}	Stocking policy S3/S4 is not suitable for better control for items under category VSM, ESM & DSM
H_{a5}	Stocking policy S3/S4 is suitable for better control for items under category VSM, ESM & DSM
H_{06}	Stocking policy S2 is not suitable for better control for items under category VFL, EFL & DFL
H_{a6}	Stocking policy S2 is suitable for better control for items under category VFL, EFL & DFL
H_{07}	Stocking policy S1/ S3 is not suitable for better control for items under category VSL, ESL & DSL
H_{a7}	Stocking policy S1/ S3 is suitable for better control for items under category VSL, ESL & DSL
H_{08}	Stocking policy S3/S4 is not suitable for better control for items under category VNL, ENL & DNL
H_{a8}	Stocking policy S3/S4 is suitable for better control for items category VNL, ENL & DNL
H_{09}	Stocking policy S0/S4 is not suitable for better control for items category VNM, ENM & DNM
H_{a9}	Stocking policy S0/S4 is suitable for better control for items under category VNM, ENM & DNM

Derived nine hypotheses to validate the suitability of integrated inventory groups carried out through statistical testing using SPSS 20.

TABLE 7.7
Reliability Test of Stocking Policy Under Hypotheses H_{01} to H_{09}

Cronbach's Alpha (Value)	"Cronbach's Alpha" based on (standardized items)	No of Items
0.963	0.968	9

Cronbach Alpha reliability test results and value is 0.963 based on survey response of nine questions pertaing to hypotheses.

TABLE 7.8
Results of Tests of Normality Based on Experts' Responses for Each Hypothesis

S. No	Description	Kolmogorov-Smirnov[a]			Shapiro-Wilk		
		Statistic	df	P	Statistic	df	P
1	L1S54-Agreement on proposed stocking policy – S1/S4 – for MCIC group – VFH, EFH & DFH	.286	70	0.001	0.715	70	0.005
2	L1S55-Agreement on proposed stocking policy S0/S4 – for MCIC group – VSH, ESH & DSH	.280	70	.002	.751	70	.004
3	L1S56-Agreement on proposed stocking policy S0/S5 – for MCIC group – VNH, ENH & DNH	.271	70	.005	.847	70	.004
4	L1S57-Agreement on proposed stocking policy S1/S2 – for MCIC group – VFM, EFM & DFM	.223	70	.006	.855	70	.005
5	L1S58-Agreement on proposed stocking policy S3/S4 – for MCIC group – VSM, ESM & DSM	.249	70	.005	.824	70	.006
6	L1S59-Agreement on proposed stocking policy S4 – for MCIC group – VFL, EFL & DFL	.338	70	.004	.768	70	.004
7	L1S60-Agreement on proposed stocking policy S1/S3 – for MCIC group – VSL, ESL & DSL	.246	70	.005	.861	70	.004
8	L1S61-Agreement on proposed stocking policy S3/S4 – for MCIC group – VNL, ENL & DNL	.221	70	.004	.844	70	.004
9	L1S62-Agreement on proposed stocking policy S0/S4-for MCIC group – VNM, ENM & DNM	.377	70	.004	.727	70	.004

Note: Significance level is $P < .05$.

It shows results of K-S and Shapiro Wilk statistical test carried out using SPSS 20 for verifying responses are not following the normality curve.

7.6.5 NON-PARAMETRIC ONE-SAMPLE TEST FOR HYPOTHESES

Non-parametric one-sample test was carried out using SPSS 20 for hypotheses H_{01} to H_{09}. Table 7.9 is obtained from SPSS software which indicates that the stocking category of each group of multi-classification is in alignment and hence, accepts alternative hypotheses Ha_1 to Ha_{09}.

TABLE 7.9

Non-Parametric Test Results of Null Hypothesis H_{01} to H_{09}

S. No	Null Hypothesis	Test	Sig.	Decision
1	L1S54-Agreement on proposed stocking policy – S1/S4 – for MCIC group – VFH, EFH & DFH	One-sample Chi-square test	0.004	Reject the null hypothesis
2	L1S55-Agreement on proposed stocking policy S0/S4 - for MCIC group- VSH, ESH & DSH	One-sample Chi-square test	0.002	Reject the null hypothesis
3	L1S56-Agreement on proposed stocking policy S0/S5 – for MCIC group – VNH, ENH & DNH	One-sample Chi-square test	0.006	Reject the null hypothesis
4	L1S57-Agreement on proposed stocking policy S1/S2 – for MCIC group – VFM, EFM & DFM	One-sample Chi-square test	0.007	Reject the null hypothesis
5	L1S58-Agreement on proposed stocking policy S3/S4 – for MCIC group – VSM, ESM & DSM	One-sample Chi-square test	0.001	Reject the null hypothesis
6	L1S59-Agreement on proposed stocking policy S4- for MCIC group- VFL, EFL & DFL	One-sample Chi-square test	0.003	Reject the null hypothesis
7	L1S60-Agreement on proposed stocking policy S1/S3 – for MCIC group – VSL, ESL & DSL	One-sample Chi-square test	0.004	Reject the null hypothesis
8	L1S61-Agreement on proposed stocking policy S3/S4 – for MCIC group – VNL, ENL & DNL	One-sample Chi-square test	0.005	Reject the null hypothesis
9	L1S62-Agreement on proposed stocking policy S0/S4 – for MCIC group – VNM, ENM & DNM	One-sample Chi-square test	0.004	Reject the null hypothesis

Note: Asymptotic significances are displayed. The significance level is 0.05.

Test results where alternative hypotheses are in line with framework and based on the survey responses.

7.7 PILOT CASES ANALYSIS: STOCKING LEVELS TRADITIONAL V/S PROPOSED, BASED ON MODEL

Two pilot cases are described below, belonging to the obtained company data from the Fertilizer and Petroleum industries of India and the Kingdom of Saudi Arabia, respectively. The proposed category and subsequent data set are part of the framework in both Tables 7.10 and 7.11.

7.7.1 CASE-I

Sustainable proposed stocking for multi-classification groups based on MCIC v/s Traditional stock: Indian Fertilizer Industry

A pilot case of spare parts inventory is described in Table 7.10 for 14 items. The column-wise parameters are item-code, description, under company data column; unit cost, consumption of last 6 years (2011–2017) and traditional stock of items as of 2018 are obtained as secondary data from industry for analysis purposes.

Multi-classification based on the framework of MCIC is indicated with an applicable stocking category and a proposed sustainable stock. The total savings of USD 68,910.0 is reflected based on current and proposed sustainable stock for all fourteen items. This can be enhanced by reviewing all applicable items. The unit price shown in USD is converted from INR based on the corresponding conversion rate during 2011 and escalated based on the year 2020.

TABLE 7.10

Case-I: Comparative Stocking of Spare Parts Inventory Traditional v/s Proposed Framework: Indian Fertilizer Industry

S. No	Item Code	Description	Company Data			Proposed MCIC Group & Stocking Category				Proposed Saving in USD
			Unit price in USD	Consumption (2011–2017)	Stock – 2018 (Traditional)	MCIC Group	Stocking category	Proposed stock		
								Essential	Sustainable.	
1	5521590038	GSKT; 11/21P52A/B; PN:S-76; DRG:2H107254R5	1347	5	8	EFH	S1/S3	2	4	5390
2	5521590028	GSKT; SEAT; 11/21P52A/B; PN:S-13; 2H107254R5	1104	4	9	EFH	S1/S3	2	4	5520
3	5509050065	FLOAT; UGA1102/2102A/B; PN:5; DRG:T3-25640	666	12	20	EFM	S1/S2	2	6	9319
4	5521550047	BSH; THRTT; 11/21P05A/B; PN:B; DRG:2H41675R3	170	4	6	EFL	S2	2	4	340
5	5503200018	RNG; MTG; 11/21P4A/B; PN:2; C409/D1094/R1	1454	1	5	ESH	S0/S4	0	2	4360
6	5509050063	O-RNG; UGA1102/2102A/B; PN:11; DRG:T3-25640	1644	2	11	ESM	S3/S4	2	4	13,152
7	5521730027	SHFT; AGA955,AGA953; PN:18400; PMP; KBL	854	3	4	ESL	S1/S3	1	2	1708
8	5521730006	SLVE; AGA955; AGA952A/B,AGA953; PN:31100	400	4	4	ESL	S1/S3	1	2	800
9	5501370032	INSRT; 11/21P21A/B,PN:2,DRG:2H-68402	1599	0	3	ENH	S0/S5	0	1	3198
10	5537950042	PMP; MOP; 11/21P02; PU04FA03; POS:1	1374	1	3	ENH	S0/S5	0	1	2746
11	5509050046	RNG; LNR; UGA1102/2102A/B; PN:107-2	956	0	24	ENM	S1/S4	1	2	21,039
12	5522710005	NUT; UGA103A/B/C; PN:922; DRG:PR17305R2	105	0	4	ENL	S3/S4	1	2	210
13	5503300016	WEARNG; CSNG; 11/21P18A/B; PN:54	334	0	3	ENL	S3/S4	1	2	334
14	5501390020	SLVE; P304; PN:10; DRG:2H-42002R1; PT-1.75"	397	2	4	ENL	S3/S4	1	2	794
									Total Saving USD →	68,910

Comparative pilot analysis of stock of 14 items based on traditional way and proposed stocking policy indicative savings USD 68910.

7.7.2 Case-II

Sustainable stock levels using stocking category S3 for MCIC group VSM, ESM & DSM v/s Traditional stock.

A pilot case of the Petrochemical industry from the Kingdom of Saudi Arabia is taken for sustainable stock levels v/s traditional stock for the spare parts of the above multiclassification group, as shown in Table 7.11. The secondary data are obtained for 18 mechanical seals having stock recommendations against each of them based on company conventional data.

Companywide interchangeability is identified among them shown as six groups carried out based on the technical attribute review from the obtained data sheets and drawings of suppliers from the industry. Proposed sustainable stock levels for each group is considered based on stocking category S3. Item wise saving is indicated in the last column and the total saving is USD 45,760.0 About 10%–15% of items could be identified as having interchangeability and may provide a huge cost saving using this stocking policy with dedicated technical attribute review for the items belonging to this multi-classification group of MCIC model.

7.8 CONCLUSIONS AND MANAGERIAL IMPLICATIONS

Petroleum and fertilizer industries have spare parts inventory ranging from 40,000 to 100,000 with associated costs ranging from USD 200 to 400 million. In this research, a decision tree model MCIC is developed by integrating selective techniques of VED, FSN and HML using the AHP process as shown in Figure 7.8. This model provides nine micro-level multi-group classifications of spare parts inventory with specific stocking category provides improved control over traditional thumb rule practice which is demonstrated through statistical testing of nine hypotheses. An in-depth review is carried out of the literature. It includes a review of research papers, reports published, petroleum handbooks and pilot analysis by experts of various industries. In the last section, a study is carried out with two pilot cases for the spares parts inventory comparing traditional and proposed sustainable stocking policies. Sustainable stock levels in these pilot cases indicate saving of USD 68,910.0 and USD 45,760.0 respectively, which further leads to the higher potential of saving with systematic review by SPRT for total spare parts inventory.

7.8.1 Managerial Implications

The framework provides a base to reduce and control excess inventory up to a level of 10%–20% and associated cost with permissible risk. Quality training is to be instituted for personnel of stores and maintenance department. It would reduce the conventional practice and provide a wide spectrum of distinguishing approaches with sustainability in spare parts inventory control. SPRT review is to be carried out for identification of applicable interchangeable parts by review of technical specification. This will lead to reduce the stocking of identical and similar items in different item codes. ERP-based materials management systems could not reveal the interchangeability of parts once codified in different item codes.

TABLE 7.11

Case-II: Economics by Using S3 Stocking Category for MCIC Group VSM, ESM & DSM-KSA Petrochemical Plant

S. No	Description–Item Mechanical seal for Pump of Tag No	Unit Price in USD	Consumption / Refurbish (2011–2017)	Recommended Stock by LSTK/OEM	Review for Interchangeability by SPRT Team	Proposed MCIC Group	Proposed stock Essential	Proposed stock Sustainable	Proposed Saving in USD
			Company Data (Stores)		Proposed S3 Stocking Category (Review for Companywide Interchangeability)				
1	P-1203 (Process side)	2060	2 (Refurbish)	1	Interchangeable (Group1)	ESM	1	2	12360
2	P1202A/B (Process side)	2060	2 (Refurbish)	2					
3	P-1204 A/B (Process side)	2060	2 (Refurbish)	2					
4	P-1217 A/B (Process side)	2060	1 (Refurbish)	2					
5	P1203 (Motor side)	1880	1 (Refurbish)	1	Interchangeable (Group 2)	ESM	1	2	5640
6	P1202A/B (Motor side)	1880	2 (Refurbish)	2					
7	P-1204 A/B (Motor side)	1880	1 (Refurbish)	2					
8	P-1217 A/B (Motor side)	1880	1 (Refurbish)	2					
9	P-1145	2080	Nil	1	Interchangeable (Group 3)	ESM	1	2	8320
10	P-1148	2080	Nil	1					
11	P-1205 A/B	2080	Nil	2					
12	P-1760 A/B	2080	Nil	2					
13	P-1147A,B	1735	2 (Refurbish)	2	Interchangeable (Group 4)	ESM	1	2	3470
14	P-1143 A/B	1735	2 (Refurbish)	2					
15	P-1250A ,B	7225	1-new	2	Interchangeable (Group 5)	ESM	1	2	14450
16	P-1650A/B	7225	1-new	2					
17	P-1142A,B	1520	1 (Refurbish)	2	Interchangeable (Group 6)	ESM	1	2	1520
18	P-1750	1520	1 (Refurbish)	1					

Pilot case indicating recommended stock and proposed stock based on 6 years cumulative consumption and indicative savings, USD 45,760.

7.8.2 FUTURE PERSPECTIVE

The framework of this research is also useful for other mega business units like steel plants, power plants and similar other industries to reduce the spare parts inventory and its associated cost. A thorough analysis and identification of various inventory items of such capital-intensive units can be undertaken shortly.

7.9 ABBREVIATIONS

ABC	Always Better Control
AHP	Analytical Hierarchy Process
CI	Consistency Index
COI	Cost of Item
CWI	Companywide Interchangeability
CR	Consistency Ratio
ECFR	Equipment Criticality and Failure Rate
EC	Exchange Curve
EOQ	Economic Order Quantity
ERP	Enterprise Resource Planning
FRMIC	Fuzzy rule-based multi-criteria inventory control
FSN	Fast, Slow and Non-moving
HML	High, Medium and Low
KSA	Kingdom of Saudi Arabia
LSTK	LumSum Turnkey
MCDM	Multi-Criteria Decision Making
MCIC	Multi-Criterion Inventory Control
MMM	Materials Management Module
OEM	Original Equipment Manufacture
P-Value	Probability of obtaining results
PV	Priority Vector
R.I.	Random Consistency Indices
RT	Replenishment Time
SC	Supply chain
SIC	Selective Inventory Control
SPIR	Spare Parts Interchangeability Record
SPRT	Spare Parts Review Team
SPSS 20	Statistical Product and Service Solutions Ver. 20
SRF	Spare part Replacement Frequency
USD	United State Dollar
VED	Vital, Essential and Desirable
XYZ	High value, medium value and low vale items at stores

ACKNOWLEDGEMENT

We are thankful to the companies' one of the Indian Fertilizer and a Petrochemical of Kingdom of Saudi Arabia and concerned officers for providing the secondary data for formulating the pilot cases with the inclusion of framework. Also, the cooperation extended from maintenance and stores personnel for in time valid relevant responses obtained through online survey from thirty-eight industries from India and Gulf. This provides an added value to this research.

REFERENCES

Bosnjakovic M. 2010. Multi-criteria inventory model for spare parts. *Technical Gazette*, 17, no. 4: 499–504.

Braglia M., Grassi A., and Montanari R. 2004. Multi-attribute classification method for spare parts inventory management. Journal of Quality in Maintenance Engineering, 10, no. 1: 55–65. doi: 10.1108/13552510410526875.

Bulletin of Petroleum Update. 2018. https://www.opec.org/opec_web/en/publications/202.htm.

Cognizant Insights. 2012. Report on spare parts pricing optimization. https://www.cognizant.com/InsightsWhitepapers/Spare-Parts-Pricing,Optimization.pdf; 20.05.2017.

Devarajan D. and Jayamohan M. S. 2016. Stock control in a chemical firm combined FSN and XYZ analysis. *Procedia Technology*, 24: 562–567. doi: 10.1016/j.protcy.2016.05.111.

Dinesh S. and Hoshiar M. 2019. A multi-item inventory model for small business a perspective from India. *International Journal of Inventory Research*, 5, no. 3: 188–209. doi: 10.1504/IJIR.2019.098856.

Directory Fertilizer Industries in India. https://www.fert.nic.in; 15.06.2017.

Directory Petroleum Industries in Gulf. http://gpca.org.ae/congulf/complete-directory/; 20.06.2016.

Donath B., Mazel J. and Dubin C. 2002. *Handbook of Logistics and Inventory Management. The Institute of Management and Administration (IOMA)*. Wiley & Sons, Inc., New York. Part II: Ch. 2, 430–455.

Duran O., Roda. I., and Macchi M. 2016. Linking the spare parts management with the total costs of ownership: An agenda for future research. *Journal of Industrial Engineering and Management*, 9, no. 5: 991–1002.

Eric P. and Rommert D. 2008. An inventory control system for spare parts at a refinery: An empirical comparison of different reorder point methods. *European Journal of Operation Research*, 184, no. 1: 101–132. doi: 10.1016/j.ejor.2006.11.008.

Fu K., Chen W., Hung L. C. and Peng S. 2012. An ABC analysis model for the multiple products inventory control: A case study of company X. *Proceedings of Asia pacific. Industrial Engineering & Management Systems*, 495–503. https://www.academia.edu/11905171/An_ABC_Analysis_Model_for_the_Multiple_Products_Inventory_Control_A_Case_Study_of_Company_X

Gurumurthy A., Nair V. K. and Vinodh S. 2021. Application of a hybrid selective inventory control technique in a hospital: A precursor for inventory reduction through lean thinking. *The TQM Journal*, 33, no. 3: 568–595. doi: 10.1108/TQM-06-2020-0123.

Jonas B., Ming Z. and Robin V. H. 2018. A thesis on "Optimizing spare-parts management", Swedish University.

Jones J. S. and David P. P. 2006. *Handbook of Petroleum Processing*, 2nd ed. Ch. 17.2: 858, Economic Analysis. Springer, Dordrecht.

Keren B. and Hadad Y. 2016. ABC Inventory Classification Using AHP and Ranking Methods via DEA. *Life Science and Operations Management (SMRLO). International Symposium on Stochastic Models in Reliability Engineering*. IEEE, 495–501. doi: 10.1109/smrlo.2016.87.

Kocaga Y. L. and Sen A. 2007. Spare parts inventory management with demand lead times and rationing. *IIE Transactions, Journal of Taylor & Francis*, 39, no. 9: 879–898. doi: 10.1080/07408170601013646.

Koen B. 2014. Spare parts management. KPMG Guide. Ch. 2: 1–2.

Kothari C. R. and Garg G. 2019. *Research Methodlogy*. New Age International Publiser, New Delhi, Ch. 9, 164–165.

Li R. and Jennifer K. R. 2011. A Bayesian inventory model using real-time condition monitoring information. *Production and Operations Management*, 20, no. 5: 754–771. doi: 10.1111/j.1937-5956.2010.01200.

Praveen M., Jay B. and Venkataram R. 2016. Techniques for inventory classification review. *International Journal for Research in Applied Science & Engineering Technology*, 4, no. 10: 508–518.

Malviya R. K., Dharmadhikari S., Choudhary S., Gupta S., and Raghuwanshi V. (2020). Study of inventory audit and control of automobile spare parts using selective inventory control techniques. *Industrial Engineering Journal*, 13, no. 1: 1–15. ISSN: 2581-4915.

Matta, K. F. 1985. A simulation model for repairable items/spare parts inventory systems. *Computers & Operations Research*, 12, no. 4: 395–409. doi: 10.1016/0305-0548(85)90037-1.

Max M. 2003. *Essentials of Inventory Management*, 10th ed. American Management Association, New York, 115–143.

Mehrotra S. and Basukala S. 2015. Management of drugs using 3D music inventory control technique in a tertiary care hospital. *International Journal of Current Research*, 7, no. 4: 15219–15223.

Mitra S., Pattanayak S. K. and Bhowmik P. 2013. Inventory control using ABC and HML analysis; A case study on a manufacturing industry. *International Journal of Mechanical and Industrial Engineering*, 3, no. 1: 76–81.

Mitra S., Reddy M. S. and Kumar P. 2015. Inventory control using FSN analysis – A case study on a manufacturing industry. *International Journal of Innovative Science, Engineering & Technology*, 2, no. 4: 322–325.

Molenaers A., Baets H., Pintelon L. and Waeyenbergh G. 2012. Criticality classification of spare parts: A case study. *International Journal of Production Economics*, 140: 570–578. doi: 10.1016/j.ijpe.2011.08.013.

Nagen N. N., Tai-san H and Baid N. K. 1994. A computer-based inventory management system for spare parts. *Industrial Management and Data Science*, 94, no. 9: 22–28.

Nareshchandra P.S. and Desai D.A. (2019). Inventory categorization techniques for effective inventory management. *Journal of Emerging Technologies and Innovative Research*, 6, no. 1: 689–700.

Roda I., Macchi M. and Fumagali L. 2014. A review of multi-criteria classification of spareparts. *Journal of Manufacturing Technology Management*, 25, no. 4: 528–549. doi: 10.1108/JMTM-04-2013-0038.

Sagar S., Wachat A. and Agrawal, K. N. 2015. Productivity improvement in a tractor-trailer manufacturing plant using selective inventory control model. *International Journal of Engineering Research*, 3, no. 2: 306–312.

Salwinder G., Paras K. and Narinder P. S. 2016. A review on various approaches of spare parts inventory management system. *Indian Journal of Science and Technology*, 9 no. 4: 1–5. doi: 10.17485/ijst/2016/v9i48/101473.

Sandeep K. V., Mekala J. K., Seshadri B. and Satyanaranya N. 2017. Application of 3D music inventory control technique for Cath Lab Store. *Journal of Dental and Medical Sciences*, 16, no. 12: 24–25. doi: 10.9790/0853-1612112425.

Sanjeev C. and Thomas, C. 2014. Use and applications of optimizing selective inventory control techniques of spares for a chemical processing plant. *International Journal of design and Manufacturing Technology*, 5, no. 3: 86–97.

Sarmah S. P. and Moharana U. C. 2015. Multi-criteria classification of spare parts inventories – A web based approach. *Journal of Quality in Maintenance Engineering*, 21, no. 4: 456–477. doi: 10.1108/JQME-04-2012-0017.

Sengottuvelu C. 2021. Multi-unit selective inventory control – Three dimensional approaches (music 3D) to inventory management, a case study. *Industrial Engineering Journal*, 16, no. 3: 19–25.

Sharda S. and Gorana V. K. 2016. Framework for spare parts inventory cost optimization and adequacy in stock control management using technique of multi unit selective inventory control: Perspective to downstream plants of petroleum industry. International Journal of Science Tech. & Management, 5 no.4: 143–153.

Sheikh A. K., Callom F. L. and Mustafa S. G. 1991. Strategies in spare parts management using reliability engineering approach. *Engineering Costs and Production Economics*, 21, no. 1: 51–57. doi: 10.1016/0167-188x(91)90018-w.

Teixeira C., Lopes I. and Figueiredo, M. 2018. Classification methodology for spare parts management combining maintenance and logistics perspectives. *Journal of Management Analytics*, 5, no. 2: 116–135. doi:10.1080/23270012.2018.1436989

Vereecke A. and Verstraeten P. 1994. An inventory management model for an inventory consisting of lumpy items, slow movers and fast movers. *International Journal of Production Economics*, 35, no. 3: 379–389.

Wild T. 2002. *Best Practices in Inventory Management*, 2nd ed. Elsevier Science Ltd, Tokyo.

Yogesh K., Janghel S., Dhiwar J. S. and Khaparde R. K. 2017. ABC & HML analysis for inventory management – Case study of sponge iron plant. *International Journal for Research in Applied Science & Engineering*, 5, no. 1: 392–397.

Zhang Y., Jedeck S., Yang L. and Bai L. 2018. Modeling & analysis of the on demand spare parts supply using additive manufacturing. *Rapid Prototyping Journal*, 25, no. 3: 473–487. doi: 10.1108/rpj-01-2018-0027.

8 Simulation of Deployment of Inflatable Structures Through Uniform Pressure Method

Aquib Ahmad Siddiqui, V. Murari, and Satish Kumar
Motilal Nehru National Institute of Technology Allahabad

CONTENTS

8.1 INTRODUCTION

Nowadays, inflatable structures are playing a crucial role in the space industry because of their lightweight, low stowage volume, and low cost. There have been many successful projects such as inflatable antennas, solar shades, solar sails, and gravity gradient booms. Even space station modules have been recently tested. A lot of literature is available on several aspects of inflatables such as the kinds of inflation systems and deployment schemes, creating agravic conditions for deployment of structure experimentally, simulation of folding the inflatables for stowage, simulation techniques of inflation, the efficient finite element modeling for effective and correct results. The concerned inflatable structure in this chapter is a one-dimensional cylindrical boom with both of its ends linearly seamed and having one z-fold in the middle. The pressure exerted by inflation gas within the structure is numerically simulated using a DLOAD subroutine in ABAQUS software. The inflation pressure is different in different pockets, and this variation regime can be decided using soft computing by stochastic methods. Data can be procured experimentally or by using heavy computation methods, e.g. SPH, CEL, CFD, etc. with different conditions like geometry, material properties, flow rate, etc. Using machine learning, these data can be processed and a relation between instantaneous angle (between the folds) and pressure distribution can be derived, as discussed in Section 8.2.

8.2   SOFT COMPUTING AND SCOPE OF ARTIFICIAL INTELLIGENCE IN GENERATIVE DESIGN

A simple Uniform Pressure Method (UPM) has been implemented for deployment. The spatial variation of the pressure with respect to time has been modeled using classical thermodynamics. The load application on the surfaces is done by a DLOAD user subroutine in ABAQUS Implicit software. The pressure distribution majorly depends upon the interim angle formed between the folds of stowed inflatable structure. This relationship is not easy to establish since it includes high computational solid mechanics theory because membrane structures can undergo large displacement which is nonlinear in nature. To overcome this complex computation, the use of soft computing can be very helpful. A large set of labeled data (experimental/computational) can be generated for the deployment with the variations of material, thickness, and inflation rate. These data can be derived either by conducting agravic experiments on zero g airplanes or with the technique prescribed by Wei et al. (2015). Also, one may obtain data through some high computational methods, e.g. Smooth Particle Hydrology (SPH), Combined Eulerian-Lagrangian (CEL), Computational Fluid Dynamics (CFD) to generate a large set of data for soft computing. Then these data will be analyzed to form correlations and patterns with respect to the aforementioned parameters to predict the best-suited relation between the pressure variation and the interim angle. This chapter is majorly focused on the development of learning cognitive skill of the inflation process. Further, the reasoning and the self-correction skills of AI can be worked upon using gathered data sets with respect to different parameters.

8.3   INFLATIONMODEL

For the precise modeling of fluid-structure interaction, one can design the membrane part as computational solid mechanics (CSM) and the fluid by Navier–Stokes equations (CFD), which require high computational application. On the other hand, we can simply treat the structure by rigid body dynamics and fluid as ideal gas homogeneously spread in the structure by classical thermodynamics (Graczykowski, 2015). The inflation gas is considered as an ideal gas, which is assumed to fill into a rigid structure. Thus, the shape and the volume of structure remain constant and the same as it is in a fully deployed state. This is the simplest model with the least complexity as mentioned in (Graczykowski, 2015). As the mass flows inside the structure the pressure builds up according to the ideal gas equation. The pressure is applied by the gas on the inner walls which varies spatially as well as with respect to time. The amount of gas is increasing with respect to time, therefore pressure exerted by the gas on the inner walls of inflatable is also increasing. During the transient state of gas filling or deployment, the pressure exerted in different regions varies. But when the cross-section area at the crease becomes big enough for the passage of gas, then these spatial variations of pressure erode away and become equal at all the sections since the gas gets equally distributed in the whole volume. During the deployment process, this variation depends on the allowability of passage of gas into different sections. The allowability depends on certain factors e.g. the interim cross-sectional area at the crease or passage, stiffness of the structure (due to material properties e.g. elastic properties and geometry e.g. span and thickness) and mass flow rate e.g. subsonic, sonic or supersonic, etc.

In the following discussed model, the structure is divided into certain finite volumes or say pockets. As the gas enters through valve, it gets distributed in various pockets according to the allowability of passage at crease. Since the slow rate of the inlet of gas is considered for the deployment of inflatable, the inertial flow characteristics of the gas are not much concerned. The pressure P_n in nth pocket is determined by the amount of gas present in it using the ideal gas equation.

$$P_n = \frac{mRT}{V_n} \tag{8.1}$$

where R is gas constant, T is temperature and V_n is the volume of the nth pocket. V_n is constant because structure is assumed rigid for the inflation model.

Since RT and V_n are constants so basically pressure variation at any given time in different pockets depend only upon the mass distribution in them. So, all we have to find is the relation between allowability (of gas passage at crease) and the mass distribution in pockets at given time. This relation can be obtained with soft computing as mentioned in Section 8.2.

Figure 8.1 shows an inflatable structure with two pockets at a certain stage of time t. The inflation valve is attached to the rear end of pocket 'b'.

V is total volume, V_a and V_b are volumes of pocket a and pocket b, respectively.

$$V = V_a + V_b \tag{8.2}$$

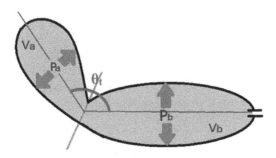

FIGURE 8.1   State of inflatable structure with two pockets certain time t.

Let m is mass flow rate, given by

$$m = \frac{dm(t)}{dt} \tag{8.3}$$

$m \cdot t$ is the total mass of gas present in structure at time t. m_{ta} and m_{tb} are mass of gas present in pockets a and b at time t. Also, the angle between the pockets a and b at this instant is θ.

The mass distribution will depend on the area of passage between the two pockets. As the fold opens up this area increases and one can notice that this area majorly depends upon the interim angle (θ). This area at the crease is directly proportional to the interim angle θ. Thus, as θ increases the allowability of mass through fold also increases.

Now relationships between the angle and the mass distribution in pockets can be obtained with correlation from big data which is organized according to the parameters of the inflation process. Polynomial regressions are being used in this case to develop relationship. For the low allow ability situations, high order of polynomial (n) will be generated, expectedly.

Gas mass in a pocket is function of time t and angle θ_t. As the time increments values of angle keep changing. Since the relation between time and angle is not predictable analytically, thus the value of angle at any time is found out using the subroutine. Angle θ_t is computed within DLOAD subroutine at every time increment. Then using the t and θ_t values, gas mass distribution in the pockets is determined through the following expressions.

$$\text{Mass in pocket 'a' at time } t\text{: } m_{ta} = mt \left(\frac{\theta_t}{\theta_o} \right)^n \quad 0 < \theta_t < \theta_f \tag{8.4}$$

$$\text{Mass in pocket 'b' at time } t\text{: } m_{tb} = mt \left[1 - \left(\frac{\theta_t}{\theta_o} \right)^n \right] \quad 0 < \theta_t < \theta_f \tag{8.5}$$

$$\theta_f = \left(\frac{\chi_a}{\chi_a + \chi_b} \right)^{1/n} \cdot \theta_o \tag{8.6}$$

θ_f is the limiting angle till which mass is distributed according to the aforementioned polynomials. When value of θ_t reaches θ_f, the mass distribution in all the pockets becomes independent of the angle, now they are distributed according to their volume fractions, which can be observed in Figure 8.2. This is because, the constriction in the passage area has now vanished, thus the pressure in the pockets will be equal from there onwards.

Since, at any instant of time, density of gas is assumed uniform and constant. Thus, the maximum amount of gas in each pocket (i.e. in a fully deployed state) is distributed as per the volume fraction as

$$\chi_a = \frac{V_a}{V} \chi_b = \frac{V_b}{V} \tag{8.7}$$

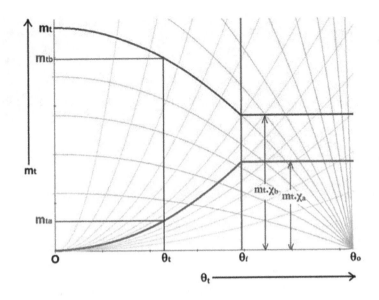

FIGURE 8.2 Mass distribution regime of gas in pockets *a* and *b* at time t.

Now the mass distributions are as follows

$$m_{ta} = mt \cdot \chi_a \tag{8.8}$$

$$m_{tb} = mt \cdot \chi_b \tag{8.9}$$

Note that, since these polynomials are the function of time thus, they keep changing with each time increment. The amount of mass in pocket 'a' can be obtained corresponding to θ_t, by following the grey curve with respect to time. The amount of mass in pocket 'b' can be obtained corresponding to θ_t, by following the black curve with respect to time.

Now, since the mass distribution functions are established, the pressures in the pockets can be computed by ideal gas equation as follows.

$$P_a(t) = \frac{m_{ta}RT}{V_a} \tag{8.10}$$

$$P_b(t) = \frac{m_{tb}RT}{V_b} \tag{8.11}$$

8.4 NUMERICAL SIMULATION

The finite element model is simulated in ABAQUS 2017 software in dynamic implicit mode. The element type of inflatable structure is M3D4R which is suitable for the membrane materials. This is a nonlinear analysis. There is no dedicated step for

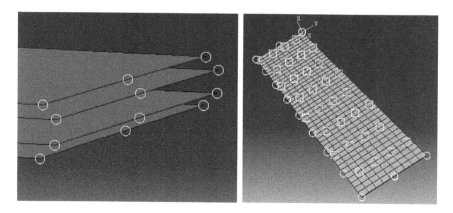

FIGURE 8.3 Depiction of all the interactions among the surfaces (squares depict friction interactions and circles depict tie constraints).

folding of structure. Rather, it is modeled as readily folded structure in its free state, made by stacking four $20 \times 9 \, cm^2$ membranes. The corresponding edges of these four membranes are joined using tie constraint. User-defined loading DLOAD is used with the amplitude of 1 for defining the pressure load which varies with respect to position and time.

8.4.1 Description of CAE model

The discussed structure is a cylindrical tube of length 21cm and width 9 cm in its flattened state, as shown in Figure 8.3. It has on z-fold in its middle. After full deployment, it acquires a length of almost 40 cm and diameter in its mid is 5.7 cm. The material is considered to be homogeneous and isotropic with Young's modulus of $18e+6 \, N/m^2$. The thickness of the membrane is 0.0125 cm. There are 1512 M3D4R membrane elements, employed for the models which do not possess any bending stiffness. A self-contact tangential behavior penalty friction is introduced between the surfaces with a coefficient of 0.01. For this model, the self-contact friction method is chosen since it produces a higher convergence rate and better deployment characteristics. The entire structure is treated as a single surface, with the self-contact norms being applied on both sides. It's a straightforward technique to deal with the connections between the layers and between the skins at the same time. This is a simple and quick approach to use. Both the pockets are of equal volume, and therefore the volume fractions of both the pockets are 0.5.

8.4.2 Concerned Inflation Models

The inflation gas enters through the rear end of the pocket 'b' as shown in Figure 8.1 with constant mass flow rate m. As the mas enters the angle between the two pockets at the fold starts increasing. This angle is assessed using the subroutine and mass is distributed accordingly.

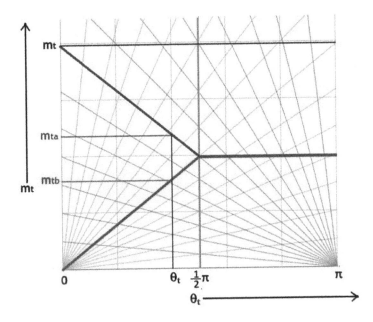

FIGURE 8.4 Mass distribution of gas in pockets *a* and *b* at time *t* using linear polynomial function.

First-order and second-order polynomial relations between mass and angle have been discussed in this chapter with the following attributes. Their respective curves are shown in Figures 8.4 and 8.5.

$\theta_o = 180°$, it is the maximum value of θ when inflatable is fully deployed.

$\chi_a = \chi_b = 0.5$, because volume of both the pockets are equal.

$\theta_f = 90°$, computed from equation 8.6. It means that mass is equally distributed after 90°.

For first-order polynomial function

$$m_{ta} = mt \, \frac{\theta_t}{\pi} \quad 0 < \theta_t < \frac{\pi}{2} \tag{8.12}$$

$$m_{tb} = mt \left(1 - \frac{\theta_t}{\pi}\right) \quad 0 < \theta_t < \frac{\pi}{2} \tag{8.13}$$

For second-order polynomial function

$$m_{ta} = mt \left(\frac{\theta_t}{\pi}\right)^2 \quad 0 < \theta_t < \frac{\sqrt{2}\pi}{2} \tag{8.14}$$

$$m_{tb} = mt \left[1 - \left(\frac{\theta_t}{\pi}\right)^2\right] \quad 0 < \theta_t < \frac{\sqrt{2}\pi}{2} \tag{8.15}$$

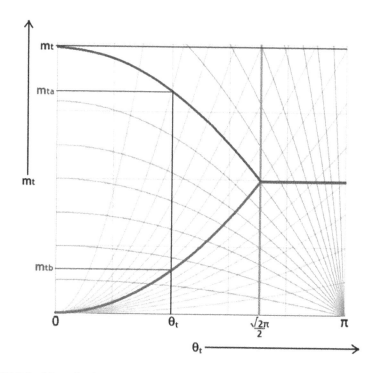

FIGURE 8.5 Mass distribution of gas in pockets a and b at time t using quadratic polynomial function.

When the value of θ hits θ_f the mass distribution in both the pockets become equal, which means that the area of gas passage at the fold has become big enough that, there is no constriction between the two pockets anymore. Thus, the load increases abruptly at this point.

Also, it is seen that, as the order increases, θ_f tends to shift towards θ_o. This suggests that higher-order polynomial functions equations 8.14 and 8.15 are suitable for more constricted (or less allowability) fold situations, where the constriction area gets open at larger angles and with a smaller rate.

8.4.3 USER SUBROUTINE

A DLOAD subroutine has been used in this dynamic implicit analysis. For every increment of time, the subroutine is called as many times as much there are elements in the model. Every time some iteration is performed and load is applied till the solution converges.

As per the proposed model, the magnitude of load acting on elements depends on the angle of fold at that instant of time. This angle is computed in two stages. In the first stage, the coordinates of a pair of elements present on each side of a pocket, one next to the crease and another a little farther away along its length are obtained, as shown in Figure 8.6a. Their respective coordinates are written in four different external database files (one file for each coordinate) at every time increment.

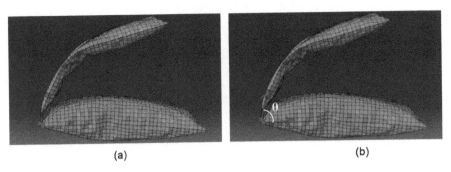

FIGURE 8.6 (a) Selected elements of registered coordinates in first stage. (b) Computing vectors and angle between them in second stage.

When coordinates of all these four elements have been registered, then comes the second stage where all the four files are opened and the coordinates of these elements are read. Two vectors can be computed using these coordinates. These vectors almost lie in the planes of the adjacent pockets. Then, using the cosine rule, the angle between these two vectors is calculated. This is the angle between the two pockets at a certain time, as shown in Figure 8.6b.

The angle at every time increment is computed and written in an external database so that their value can be procured to compute the magnitude of load P_a and P_b by equations 8.10 and 8.11 as discussed in the inflation model in Section 8.2. Since the range of elements of each pocket is known, so P_a and P_b can be applied to those elements of pocket 'a' and pocket 'b' respectively.

The flow chart of the complete methodology is as follows (Figure 8.7).

8.5 RESULTS AND DISCUSSION

8.5.1 SIMULATION RESULT

The uncertainty observed during the analysis of the mechanical behavior of inflatable elements, is mainly due to the strong nonlinear phenomena, both in the material and the geometric since it is a large displacement problem. The mechanical behavior of inflatable structures shows a strong nonlinear dependence of the internal pressure because it is the internal pressure, due to which the deformation of the membrane is happening (Barsotti and Ligarò, 2014). As the internal pressure keeps growing up, the overall stiffness of the structure also keeps increasing. Also due to variation of internal pressure with respect to time and position, during the inflation process, one can notice that the structure undergoes more perturbation and displacement in space.

Deployment using first-order polynomial functions (Figures 8.8 and 8.9).

The deployment starts with stress-free configuration where the structure is in a folded state. Thus, there is no stiffness initially in the structure. Then gas starts to rush in at a constant rate. It is the time when stiffness in the structure starts building up but differently at different positions. Initially, the pocket 'b' (attached to the valve) gets pressurized/stiffened at a faster rate due to more allowability to gas in this region, but the pressure in the farther pocket i.e. 'a' increases with a very slow

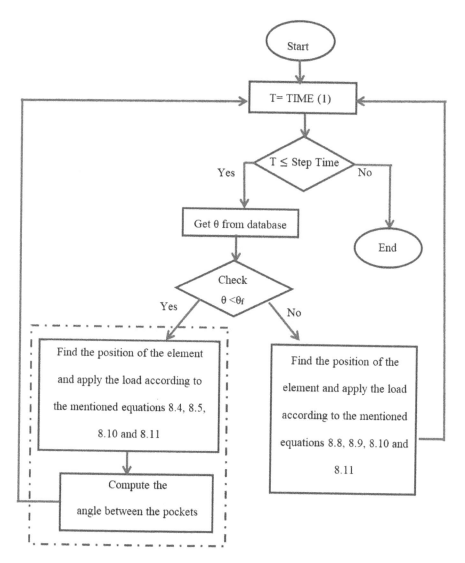

FIGURE 8.7 Flowchart of complete methodology.

rate because of the large constriction present at the crease. As the inflation proceeds, the angle between the pockets grows, and thus the constriction area grows. Hence, increasing allowability of gas into pocket 'a'. Later, pressure in 'a' also starts catching up with 'b'. According to the model discussed in Section 8.3, when the θ hits the value of θ_f, the constriction comes to end. This is the point when pressures in both pockets become equal. Now the deployment starts to happen with uniform pressure throughout the internal surface of structure. Finally, when θ hits θ_o the structure gets fully deployed. Further to this point with an increase in the gas inlet, internal pressure increases which start causing pre-tension in the membrane walls.

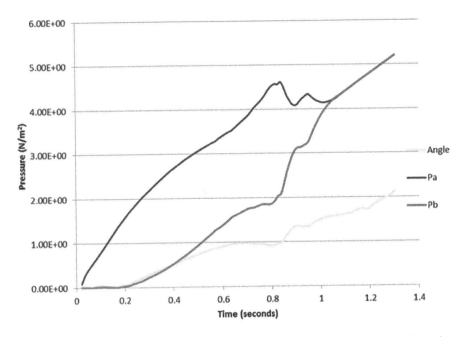

FIGURE 8.8 Pressure variations in pockets *a* (black) and *b* (grey) with respect to time using first-order polynomial function

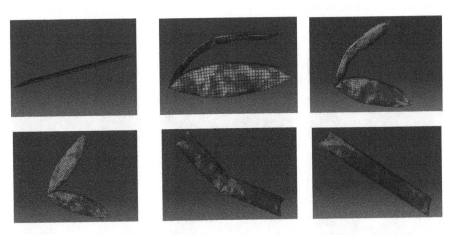

FIGURE 8.9 FE simulation results in sequence with first-order polynomial function.

Deployment using second-order polynomial functions (Figures 8.10 and 8.11).

The qualitative trends in both the cases are similar, i.e., in both the graphs the initial pressure rises in pocket 'a' is higher than 'b'. Later, the pressure of 'a' catches up with 'b'. Finally, when the θ becomes θ_f, both the pressures become equal. The ups and downs in the trends are also observed in the deployment process. This is incurred due to the variation in stiffness at the crease portion in the structure. This variation of stiffness is quantified by finding the angle between the pockets. Also, one can clearly

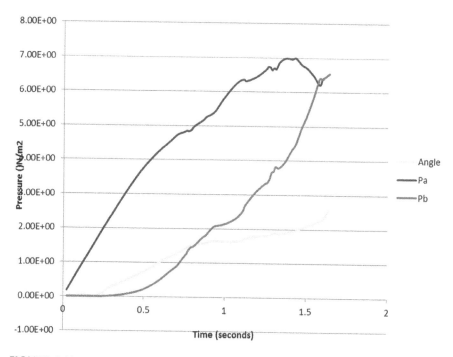

FIGURE 8.10 Pressure variations in pockets *a* (black) and *b* (grey) with respect to time using second-order polynomial function.

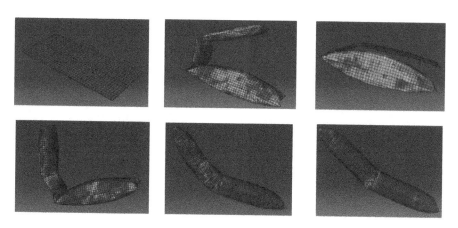

FIGURE 8.11 FE simulation results in sequence with second-order polynomial function.

notice that the gap in the first-order polynomial function is relatively lower than in the second-order polynomial function. This happens due to the use of higher-order polynomial; thus, the appropriate formulation must be implemented according to the features of the structure and process, as discussed in Section 8.2.

8.5.2 VALIDATION EXPERIMENT

The experimental results of Salma et al. (Salama, Kuo and Lou, 2000) have been taken for validation. They have considered a structure of the same geometric attributes. The structure is folded in its middle in the stowed state. Deployment is done by a pneumatic pump attached to pressure regulator and flow meter. Pressure in each pocket is monitored by separate pressure gauges. The simulation results have a resemblance with their experimental results. However, some difference also shows up due to the following reasons.

There are quite some differences between the conditions of experiment and simulation, experiment is carried out with slow inflation of structure for 1.5 minutes. This is computationally difficult to conduct in CAE analysis. Also, liberty in analysis has been taken in considering comparatively small Young's modulus in order to reduce stiffness of the structure, to reduce computational difficulty. Gravity and ambiance pressure are neglected in the analysis. The membrane element considered in analysis M3D4R does not have bending stiffness but actually the membrane structures do possess very small bending stiffness. The pressure variation model is of very primitive level that uses rigid body analysis and ideal gas equation.

Even after these limitations, a good agreement between the pressure curves in experiment and simulation is seen. So only a qualitative comparison between experiment and simulation can be seen which shows that the trend of pressure variation looks very alike.

8.6 CONCLUSION AND FUTURE SCOPE

An FE analysis for the deployment of simple inflatable structure has been done in this chapter. All the complexity of large displacement problem which is nonlinear in nature can be handled using soft computing and AI. Computing the cross-sectional area (at the crease) is cumbersome, so in place of that, an interim angle between folds has been employed during deployment. As this angle changes, the mass flow and thus the pressure across the crease also changes. In this chapter, the relation between this rate of change of pressure across the crease with respect to the interim angle has been successfully discussed. With the full development of artificial intelligence algorithm, correct function for pressure variation can be judicially selected as per the material properties and inflation conditions. This will be very helpful for generative designing of inflation process and will be more sustainable because it will reduce a lot of experimental and computational consumption of resources without compromising much with the result.

ABBREVIATIONS

Notation	Definition
P_n	Pressure in the nth pocket of the inflatable using the ideal gas equation (N/m²)
m	Amount of mass of gas in nth pocket (kg)
R	Gas constant of air ($= 287$ J/kg·K)
T	Ambient temperature (K)
V_n	Volume of the nth pocket (m³)
V	Total volume (m³)
V_a	Volume of the ath pocket (m³)
V_b	Volume of the bth pocket (m³)
$m(t)$	Mass inlet flow function (kg)
t	Time (seconds)
n	Order of the polynomial function
χ_a	Volume fraction of pocket a
χ_b	Volume fraction of pocket b
m_{ta}	Amount of gas present in pocket a at time t (kg)
m_{tb}	Amount of gas present in pocket b at time t (kg)
θ_t	Angle between the pockets at time t
θ_o	Limiting angle for the polynomial functions
θ_f	The angle beyond which masses in both pockets get distributed according to their respective volume fractions
P_a	Pressure in pocket a at time t (N/m²)
P_b	Pressure in pocket b at time t (N/m²)

REFERENCES

Barsotti, R. and Ligarò, S. S. (2014) 'Thin-Walled structures numerical analysis of partly wrinkled cylindrical in flated beams under bending and shear', *Thin Walled Structures*, 84, pp. 204–213. doi: 10.1016/j.tws.2014.06.009.

Graczykowski, C. (2015) 'Mathematical models and numerical methods for the simulation of adaptive inflatable structures for impact absorption', *Computers and Structures*. doi: 10.1016/j.compstruc.2015.06.017.

Salama, M., Kuo, C. P. and Lou, M. (2000) 'Simulation of deployment dynamics of inflatable structures', *AIAA Journal*, 38(12), pp. 2277–2283. doi: 10.2514/2.896.

Wei, J. et al. (2015) 'Deployable dynamic analysis and on-orbit experiment for inflatable gravity-gradient boom', *Advances in Space Research*, 55(2), pp. 639–646. doi: 10.1016/j.asr.2014.10.024.

9 Experimental and Machine Learning Approach to Evaluate the Performance of Refrigerator and Air Conditioning Using TiO$_2$ Nanoparticle

Harinarayan Sharma
Netaji Subhas Institute of Technology

Aniket Kumar Dutt
CSIR-National Metallurgical Laboratory

Pawan Kumar
University of Johannesburg

Mamookho Elizabeth Makhatha
University of Johannesburg

CONTENTS

DOI: 10.1201/9781003154518-9

159

9.1 INTRODUCTION

In a refrigeration system, the Coefficient of performance (COP) is termed as the ratio of desirable effect in the evaporator and work input to the compressor [1]. It can be depending upon fluids used in the vapour compression refrigeration (VCR) cycle. In refrigeration and air conditioning system (RAC), two types of fluid are used: one is refrigerant used as a cooling gas and the other is compressor oil to lubricate and cool the compressor as possible [2–6]. In RAC system including home refrigerator, chiller and automobile refrigeration, R134a is a commonly used alternative refrigerant. This refrigerant has been accepted in many countries as an alternative refrigerant. The polyolester (POE) oil, mineral oil and PAG oil are used as compressor oil but POE oil has great chemical polarity with R134a refrigerant. In order to enhance COP, heat transfer in the used fluid plays an important role. The heat transfer is enhanced to increase the transport properties of the fluid. Nanoparticles are introduced in the base fluid, either refrigerant or lubricant, to modify the transport properties of heat transfer flow [7–9]. The nanoparticle (range between 1 and 100 nm) is suspended in the base fluid to engineer a new class of fluid having good thermal properties called nanofluids. Choi and Eastman first introduced the concept of nanofluid in 1995 [10–12]. Bi et al. [13] took TiO_2-R600 as a nano refrigerant and found that the system works efficiently and smoothly. The energy is saved 9.60% when using 0.5 g nanoparticles per liter of refrigerant. Hussen [14] took R22 refrigerant and investigated the effect of titanium-based mineral nano lubricant in a window-type RAC system. The result shows that the network on compressor is decreased and improved the performance. Kumar et al. [15] did work on PAG-Al_2O_3 nano lubricant and R134a-Al_2O_3 as a nano refrigerant in a VCR system. When 0.2% volume of concentration of aluminum dioxide is used in oil, then 10.32% less energy is required in comparison to simple PAG oil. Bi et al. [16] studied the performance of home refrigerators and used nano TiO_2 embedded mineral oil and R134a refrigerant. The functionality in this condition works safely and a decrement of 26.1% energy consumption when using a TiO_2 of 0.1% mass fraction with mineral oil in the context of without nanoparticles.

Manivannan et al. [17] use different machine learning algorithms to predict the air-conditioning load of a residential building on an hourly and daily basis. The data is taken from conventional smart meters and past weather data for training and testing. The result shows that Random Forests gives the best result in terms of prediction in the context of other different algorithms. The value of R^2 was founded at 87.3% and 83.2% on an hourly and daily basis, respectively. Reddy et al. [18] investigated the domestic refrigerator performance in which a propane/butane mixture as a refrigerant in place of R134a refrigerant and got COP of a system. He used ANN and Fuzzy logic to get enthalpy at different point as a output and pressure as well as temperature as a input to get the maximum COP.

9.2 EXPERIMENTAL SETUP

9.2.1 SET UP AND PERFORMANCE TEST

Our experiment was conducted on vapour compression test rig that is placed in RAC lab, which is shown in Figure 9.1. The test rig encompasses mainly four components.

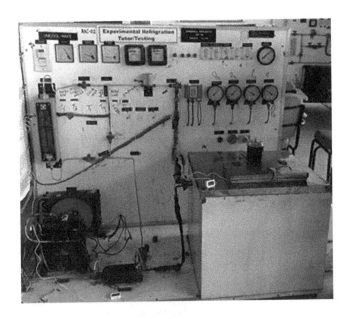

FIGURE 9.1 Setup of vapour compression refrigeration system.

These components are hermetically sealed compressor, air-cooled condenser, capillary tube and evaporator. Fan is used to cool the condenser for heat transfer. The spiral coil of copper in the cylindrical form is used in the evaporator for cooling. Heat transfer in the condenser and evaporator is done through phase change. This type of heat transfer is known as latent heat transfer. Capillary tube is used as a throttling device in the RAC system. Copper is used for capillary tube. It is a long tube with a smaller inner diameter. It takes up less space due to several turns.

The turn is typically used as a circular shape, but in our experiment, we used as a cubic shape, as shown in Figure 9.2. The main objective of a capillary tube is to reduce refrigerant pressure from the higher side, resulting in a decrease in temperature.

The instalment of the pressure gauge and digital thermocouple has been done at the appropriate point to measure the pressure and temperature, respectively.

The spiral coil of the evaporator is immersed in water. Water is treated as a cooling load. The heat flux is constantly supplied by a heating rod of 2000 W capacity, and water is agitated to get desire and uniform temperature. The test is carried out with different prepared samples of POE-TiO$_2$ nano lubricant and R134a refrigerant. The nano

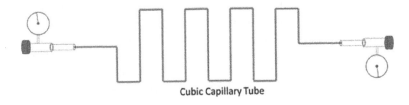

Cubic Capillary Tube

FIGURE 9.2 Shape of capillary tube.

lubricant is filled in the compressor through the service port firstly then R134a gas is charged in the VCR system. The system is allowed to stabilize for 15 minutes every time.

9.2.2 Preparation of Nano Lubricant

Many input and output parameters are there in the area of RAC system. These parameters were related to lubricant used in the compressor and refrigerant used in the VCR system. The combination of nanoparticles and compressor oil is termed as nano lubricant. The methods used to achieve this combination are very important. There are mainly two methods to prepare nano lubricant: one is one-step method and other is two-step method. One-step method is very costly and is not used for commercial purpose. So, in this case, we used a two-step method to prepare nano lubricant, which is a versatile technique. The compressor oil used in this experiment was polyolester (POE) oil and nano particle titanium dioxide (TiO_2) was taken i.e. manufactured by Reinste Nano venture Pvt. Ltd. New Delhi. In this method, ultrasonic vibrator is used for uniform distribution of nano particle and prepared sample is then kept for ultrasonic bath about 24 hours for agitation. Three samples of 0.5, 1.0 and 1.5 g of TiO_2 and 1 L of POE oil are prepared for the experiment. The nano particle is weighted by digital weighing machine.

9.3 MACHINE LEARNING MODELS

9.3.1 Gaussian Process Regression

It is a robust tool of machine learning to make a model of unknown functions. It is used to solve the regression problem which is non-parametric and kernel-based Bayesian approach.

9.3.2 Support Vector Regression

It is a supervised learning algorithm of machine learning which is based on statistical theory. It is a technique to solve the regression as well as pattern recognition problems. A fit line is generated between the predicted and actual data in SVR.

9.4 RESULTS AND DISCUSSION

Research deals the study of COP of the VCR system with pure form of basic refrigerant R134a with POE oil and nano lubricant POE-TiO_2 with cubic capillary tube shape of copper. Titanium Dioxide (TiO_2) of different concentration i.e. 0.5, 1.0 and 1.5 g is mixed in the POE oil. The VCR system starts above combination at different heat flux load i.e. 298, 303, 308, 313 and 318 K to check the effect of COP of the refrigeration system. Figure 9.3 shows the effect of different load conditions, concentration of TiO_2 on the COP of VCR system of the actual experimental data.

Figure 9.3 revels the influence of COP on the basis of evaporative load and concentration of titanium dioxide. The combination of R134a and POE oil, the COP of the system increases as the evaporative load rises from 295 to 318 K monotonically.

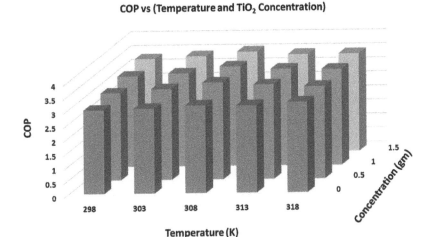

FIGURE 9.3 Experimental COP with varying temperature (K) and concentration (g).

When added titanium dioxide nano particles in the POE oil in the concentration of 0.5, 1.0 and 1.5 g, the COP of the VCR system increases when evaporative load increases from 298 to 308 K after that it decreases to 318 K. The rate of increment in COP differs according to heat flux and concentration of nano particles.

For prediction purpose, different soft computing techniques are used in worldwide today. However, in our study, the most emerging technique machine learning is used to predict the outcomes. In machine learning, there are different regression algorithms for predictions, but here support vector machine and Gaussian process regression with different kernel functions are used. PUK and RBF are kernel functions which are used with above algorithms to predict the COP of experimental data. Hence, a machine learning model was developed with different combinations of algorithms and kernels for predictions. The COP of predicted data verses actual data with ML models such as GPR_RBF, GPR_PUK, SVR_RBF and SVR_PUK of training and testing results are shown in the Figures 9.4 and 9.5, respectively. The developed models perform better performance in terms of prediction; kernel parameters are optimized, as shown in Table 9.1, and performance parameters such as coefficient of correlation (CC) and root mean square error (RMSE) are shown in Table 9.2.

Figure 9.4 gives the information of predicted COP and actual COP with different developed ML models of training set. Total twenty experimental data are taken for model development. The predicted COP is obtained from training of 75% of experimental data (fifteen data points) of discussed models and these models are tested by 25% experimental data (five data point), then these models are developed to work accurately. After testing the models, the predicted COP is obtained, as shown in Figure 9.5.

The value of CC and RMSE of different trained as well as tested developed ML models are shown in Table 9.2. It is concluded that Gaussian process regression with PUK kernel works better in comparison to support vector regression with RBF kernel.

The predicted COP is very close to the experimental COP in training as well as testing data set. The intake parameter like concentration of titanium dioxide and

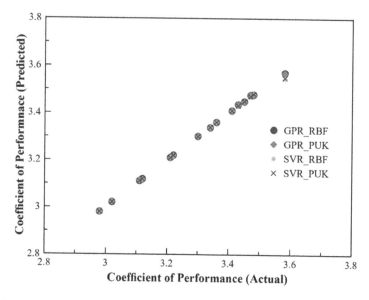

FIGURE 9.4 Predicted coefficient of performance versus actual coefficient of performance for the training data.

evaporative load is a non-linear relationship of COP of VCR system. To perform better non-linear relation, GPR and SVR with PUK kernel is most promising ML model. The value of CC = 0.9697 (RMSE = 0.0899) and CC = 0.9699 (RMSE = 0.0879) is obtained in GPR as well as SVR with PUK kernel function. In context of GPR and SVR, SVR with PUK performs better to obtain the predicted COP.

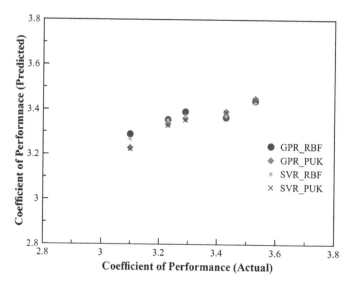

FIGURE 9.5 Predicted coefficient of performance versus actual coefficient of performance for the testing data.

TABLE 9.1

User-Defined Parameter for GPR and SVR Using RBF and PUK Kernel Function

Kernels	GPR	SVR
PUK	Gaussian noise = 0.01, $\sigma = 2$, $\omega = 2$	$C = 80$, $\sigma = 1.3$, $\omega = 80$
RBF	Gaussian noise = 0.002, $\gamma = 0.7$	$C = 380$, $\gamma = 1.1$

TABLE 9.2

Performance Characteristics for COP

Machine Learning Approach	Training Data Set		Testing Data Set	
	CC	RMSE	CC	RMSE
GPR_PUK	0.9996	0.0051	0.9697	0.0899
GPR_RBF	0.9998	0.0032	0.8838	0.1215
SVR_PUK	0.9991	0.0081	0.9699	0.0879
SVR_RBF	0.999	0.0086	0.9283	0.1119

9.5 CONCLUSION

In this research, the experimental and machine learning study reveals the performance of VCR system with respect to application of nano lubricant with varying concentration of TiO_2 and different heat flux in the evaporator. It is noted that with different concentration of titanium dioxide with POE oil as well as evaporative load, the COP of RAC is increased from 298 to 308 K after that it decreases to 318 K. To forecast the COP, the machine learning technique is used, and different ML models such as GPR_RBF, GPR_PUK, SVR_RBF and SVR_PUK are developed from experimental data. The performance of these models is expressed in terms of CC and RMSE value. From these CC and RMSE value, it can be said that SVR with PUK performs well to predict the COP of the system from experimental data.

REFERENCES

1. D. Yang, B. Sun, H.W. Li, X.C. Fan, "Experimental study on the heat transfer and flow characteristics of nanorefrigerants inside a corrugated tube", *Int J Refrig*, Vol. 56, pp. 213–223, 2015.
2. D. Wen, G. Lin, S. Vafaei, K. Zhang, "Review of nanofluids for heat transfer applications", *Particuology*, Vol. 7, pp. 141–150, 2007.
3. J. X. Liu, R. Bao, "Boiling heat transfer characteristics of nanofluids in a flat heat pipe evaporator with micro-grooved heating surface", *Int J Multiph Flow*, Vol. 33, pp. 1284–1295, 2007.
4. D. Wen, Y. Ding, "Experimental investigation into the pool boiling heat transfer of aqueous based-Al2O3 nanofluids", *J Nanopart Res*, Vol. 7, pp. 265–274, 2005.

5. S. Torii, "Experimental study on thermal transport phenomenon of nanofluids as working fluid in heat exchanger". *Int J Air Cond Refrig*, Vol. 22, pp. 1–6, 2014.

6. A. Sözen, E. Özba, T. Menlik, T. Çakır, M. Gürü, K. Boran, "Improving the thermal performance of diffusion absorption refrigeration system with alumina nanofluids: An experimental study", *Int J Refrig*, Vol. 44, pp. 73–80, 2014.

7. O. A. Alawi, N. A. C. Sidik, M. Beriache, "Applications of nanorefrigerant and nano-lubricants in refrigeration, air-conditioning and heat pump systems: A review", *Int Commun Heat Mass Transf*, Vol. 68, pp. 91–97, 2015.

8. C. S. Jwo, L.Y. Jeng, T. P. Teng, H. Chang, "Effects of nanolubricant on performance of hydrocarbon refrigerant system", *J Vac SciTechnol B*, Vol. 27, pp. 1473–1477, 2009.

9. A. Celen, A. Çebi, M. Aktas, O. Mahian, A. S. Dalkilic, S. Wongwises, "A review of nanorefrigerants: Flow characteristics and applications", *Int J Refrig*, Vol. 44, pp. 125–140, 2014.

10. M. A. Kedzierski, "Viscosity and density of CuO nanolubricant", *Int J Refrig*, Vol. 35, pp. 1997–2002, 2012.

11. J. B. Youbi, "The effect of oil in refrigeration: Current research issues and critical review of thermodynamic aspects", *Int J Refrig*, Vol. 31, pp. 165–179, 2008.

12. O. A. Alawi, N. Sidik, M. Beriache, "Applications of nanorefrigerant and nanolubricants in refrigeration air-conditioning and heat pump systems: A review", *Int Commun Heat Mass Transf*, Vol. 68, pp. 91–97, 2016.

13. S. Bi, K. Guo, Z. Liu, J. Wu, S. Bi, L. Shi, Z. Li, "Performance of a domestic refrigerator using TiO_2-R600a nano-refrigerant as a working fluid", *Energy Convers Manag*, Vol. 52, pp. 733–737, 2010.

14. H. A. Hussen, "Experimental investigation for TiO_2 nanoparticles as a lubricant-additive for a compressor of window type air-conditioner system", *J Eng*, Vol. 20, pp. 61–72, 2014.

15. D. Kumar, R. Sendil, "Experimental study on Al_2O_3-R134a nano refrigerant in refrigeration system", *Int J Modern Eng Res*, Vol. 2, pp. 3927–3929, 2012.

16. S. Bi, L. Shi, Z. Li, "Application of nanoparticles in domestic refrigerators" *Appl Therm Eng*, Vol. 28, pp. 1834–1843, 2008.

17. M. Manivannan, B. Najafi, F. Rinaldi, "Machine learning based short term prediction of air conditioning load through smart meter analytics", *Energies*, Vol. 1905, pp. 1–17, 2017.

18. D. V. Reddy, P. Bhramara, K. Govindarajulu, "Application of soft computing techniques for analysis of vapour compression refrigeration system", *International Conference on Advances in Mechanical Sciences*, Vol. 2, pp. 368–373, 2014.

10 Numerical and Experimental Investigation on Thinning in Single-Point Incremental Sheet Forming

Sahil Bendure, Rahul Jagtap, and Malaykumar Patel
Dr. Vishwanath Karad MIT World Peace University

CONTENTS

10.1 INTRODUCTION

SPIF entails a set of layer-by-layer plastic deformations that are used to shape a sheet into the desired component. To clamp the sheet rigidly, a fixture is used and the tool travels over the sheet as per the program command to achieve the final design of the component. The benefits of traditional sheet metal forming are that the process can be directly operated by CNC machines. As in traditional sheet metal forming, no die is needed. In the manufacturing phase, the removal of the die decreases the price per piece and rises the improvement in time for small manufacture runs as the need to create a die is excluded. Since its inception, the ISF process has seen many developments. Industries, such as Honda Motor Co., Ltd. & Amino Corp., teamed up to investigate die-less shaping as a

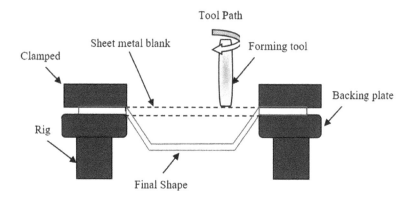

FIGURE 10.1 Schematic representation of symmetric SPIF.

potential manufacturing process for car replacement panels. Toyota Motor Corporation & Amino Corporation collaborated to manufacture a high-style logo mark and sharp feature lines on the door panels of TOYOTA supercharger model iQ-GRMN using the ISF process [1]. Vanhove et al. [2] created thin shell clavicle implants using SPIF. Potran et al. [3] compared the denture geometry of casted and SPIF-based dentures, and the SPIF process gives the desirable and comfort fitting as per patient requirements.

The SPIF method is schematically represented in Figure 10.1. Thickness of the formed part using this process follows the sine law of thinning as given in equation 10.1:

$$t_f = t_i \cdot \sin(\pi/2 - \alpha) = t_i \cdot \sin\alpha \qquad (10.1)$$

where t_i – initial thickness and t_f – final thickness, and α is the semi cone angle [4].

Thickness strain in the formed parts using the SPIF process is estimated more efficiently using the FEM. The thickness of the saturation point is measured using the thickness strain of the final triangular mesh elements [5]. Yang et al. [6] investigated and validated the efficacy of various finite element techniques for predicting sheet thinning in formed parts. Yamashita et al. [7] used a dynamic explicit finite element program called DYNA3D to numerically evaluate the deformation behavior utilizing multiple tool paths. They noticed that a spiral tool path produces a more consistent thickness distribution in the result. Blaga and Oleksik [8] investigated the impact of the forming method by selecting the location of forming tool in the first step in three distinct trajectories. The most critical element in thinning ratio is determined to be the forming angle. Using a tool path with consistently spaced pressing points, thinning may be effectively reduced. Sequential limit analysis was utilized by Mirnia et al. [9] to analyze thickness distribution in SPIF. They conclude that more increases in pitch can reduce the minimum thickness. The innovative hybrid incremental sheet forming (HISF) technique demonstrated promising results in terms of improving thickness distribution. Researchers, such as Jagtap and Kumar [10], proposed a two-step hybrid incremental sheet forming (HISF) procedure. Experiments on the thinning and formability of Al-1050 material sheets are carried out. They observed that the shape of the preform tool has a major impact on thickness distribution [11]. It is concluded that in the HISF process, the amount of stretching and preform tool radius also have a considerable impact on thickness distribution. Stretching causes greater plastic deformation, which leads to more local thinning [12]. Joseph [13] studied the thickness deformation and formability of aluminum 5052. The authors performed an FLD analysis for the formability of sheet. There is an influence of temperature on the formability and thickness distribution sheet. It was found that sheet annealed at higher than room temperature results in better thickness distribution. Salem et al. [14] studied the effect of tool path on thickness and formability of sheet. The impact of the tool path on total strain along the formed part is determined using experimental and simulation models. A bending zone is visible near the clamed sheet at the cone forming process, with constant thickness reduction followed by severe thinning region. Nirala and Agrawal [15] found that ISF result in improved formability as compared to the forming or deep drawing methods. A thickness prediction model was also developed to predict the thickness of formed parts. More et al. [16] discussed the influence of process parameters on performance characteristics such as sheet formability, thickness and surface finish.

From the reviewed literature, it is found that the FEM method is useful to predict the localized thinning and thickness spread in the formed parts using the SPIF process. It helps in planning the SPIF process which increases the process performance and results in forming accurate and sound sheet metal parts. The present work involves numerical analysis of thinning in part formed using the SPIF technique. Experiments are performed to confirm the results of the FEM analysis. The simulation plan is designed according to the Box–Behnken experimental design. Analysis of variance (ANOVA) is used for statistical analysis. The finding of the simulation results is validated by the experimental results.

10.2 MATERIALS AND METHODOLOGY

In the current work, experiments are implemented on the aluminum alloy Al-6061 blanks. The blank sheet dimensions are 85 mm × 85 mm × 0.8 mm. Because of its excellent strength-to-weight ratio and formability, aluminum is widely utilized in the automotive and aerospace industries. Table 10.1 lists the mechanical properties of the aluminum blank. 3D model of the conical frustum to be formed is designed using Autodesk Fusion 360 software. Helical tool path is generated for forming conical frustum using the SPIF process.

10.2.1 FEA Modeling

ABAQUS/Explicit platform was used for the FEA modeling, which is well known in the industry for nonlinear analysis. The sheet is assumed to be a deformable shell, and the tool is assumed to be analytical rigid. Import G-code from Fusion 360's CAM tools. Isotropic and elastic-plastic sheet materials were assumed [7]. In all nonlinear simulations, the boundary condition must be defined. In this case, as shown in Figure 10.3, the sheet edges were encastre in all DOF, and the analytical rigid body forming tool was given displacement/rotation in X, Y, and Z smooth step directions. For the study, an explicit linear S4R 4-node thick shell type 1 mm element size mesh was used. Scale to target time increment 0.01 and scale factor mass uniformly to satisfy target was used to minimize CPU time in mass scaling.

TABLE 10.1
Material Property

Properties	Value
Sheet material	Al-6061
Density	2.7 g/cm³
Young's modulus (E)	68,000 MPa
Tensile yield strength	370 MPa
Poisson's ratio	0.33
Thermal conductivity	166 W/m/K
Elongation	10.280%
Sheet thickness	0.8 mm

10.2.2 EXPERIMENTAL SETUP

The experiment was carried out on an AMS mcv-350 three-axis vertical milling machine with a FANUC 0I-MF numeric control machine, as shown in Figure 10.4. Al 6061 material sheet sizes of 85 mm×85 mm×0.8 mm was used according to fixture specification. A hemispherical end headed 8 mm diameter tool made of HSS is used to form the perfect shape according to the tool direction. The spindle speed was set to 2000 rpm and the tool and ramp feed rate was set to 300 mm/min. Figure 10.2 shows a spiral tool path that was used to save time. In Table 10.2, there are more input process parameters.

10.2.3 FEA SIMULATION PLAN

The response surface method (RSM) is used to plan the FEA simulation in this chapter [17]. The optimum parameters of the SPIF process should be chosen to create

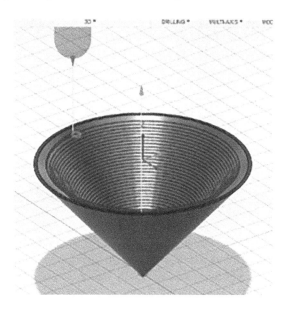

FIGURE 10.2   Cone shape geometry.

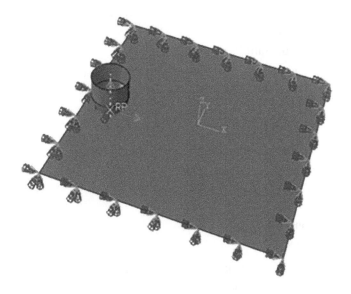

FIGURE 10.3   Boundary condition applied on sheet and tool.

FIGURE 10.4   Experiment setup.

conical frustum sufficient quality of final sheet thickness without failures. The simulation plan employs a three-level Box–Behnken DOE method. Higher-order response
surfaces are created using Box–Behnken designs, which need fewer runs than a traditional factorial technique [18]. The thickness of the formed part is measured using
ABAQUS/Explicit software [19]. The minimum thickness along formed surface is
used as the response. Table 10.2 lists the constant parameters. Table 10.3 shows the
factors and their level, which are utilized in the experiment design.

TABLE 10.2
Constant Parameters

Parameters	Dimensions
Cone Diameter	45 mm
Wall angle	48°
Height of cone	25 mm
Spindle speed	2000 rpm
Tool path	Spiral

TABLE 10.3
Process Parameters

Process Parameters		Actual values		
Levels	Unit	1	2	3
Tool diameter	(mm)	5	6.5	8
Pitch	(mm)	0.35	0.55	0.75
Feed	(mm/min)	300	450	600

10.3 RESULT AND DISCUSSION

10.3.1 FEA SIMULATION

The thickness of parts formed by the SPIF process can be approximately predicted using the traditional spinning process' sine law of thinning (equation 10.1). The thickness of the conical frustum is measured along the formed wall in the FEA simulation, as presented in Figures 10.5 and 10.6. Figures 10.5 and 10.6 show the thickness along the formed wall from the clamped edge to the center of the conical frustum. As presented in Figure 10.5, to determine the minimum thickness of the formed part, a path is generated by collecting points along the edges of the mesh and determining the sheet thickness at a specific point. During the simulation, points were monitored to determine the final sheet thickness of formed parts [20]. Simulated part thickness ranges between 0.49 and 0.53 mm along the formed wall, which is approximately validated by the sine law of sheet thinning. As a result, the simulations results are in good accord with the sine law predictions. Simulated thickness is smaller than the thickness anticipated by the sine law of thinning. Similar outcomes were presented by Yang et al. [6].

The maximum forming height of the formed conical frustum is 23.2 mm. In the FEA simulation, the maximum height was found to be 22.79 mm, which is very close to the actual value. The maximum height of the part formed using simulation is depicted in Figure 10.7 and forming height achieved experimentally is shown in Figure 10.8.

10.3.2 INFLUENCE OF CONTROL PARAMETERS ON MINIMUM THICKNESS

Simulations were planned using Box–Behnken DOE method. The influence of three-process parameters specifically pitch (p), tool diameter (d) and feed (f) on minimum thickness is studied. The results are analyzed using ANOVA. ANOVA is done using

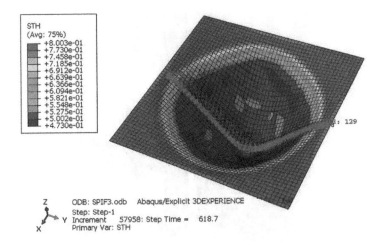

FIGURE 10.5   Thickness distribution.

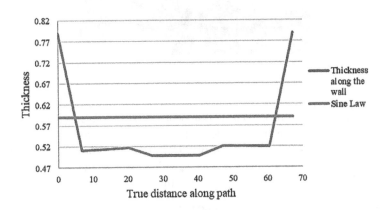

FIGURE 10.6   Thickness vs true distance along path plot.

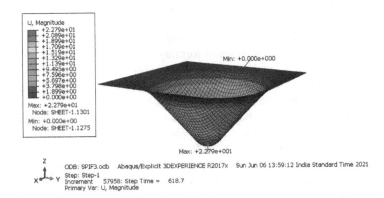

FIGURE 10.7   Maximum deformation.

FIGURE 10.8 Height gauge.

the statistical software tool Minitab 19.0 student's version. The analysis is conducted with a 95% confidence interval. Table 10.4 displays the results of an ANOVA for minimum thickness (t). The R^2 value of 99.66% and the normal probability plot demonstrate that regression fitness is a statistically significant measurement.

The final regression equation to predict minimum thickness is given as follows:

$$t = 0.4507 + 0.7321\,p - 0.02372\,d - 0.000257\,f - 0.5928\,p*p + 0.001461\,d*d$$

$$+ 0.000001\,f*f + 0.00458\,p*d - 0.000225\,p*f - 0.000006\,d*f \qquad (10.2)$$

Figure 10.9 shows the normal probability plot graph. Figures 10.10a and 10.11a demonstrate the effect of tool size as well as pitch on thickness. From the figures, it is found that a small value of tool diameter and intermediate value of pitch results in maximum thickness. In incremental forming, smaller tools are combined with small pitch values, which results in less rubbing against the blank sheet. As tool size increases, the tool rubs more frequently against the blank sheet which reduces the sheet thickness. Similar results are also presented by Jagtap et al. [20].

Figures 10.10b and 10.11b show the result of pitch and feed on minimum thickness. It is found that intermediate values of pitch and maximum value of feed result in maximum thickness. While using small tools and small pitch values, the rubbing of tool against the sheet is more. As the pitch goes on increasing, vertical tool travel after every layer formed is more. For the intermediate pitch value, the repeated rubbing of the tool against sheet in the same area is considerably reduced resulting in

TABLE 10.4
ANOVA Table for Minimum Thickness

Source	Degrees of freedom	Adjusted SS	Adjusted MS	F-Value	P-Value
Parameter	9	0.004031	0.000448	161.73	0.000
Linear	3	0.000998	0.000333	120.16	0.000
p	1	0.000023	0.000023	8.47	0.033
d	1	0.000434	0.000434	156.58	0.000
f	1	0.000541	0.000541	195.42	0.000
$p*p$	1	0.002076	0.002076	749.64	0.000
$d*d$	1	0.000040	0.000040	14.41	0.013
$f*f$	1	0.000520	0.000520	187.61	0.000
$p*d$	1	0.000008	0.000008	2.73	0.159
$p*f$	1	0.000182	0.000182	65.81	0.000
$d*f$	1	0.000007	0.000007	2.63	0.166
Error	5	0.000014	0.000003		
Pure error	2	0.000000	0.000000		
Total	14	0.004045			
		R^2	99.66%		
		Adj – R^2	99.04%		

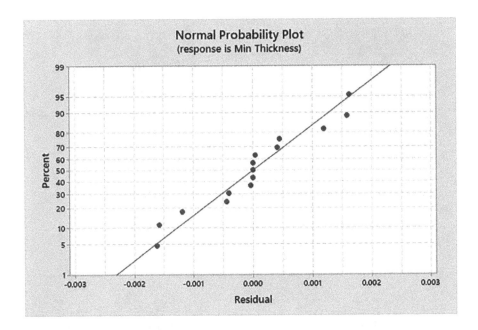

FIGURE 10.9 Normal probability plot.

less thickness reduction. Further, as pitch value goes on increasing, the vertical tool travel is more. The increased vertical tool movement results in more plastic strain in the blank sheet, which further reduces the wall thickness of the formed part. Figures 10.10a, 10.11a and b, and 10.10b confirm the trends. At lower feed values, more thickness reduction is observed, as shown in Figures 10.10c and 10.11c.

10.4 CONCLUSION

A conical frustum of aluminum alloy 6061 was formed using the SPIF method. The thickness reduction and formation height of the conical frustum are studied using a FEM simulation model created in ABAQUS/Explicit software. Using the Box–Behnken DOE technique, the influence of process parameters is studied. Experiments and published results are used to validate the results. From the research, the subsequent conclusions can be derived:

1. The thickness of the formed part is influenced by all process factors, including pitch, tool size, and feed.
2. Maximum thickness is obtained with a small tool size, intermediate pitch, and maximum feed value.
3. The simulated model's results are substantially close to the experimental results. As a result, a similar model will be beneficial in analyzing the influence of various process parameters and responses.

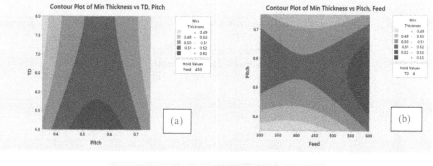

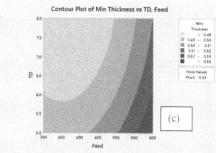

FIGURE 10.10 Contour plots (a) Minimum thickness vs TD, pitch. (b) Thickness vs pitch, feed. (c) Thickness vs TD, feed.

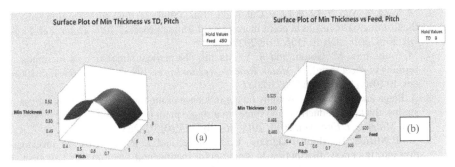

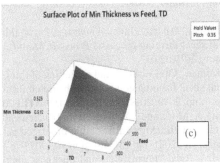

FIGURE 10.11 Surface plots (a) Minimum thickness vs TD, pitch. (b) Minimum thickness vs pitch, feed. (c) Minimum thickness vs TD, feed.

ABBREVIATION

SPIF	Single-point incremental forming
CNC	Computer numerical control
FEM	Finite element method
ANOVA	Analysis of variance
DOF	Degree of freedom
RSM	Response surface method

REFERENCES

1. M. Amino, M. Mizoguchi, Y. Terauchi, and T. Maki, "Current status of 'dieless' amino's incremental forming," *Procedia Eng.*, vol. 81, pp. 54–62, 2014, doi: 10.1016/j.proeng.2014.09.128.
2. H. Vanhove, Y. Carette, S. Vancleef, and J. R. Duflou, "Production of thin shell clavicle implants through single point incremental forming," *Procedia Eng.*, vol. 183, pp. 174–179, 2017, doi: 10.1016/j.proeng.2017.04.058.
3. M. Potran, P. Skakun, and M. Faculty, "Application of single point incremental," *J. Technol. Plast.*, vol. 39, no. 2, pp. 16–23, 2014.
4. S. Kobayashi, I. K. Hall, and E. G. Thomsen, "A theory of shear spinning of cones," *J. Manuf. Sci. Eng. Trans. ASME*, vol. 83, no. 4, pp. 485–494, 1961, doi: 10.1115/1.3664573.
5. P. A. F. Martins, N. Bay, M. Skjoedt, and M. B. Silva, "Theory of single point incremental forming," *CIRP Ann. Manuf. Technol.*, vol. 57, no. 1, pp. 247–252, 2008, doi: 10.1016/j.cirp.2008.03.047.

6. M. Yang, Z. Yao, Y. Li, P. Li, F. Cui, and L. Bai, "Study on thickness thinning ratio of the forming parts in single point incremental forming process," *Adv. Mater. Sci. Eng.*, vol. 2018, 2018, doi: 10.1155/2018/2927189.

7. M. Yamashita, M. Gotoh, and S. Y. Atsumi, "Numerical simulation of incremental forming of sheet metal," *J. Mater. Process. Technol.*, vol. 199, no. 1, pp. 163–172, 2008, doi: 10.1016/j.jmatprotec.2007.07.037.

8. A. Blaga and V. Oleksik, "A study on the influence of the forming strategy on the main strains, thickness reduction, and forces in a single point incremental forming process," *Adv. Mater. Sci. Eng.*, vol. 2013, 2013, doi: 10.1155/2013/382635.

9. M. J. Mirnia, B. Mollaei Dariani, H. Vanhove, and J. R. Duflou, "An investigation into thickness distribution in single point incremental forming using sequential limit analysis," *Int. J. Mater. Form.*, vol. 7, no. 4, pp. 469–477, 2014, doi: 10.1007/s12289-013-1143-x.

10. R. Jagtap and S. Kumar, "An experimental investigation on thinning and formability in hybrid incremental sheet forming process," *Procedia Manuf.*, vol. 30, pp. 71–76, 2019, doi: 10.1016/j.promfg.2019.02.011.

11. R. Jagtap and S. Kumar, "Optimisation and modelling of thinning and geometric accuracy in incremental sheet forming combined with stretch forming," *Int. J. Mater. Eng. Innov.*, vol. 10, no. 1, pp. 2–19, 2019, doi: 10.1504/IJMATEI.2019.097888.

12. R. Jagtap, V. Sisodia, K. More, and S. Kumar, "Hybrid incremental forming: Investigation on localized thinning and thickness distribution in formed parts," In *Lecture Notes in Mechanical Engineering*, 2021, pp. 151–161, doi: 10.1007/978-981-15-6619-6_16.

13. S. Selvaraju and J. I. Raja, "Formability and thickness distribution analysis on aluminium alloy 5052 using single point incremental forming", TJPRC Pvt. Ltd., 306–315, May, 2018, ISSN (P): 2249-6890.

14. E. Salem, J. Shin, M. Nath, M. Banu, and A. I. Taub, "Investigation of thickness variation in single point incremental forming," *Procedia Manuf.*, vol. 5, pp. 828–837, 2016, doi: 10.1016/j.promfg.2016.08.068.

15. H. K. Nirala and A. Agrawal, *Sheet Thinning Prediction and Calculation in Incremental Sheet Forming*, Springer, Singapore, 2018, doi: 10.1007/978-981-10-8767-7_15.

16. K. R. More, V. Sisodia, S. Kumar, *A Brief Review on Formability, Wall Thickness Distribution and Surface Roughness of Formed Part in Incremental Sheet Forming*, Springer, Singapore, 2020, doi: 10.1007/978-981-15-9117-4_11.

17. M. D. Vijayakumar, D. Chandramohan, and G. Gopalaramasubramaniyan, "Experimental investigation on single point incremental forming of IS513Cr3 using response surface method," *Mater. Today Proc.*, vol. 21, pp. 902–907, 2020, doi: 10.1016/j.matpr.2019.07.74.

18. J. S. Rao and B. Kumar, *3D Blade Root Shape Optimization*, Woodhead Publishing Limited, New Delhi, 2012.

19. M. Sbayti, A. Ghiotti, R. Bahloul, H. Belhadjsalah, and S. Bruschi, "Finite element analysis of hot single point incremental forming of hip prostheses," *MATEC Web Conf.*, vol. 80, 2016, doi: 10.1051/matecconf/20168014006.

20. R. Jagtap, S. Kashid, S. Kumar, and H. M. A. Hussein, "An experimental study on the influence of tool path, tool diameter and pitch in single point incremental forming (SPIF)," *Adv. Mater. Process. Technol.*, vol. 1, no. 3–4, pp. 465–473, 2015, doi: 10.1080/2374068X.2015.1128171.

11 Smart Manufacturing
Opportunities and Challenges Overcome by Industry 4.0

Ishan Mishra, Sneham Kumar, and Navriti Gupta
Delhi Technological University

CONTENTS

11.1 INTRODUCTION

The fourth industrial revolution and the introduction of sustainable production methods are two major changes that will affect all consumption and production prospects in this century. This began historically with the use of steam energy and mechanical mechanisms in the first industrial revolution. Then various industries adopted the concept of mass production and assembly lines. With the introduction of Robotics technology in various stages of production in 1969, automation and information technology became the focus of the third industrial revolution. Current revolution is based on the technology as shown in Figure 11.1.

DOI: 10.1201/9781003154518-11

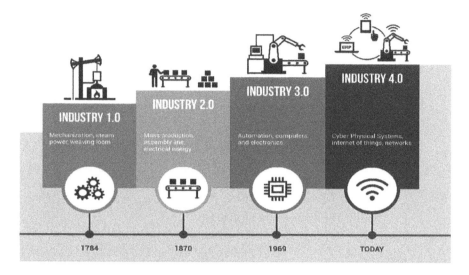

FIGURE 11.1   A timeline of industrial revolution.

11.2   DEFINITION AND FRAMEWORK

11.2.1   INDUSTRY 4.0

Industry 4.0, also known as fourth industrial revolution, is the constant automated application of advanced smart technology in the conventional industrial and manufacturing process. Communication between machines on an industrial scale reinforced with the Internet of Things brings about more automation, connectivity and self-control. Intelligent gadgets are being implicated which can completely analyze and diagnose problems without the need for human involvement.

11.2.2   SMART MANUFACTURING

Intelligent manufacturing includes a variety of technologies, including cyber-physical manufacturing systems, Internet of Things, robotics/automation, big data analysis, turning the concept of data-driven networks into reality. But, it does not replace people with machines and AI in the workshop, rather it empowers them by intelligent design of solutions tailored to specific areas.

11.3   MODERN TECHNOLOGIES ASSISTING SMART MANUFACTURING

For manufacturing to be smart, it must incorporate modern technological advances in its production process. Some of the basic parameters of a brilliant system, and its role in smart manufacturing is shown below.

11.3.1 Digital Manufacturing

It is defined as a combined and comprehensive approach to manufacturing which revolves around computer systems and automation. It allows virtual simulation on digital models without any experiment or prototypes and hence assisting in decision-making. It affects every facet of manufacturing from design and production to service and feedback.

11.3.2 Artificial Intelligence and Machine Learning

With the onset of the augmented age, biological intuition combined with powerful algorithms and high-performance computers have the capability of transforming the entire process of design, manufacturing, logistics and consumer feedback mechanisms. Generative design is one such technique that allows detailed descriptions created by humans to be incorporated into artificial intelligence algorithms as presented in Figure 11.2. The information can include various parameters, such as available production resources, budget, and time. The algorithm checks all possible options and generates several optimal solutions. Right now, Artificial intelligence is completely objective and has to start from ground zero every time. There are no unproven assumptions, which are different from what humans might have. But they have shown unparalleled ability of optimization, decision making and to respond to various types of physical input.

11.3.3 Internet of Things

The Internet has been around for a while, and in its entire lifespan it has been mostly about connecting computers and through that connecting people, hence it may be termed as Internet of people. A smart factory incorporates IoT by linking every entity, every piece of machinery into an internet cloud letting them interact with each other allowing the entire factory to behave like one single unit with various parts working in synergy to complete a given task.

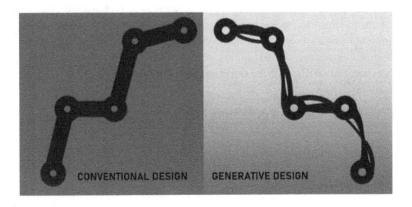

FIGURE 11.2   Representational image comparing conventional and generative design.

11.3.4 BIG DATA AND ANALYTICS

Big data analysis can help manufacturers determine the current status and product defects in real time, making products more consumer-friendly, understanding the buying habits of the population at large and unleashing the potential of data-driven predictive production and marketing. To fulfil the demands of a wide variety of clients, the manufacturers want to tailor their product designs based on this knowledge.

11.4 CHALLENGES OF SMART MANUFACTURING AND FOURTH GENERATION INDUSTRIES

11.4.1 SECURITY OF COMPUTER-BASED SYSTEMS

Smart system requires a network connection and is especially organized through the Internet. It is necessary to implement system-wide data and information security in multiple places, with a universally unique identification number and full-proof data encryption and protection. Therefore, every connection in the network must be shielded from external attacks and data abuse.

11.4.2 MULTILINGUALISM AND DIVERSITY

In a diverse world like ours, smart manufacturing processes should be capable of managing multilingual operations, interpreting any type instruction supplied in any language into machine language, thus allowing it to function without excluding any demographic.

11.5 CONCLUSION

Fouth-generation industries are bringing about an advancement of manufacturing capacity and are improving the operations via sturdy integration of physical and network capabilities, compounded by the evolution of big data and its analysis. One of the challenging factors of intelligent manufacturing systems is the compatibility between old machinery and systems with new technology. The effective deployment of smart technologies in the actual industrial area requires appropriate development of intuitive artificial intelligence augmented with big data processing, CP systems, augmented, virtual reality, IoT, automated machines and other related technologies. This will optimize the manufacturing thus putting less burden on the environment as well.

12 Multi-Response Optimization of Input Parameters in End Milling of Metal Matrix Composite Using TOPSIS Algorithm

A. Singhai and K. Dhakar
Shri G.S. Institute of Technology and Science

P.K. Gupta
Malaviya National Institute of Technology

CONTENTS

12.1 INTRODUCTION

Metal matrix composites (MMCs) play a significant role in the manufacturing sector's growth because of their excellent properties such as high strength, toughness, corrosion resistance, stiffness, etc. These materials' demand is increasing progressively in

DOI: 10.1201/9781003154518-12

many sectors viz defence, aerospace, medical and automobile industries [1]. In general, in MMCs, abrasive materials are used as a reinforcement material that causes severe tool wear in conventional machining [2]. Consequently, machining of MMCs is very expensive.

End milling machines are used for light milling operations, producing small holes, and cutting slots. The end milling operation is preferably performed on a vertical milling machine. A multi-tooth cutter known as end mill, rotates along the axis with respect to the workpiece. This milling operation is one of the most utilized material removal operations in various manufacturing industries due to its faster metal removal ability and reasonably fine surface finish [1–2]. Numerous machining factors affect the surface finish and tool flank wear. The surface integrity of the work part is most significant in the functional behaviour of the components undergone in the milling process. Surface finish is an imperative factor as it affects the practical properties of the machined component. Here is the need for advanced materials that can fulfil the requirement of automotive and aerospace industries, High-performance applications in these manufacturing industries have been significantly increased using MMCs. These are the new class of materials that are being preferred for their improved properties as compared to conventional metals and alloys [3–7].

To obtain a fine surface, the selection of machining parameters is the most vital part of the machining method. This experimental study observes the cut quality of machined part, based on three machining parameters by the combined effect of the analysis of variance (ANOVA) and multi-criterion-decision-making methodology (MCDM). The aluminium alloy LM24 reinforced with 2 wt.% of B_4C fabricated by using an ultrasonic-assisted stir casting technique. LM24/2%B_4C composite is used as workpiece material for end milling operation. Composite material is a combination of base alloy and reinforced particulates of material, which is composed of two or more elements that are dissimilar in shape and chemical composition and are insoluble in each other. In this investigation, the "Technique for Order Preference by similarity to Ideal Solution" (TOPSIS) approach was utilized to optimize the multi-response characteristic of end milling of LM24/2%B_4C composite material.

The Taguchi methodology is a frequently used optimization technique for improving quality. However, this method has limitation that it can optimize only one-response characteristic. There are many MCDM methods available, such as TOPSIS, utility concepts and grey relational analysis, etc. However, it was observed that these techniques were applied by a few researchers for different manufacturing processes. Further, a few studies are available on the optimization of end milling machining parameters with MCDM. Thus, this investigation intended to examine end milling machining parameters by changing the level of the spindle speed, feed rate, and depth of cut (DOC) while machining of LM24/2%B_4C composite material, the output MRR and Ra were measured as a response characteristic.

Among the different MCDM methods, TOPSIS is found to be the most effective technique. Ravikumar et al. predicted optimal drilling condition by using Grey Taguchi-based TOPSIS technique (GT-TOPSIS) [8]. Kasdekar and Vishal solved the multi-response parameter optimization problem in electrical discharge machining by using entropy-based TOPSIS [9]. Yuvaraj and Kumar utilized TOPSIS for the optimization of multi-response characteristics in an abrasive water jet (AWJ) machine.

It was reported that multi-response characteristics can be enhanced by the TOPSIS approach [10]. Sivapirakasam et al. implemented the combination of Taguchi and fuzzy TOPSIS to optimize electrical discharge machining parameters for green manufacturing [11]. Asokan and Senthil Kumar reported that TOPSIS with AHP is helpful in selecting the optimal parameters setting for turning the Inconel 718 [12].

12.2 MATERIALS AND METHOD

12.2.1 FABRICATION OF COMPOSITE MATERIAL

LM-24 (Al-Si8Cu3.5), as given in Table 12.1, is utilized as an alloy material for matrix of composite. Small pieces of LM-24 square rod were used for easily placing the alloy inside the crucible. A very hard boron–carbon ceramic material, Boron carbide (B_4C), was used as reinforcement particulates (Table 12.2). Metal matrix composites are formed by using the stir casting technique. Approximately 1.430 kg of aluminium alloy LM24 were cut into pieces by using Grinder. Heating of base aluminium alloy in ceramic crucible at a temperature of 700°C and allowed into the molten form. A thermocouple is used for measuring the raised temperature of furnace. At 570°C, the alloy started melting measuring the temperature using thermocouple. Now, the reinforcement particle 28 g weighted by digital weighing machine preheated at 400°C in pre-heater to extract gases and moisture content present in the particles. Base alloy was completely melt at 670°C. 2 wt.% of magnesium wrapped in aluminium foil in like small capsules, as shown in Figure 12.1a, approximately 14 g. To increase the wettability, it was added to the molten metal. Stirring was started to homogenize the temperature and at every stage before and after adding the reinforcement into the molten alloy took place. The mechanical stirring was performed up to

TABLE 12.1

Properties of LM 24 Alloy

1	Density	2.7 g/cm³
2	Melting point	580°C
3	Poisson's ratio	0.3
4	Modulus of elasticity	70–80 GPa

TABLE 12.2

Properties of Boron Carbide

Properties	Description
Chemical formula	B_4C
Molar mass	55.255 gm/mole
Appearance	Black powder (greyish black)
Density	2.45 gm/cm³
Particle size	400 mesh or 37 microns

10 minutes. The rotational speed of stirrer was constant at 250 rpm, and it can stir the melted metal from the bottommost of the crucible, as shown in Figure 12.1(b). The reinforcement particles that were preheated, mixed at the rate of 10–20 g/min into molten metal. The molten metal was then kept in a crucible in a static condition for approximately 30 seconds, and later, it was transferred into the flat mold.

12.2.2 EXPERIMENTAL PROCEDURE

LM24/B_4C was utilized as a workpiece material and carbide as a tool material. Feed rate, speed, and DOC were noted down as input factors, whereas MRR and RA were noted down as output parameters. Various input process parameters (Table 12.3) were selected by extensive evaluation of the literature review. Literature review and subsequent pilot experimentation were the basis of the selection of input machining parameters. Parameters such as speed, feed rate, and DOC are vastly used among milling researchers. Experiments are carried out in accordance with the RSM technique utilized in experimental design. The computation of the codes as functions of range of interest with each factor having a central composite design where in the three input variables have five levels between ±2 coded values. We performed twenty experimental runs. The number of tests needed to perform is selected with the standard 2k full factorial central composite design. Value of α is taken as 1.682 throughout the work.

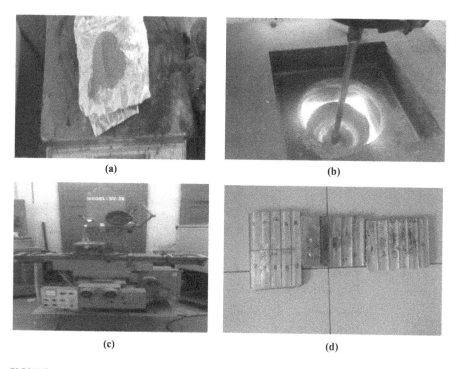

(a)

(b)

(c)

(d)

FIGURE 12.1 (a) Show a physical picture of magnesium powder. (b) Show a physical process of mechanical stirring with crucible. (c) Show a physical picture of vertical milling machine. (d) Show a physical picture of work samples made by ultrasonic-assisted stir casting technique.

TABLE 12.3
Input Parameters and Level

Parameters	L1	L2	L3	L4	L5
Speed (rpm)	248.75	380	572.50	765	896.25
Feed (mm/min)	26.14	50	85	120	143.86
Depth cut (mm)	4.32	5	6	7	7.68

The end milling operation was performed on a vertical milling machine, as shown in Figure 12.1c. The tool used is the carbide tool having 8 mm diameter with four flutes. The workpiece composite material in the form of a rectangular shape is shown in Figure 12.1d. Measurement of surface roughness is computed using Surtronic 3+ instrument at 0.4 mm cut off. Ra, which is the universally recognized and vastly utilized international parameter of roughness.

12.3 METHODOLOGY

The standard procedure of the TOPSIS methodology for narrowing down the best substitute from the ones available is as follows:

- First, the objective is determined, and following those the pertinent appraisal attributes are identified.
- From the normalized decision matrix. R_{ij}, the corresponding normalized value, can be denoted as:

$$R_{ij} = \frac{a_{ij}}{\sqrt{\sum_{i=1}^{m} a_{ij}^2}} \qquad (12.1)$$

- A set of weights w_j (for $j = 1 \ldots n$) is used for deciding on the comparative rank of varying attributes with respect to the objectives. Such that $\sum w_j = 1$.
- Next, the weighted normalized matrix V_{ij} was calculated by

$$V_{ij} = R_{ij} \times w_j \qquad (12.2)$$

- Next, the ideal (best) and ideal (worst) solutions were obtained by

$$V^+ = \left\{ \left(\max V_{ij} / j \in J \right), \left(\min V_{ij} / j \in J' \right) / i = 1, 2, \ldots m \right\}$$

$$= \left\{ V_1^+, V_2^+, V_3^+, V_4^+, \ldots V_m^+ \right\} \qquad (12.3)$$

$$V^- = \left\{ \left(\min V_{ij} / j \in J \right), \left(\max V_{ij} / j \in J' \right) / j = 1, 2, \ldots n \right\} \qquad (12.4)$$

where beneficial attributes are linked with $J^+ = \left(1, 2, \ldots N\right)\big/ j$ and non-beneficial attributes are linked with $J^- = \left(1 = 1, 2, \ldots N\right)\big/ j$.

V_j^+ = ideal (best) value, V_j^- = negative ideal (worst) value.

- The Euclidean distance is used to show separation of each alternative from the ideal one and was calculated as.

$$S_i^+ = \sqrt{\sum_{i=1}^{m}(V_{ij} - V_j^+)^2} \quad i = 1,\ 2 \ldots m \tag{12.5}$$

$$S_i^- = \sqrt{\sum_{i=1}^{m}(V_{ij} - V_j^-)^2} \quad i = 1,\ 2 \ldots m \tag{12.6}$$

- The relative proximity, P_i, of a given alternative to the ideal solution may be obtained by:

$$P_i = \frac{S_i^-}{S_i^- + S_i^+} \tag{12.7}$$

- A set of alternatives was obtained in the downward order, according to the value of P_i. This indicates the most ideal and least ideal solution. P_i may also be known as composite performance alternative [13–14].

12.4   RESULT AND DISCUSSION

End milling due to conventional machining procedures undoubtedly gives better outcomes than other conventional machining methods. Through better results, the high initial cost is compensated. It was performed on LM24/B$_4$C workpiece using a carbide cutting tool. The influence of the selected machining parameters on responses was evaluated and is explained in the following sections.

12.4.1   EXPERIMENTAL RESULT

The experiments of milling machining on LM24/2%B4Cp composite metal matrix in automatic vertical milling machine were investigated.

12.4.2   ANOVA RESULT FOR RESPONSE MRR

The results were examined for ANOVA for the tailored RSM quadratic model and ANOVA for each individual term on the performance characteristics are presented in Table 12.4 The examination of variance was used to understand the significance and influence of the cutting parameters on output characteristic MRR.

F-value of the model suggests that the model is significant, as given in Table 12.4. In this analysis feed, DOC and interaction between feed*doc, are significant for MRR. The "Lack of Fit" F-value of 4.48 exhibits that there is very less noise in the process.

TABLE 12.4
ANOVA for Quadratic Model

Source	Sum of Squares	Df	Mean Square	F Value	p-value Prob > F	
Model	3.858E+006	9	4.287E+005	229.11	<0.0001	Significant
A-A	322.36	1	322.36	0.17	0.6869	
B-B	2.911E+006	1	2.911E+006	1556.00	<0.0001	
C-C	5.230E+005	1	5.230E+005	279.52	<0.0001	
AB	514.40	1	514.40	0.27	0.6115	
AC	279.31	1	279.31	0.15	0.7073	
BC	84569.45	1	84569.45	45.20	<0.0001	
A^2	9443.61	1	9443.61	5.05	0.0485	
B^2	3.342E+005	1	3.342E+005	178.60	< 0.0001	
C^2	172.44	1	172.44	0.092	0.7677	
Residual	18711.19	10	1871.12			
Lack of fit	15297.29	5	3059.46	4.48	0.0627	Not significant
Pure Err	3413.90	5	682.78			
Cor total	3.877E+006	19				
Std. Dev	43.26			R^2	0.9952	
Mean	983.19			Adj R^2	0.9908	
C.V.%	4.40			Pred R^2	0.9680	
PRESS	1.242E+005			Adeq Prec	51.900	

In this analysis, it was found that R^2 is 0.9952, it means the mathematical model is 99% efficient. "Adeq Prec" calculates the S/N ratio. This ratio can be desirable if it is greater than 4.

12.4.3 ANOVA for RA

The outcomes were studied for ANOVA to suited RSM linear model and ANOVA for each term on the responses are presented in Table 12.5. The examination of variance was utilized to know the significance and influence of the cutting parameters on the response variable RA.

F-value of the model suggests that the model is significant as given in Table 12.5. In this analysis, speed and DOC are significant for RA.

12.4.4 The Effect of Machining Parameters on the Responses

The nature of surface plot as shown in Figure 12.2 depends on the moment of feed and DOC. Upon increasing the DOC and the feed leads to MRR increased. Whenever DOC is fixed at any point, then MRR varies according to the variation of feed for the range of 50–120 mm/rev. Also, when feed is fixed at any point, then MRR varies according to the variation of DOC 5–7 mm. When one parameter is fixed, the moment of MRR is slow but when both the parameters that is DOC and

TABLE 12.5
ANOVA for RA

Source	Sum of Squares	Df	Mean Square	F Value	p-value Prob > F	
Model	7.23	3	2.41	13.83	0.0001	significant
A-A	3.37	1	3.37	19.37	0.0004	
B-B	0.37	1	0.37	2.13	0.1638	
C-C	3.48	1	3.48	20.00	0.0004	
Residual	2.79	16	0.17			
Lack of fit	2.14	11	0.19	1.49	0.3455	Not significant
Pure Err	0.65	5	0.13			
Cor Total	10.02	19				
Std. Dev.			0.42	R²		0.7217
Mean			1.85	Adj R²		0.6695
C.V. %			22.54	Pred R²		0.5362
PRESS			4.65	Adeq Prec		12.504

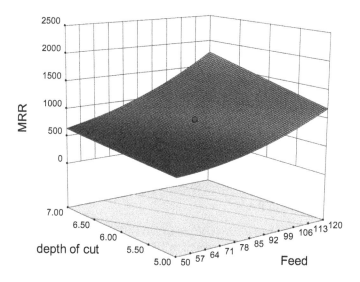

FIGURE 12.2   A three-dimensional graph showing surface plot in which increment of MRR on Y-axis, decrement of depth of cut on X-axis and increment of feed on Z-axis.

feed increase MRR increases rapidly to the maximum. From Figure 12.3 surface plot shows the outcome of the rotational speed and DOC on the surface finish. The surface roughness is seen to be very sensitive to DOC. As DOC in the range of 5–7 mm increased the roughness increased to maximum then by speed. The surface roughness slightly affected by cutting speed. When the cutting speed is increased to maximum and DOC at minimum value RA is minimum. Thus, to get better surface finish the machining parameters at a speed 380 rpm, DOC at 5 mm.

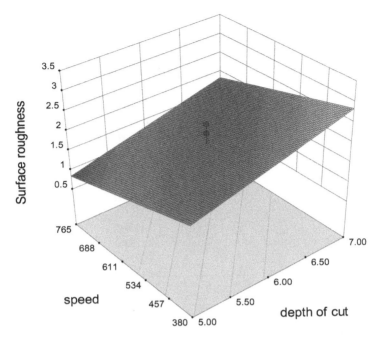

FIGURE 12.3 A three-dimensional graph showing surface plot in which increment of surface roughness on Y-axis, decrement of speed on X-axis and increment of feed on Z-axis.

12.5   OPTIMIZATION OF MILLING PARAMETERS

12.5.1   TOPSIS Algorithm

1. First, determine the purpose and found the appropriate evaluation attributes. Taking the responses from experimental results as MRR and surface roughness known as Attributes. Experimental run and experimental result data are identified in column as attributes. It is in the non-normalized form and units.
2. Obtained the normalized decision matrix and it can be shown as follows:

$$R_{ij} = \frac{a_{ij}}{\sqrt{\sum\limits_{i=1}^{m} a_{ij}^2}}$$

3. Using this formula obtained a normalized decision matrix for MRR and RA. As shown in Table 12.6.
4. Decided on the comparative rank (*i.e.* weights) equally as 0.05 for different 20 attributes with respect to the objective. Attain the weighted normalized matrix V_{ij} (Table 12.7). It is calculated through the multiplying of every single component of column of the matrix both for MRR and RA with its corresponding weight w_j (0.05). The weighted normalized matrix V_{ij} is calculated by equation 12.2.

TABLE 12.6
Normalized Decision Matrix

Run	MRR	Ra	Normalized MRR	Normalized Ra
18	825	1.692	0.171244	0.190817
14	1187.62	3.385	0.246513	0.381747
6	700	2.064	0.145298	0.23277
8	1773.34	2.025	0.36809	0.228371
12	2127.2	1.828	0.44154	0.206155
16	868.54	1.304	0.180282	0.14706
1	500	1.564	0.103784	0.176382
3	1130	2.36	0.234552	0.266151
13	576	1.32	0.119559	0.148864
15	838	1.648	0.173942	0.185855
10	912	0.88	0.189302	0.099243
7	1789.9	2.22	0.371527	0.250363
5	685.71	2.75	0.142332	0.310134
17	848	2.1	0.176018	0.23683
20	894.28	2.33	0.185624	0.262768
2	475	0.55	0.098595	0.062027
4	1200	1.16	0.249082	0.13082
9	976.86	3.076	0.202765	0.346899
11	478.28	0.987	0.099276	0.11131
19	878	1.8	0.182245	0.202997

5. The best and worst ideal solutions are obtained by equations 12.3 and 12.4 respectively.

   Ideal (best) solution for MRR, in this case, higher MRR is appreciated ("higher-is-better"), max. value of MRR is considered the best solution. In the case of RA, ideal (best) solution is minimum RA value. It means "lower is better" is considered the best solution for RA. The ideal (worst) solution will be vice-a-versa for both cases. The best and worst ideal solution of responses is given in Table 12.8.

6. The difference in measures is obtained. Euclidean equation is used to give the difference of each alternative from the ideal one.

$$S_i^+ = \sqrt{\sum_{i=1}^{m}(V_{ij} - V_j^+)^2} i$$

$$S_i^- = \sqrt{\sum_{i=1}^{m}(V_{ij} - V_j^-)^2} i$$

7. Calculate the comparative closeness of a certain substitute to the ideal answer, P_i is measured by:

TABLE 12.7
Weighted Normalized Decision Matrix

Run	Normalized MRR	Weighted Normalized 0.05 × MRR	Normalized Ra	Weighted Normalized 0.05 × Ra
18	0.171244	0.008562	0.190817	0.009541
14	0.246513	0.012326	0.381747	0.019087
6	0.145298	0.007265	0.23277	0.011638
8	0.36809	0.018404	0.228371	0.011419
12	0.44154	0.022077	0.206155	0.010308
16	0.180282	0.009014	0.14706	0.007353
1	0.103784	0.005189	0.176382	0.008819
3	0.234552	0.011728	0.266151	0.013308
13	0.119559	0.005978	0.148864	0.007443
15	0.173942	0.008697	0.185855	0.009293
10	0.189302	0.009465	0.099243	0.004962
7	0.371527	0.018576	0.250363	0.012518
5	0.142332	0.007117	0.310134	0.015507
17	0.176018	0.008801	0.23683	0.011841
20	0.185624	0.009281	0.262768	0.013138
2	0.098595	0.00493	0.062027	0.003101
4	0.249082	0.012454	0.13082	0.006541
9	0.202765	0.010138	0.346899	0.017345
11	0.099276	0.004964	0.11131	0.005565
19	0.182245	0.009112	0.202997	0.01015

$$P_i = \frac{S_i^-}{S_i^- + S_i^+}$$

8. In this step, a set of substitutes is articulated in a downward manner. The P_i showing the most favoured and least favoured possible solution (Table 12.9).

The proximity coefficient values of input parameters are given in Table 12.10. The optimum level of process parameters will be a number with the larger proximity coefficient value. According to the closeness of coefficient values, the most preferred feasible solution is **0.768316,** and the least preferred feasible solution **0.106092.** The comparative proximity is used to decide the optimal combination of machining

TABLE 12.8
Best and Worst Ideal Solution

	Ra	MRR
V^+	0.003101	0.018576
V^-	0.019087	0.00493

TABLE 12.9
Separation Decision Matrix

Run	S_i^+	S_i^-
18	0.01190604	0.0102135
14	0.01716434343	0.007396
6	0.01417	0.007806
8	0.008319	0.0155
12	0.008012356	0.001926
16	0.010464766	0.001242
1	0.014557035	0.01090
3	0.01229	0.01494
13	0.01332526	0.01169
15	0.011659	0.010493
10	0.009299	0.014835
7	0.009417	0.015144
5	0.01688	0.004195
17	0.01311252	0.008215
20	0.012758	0.00737
2	0.013646	0.015986
4	0.007022848	0.014629
9	0.0016555	0.00549
11	0.013833	0.013522
19	0.011800665	0.009867

parameters for maximizing of MRR and minimizing the RA. The ideal best input parameters optimized by the TOPSIS algorithm is experimental run 9. The optimized multi-response milling parameters were obtained as which corresponds to design variables speed 248.75 rpm (L1), feed 85 mm/min (L3), and DOC 6 mm (L3).

12.6 CONCLUSION

This work proposed to solve the multi-response parameter such as RA and MRR in end milling of LM24/2%B$_4$C composite metal matrix using the TOPSIS Algorithm. ANOVA was performed to examine the important parameters for the multi-response characteristics in end milling operation. The following deductions were concluded from the study presented:

1. The study helped in concluding that B$_4$C particles can be used as reinforcement material along with LM24 aluminium as a material of matrix for stir casting process.
2. RSM was successfully applied to optimize the MRR and RA for selected input process parameters. It also reduces the total number of experiments quite significantly.

TABLE 12.10
Closeness Coefficient Table

Run	P_i	Rank of Order
18	0.461741	10
14	0.301136	17
6	0.355206	16
8	0.650741	3
12	0.193795	19
16	0.106092	20
1	0.428172	13
3	0.54866	6
13	0.467315	10
15	0.473682	9
10	0.614693	5
7	0.616587	4
5	0.199051	18
17	0.385183	14
20	0.366157	15
2	0.539484	7
4	0.675647	2
9	0.768316	1
11	0.494315	8
19	0.455379	12

3. This analysis was carried out by developing RA and MRR models using RSM. TOPSIS algorithm is used for optimizing the output characteristics.
4. It was observed that speed and DOC were the significant parameters for RA, while feed and DOC kept a significant effect for MRR.
5. For RA, the combined effect of DOC and speed was significant, whereas for MRR, the combined effect of feed and DOC was significant.
6. The optimum parameters setting of end milling of LM24/2%B_4C for min. RA and max. of MRR were cutting speed 248.75 rpm (L1), feed 85 mm/min (L3), and DOC 6 mm (L3).

REFERENCES

1. B. Stalin, C. Murugan. (2016) "Evaluation of Mechanical Behavior of Aluminium Alloy Boron Carbide MMC" *International Conference on Emerging Engineering Trends and Science (ICEETS)*, Madurai, pp. 32–41.
2. A. Anarghya, B. M. Gurumurthy, S. S. Sharma, R. Nitish and R. B. Yatheesha (2014) "Manual Stir Cast Processing Method, Hardness and Compression Characteristics of Quartz Reinforced Al Metal Matrix Composite" *International Journal of Engineering Sciences &Research Technology* Vol. 3(10) pp. 6–16.
3. M. S. Karakas, A. Adam, U. Mustafa, O. Bilgehan (2006) "Effect of Cutting Speed on Tool Performance in Milling of B4Cp Reinforced Aluminium Metal Matrix Composites" *Journal of Materials Processing Technologies* Vol. 178 pp. 241–246.

4. S. T. Warghat, T. R. Deshmukh (2015) "A Review on Optimization of Machining Parameters for End Milling Operation" *International Journal of Engineering Research and Applications (IJERA)* pp. 31–35 ISSN: 2248-9622.

5. V. V. K. Lakshmi, K. V. Subbaiah (2012) "Modelling and Optimization of Process Parameters During End Milling of Hardened Steel" *International Journal of Engineering Research and Applications (IJERA)* Vol. 2 pp. 667–674.

6. R. Arokiadass, K. Palaniradja, N. Alagumoorthi (2012) "Prediction and Optimization of End Milling Process Parameters of Cast Aluminium Based MMC" *Transaction of Nonferrous Metals Society of China* Vol. 22 pp. 1568–1574.

7. V. Kumar, S. Jatti, R. Sekhar, R. K. Patil (2013) "Study of Ball Nose End Milling of LM6 Al Alloy: Surface Roughness Optimization using Genetic Algorithm" *International Journal of Engineering and Technology (IJET)* Vol. 5 (3) pp. 2859–2865.

8. H. Ravikumar, P. L. Arun, S. Thileepan (2015) "Analysis in Drilling of Al6061/20%SiCp Composites Using Grey Taguchi Based TOPSIS (GT-TOPSIS)" *International Journal of Chem Tech Research CODEN (USA)* Vol. 8 (12) pp. 292–303.

9. D. K. Kasdekar, V. Parashar (2015) "MADM Approach for Optimization of Multiple Responses in EDM of En-353 Steel" *International Journal of Advanced Science and Technology* Vol. 83 pp. 59–70.

10. N. Yuvaraj, M. P. Kumar (2015) "Multi Response Optimization of Abrasive Water Jet Cutting Process Parameters Using TOPSIS Approach" *Materials and Manufacturing Processes* Vol. 30 (7) pp. 882–889.

11. S. P. Sivapirakasama, J. Mathewa, M. Surianarayana (2011) "Multi-Attribute Decision Making for Green Electrical Discharge Machining" *Expert Systems with Applications,* Vol. 38 pp. 8370–8374.

12. P. Asokan, S. Kumar (2010) "Intelligent Selection of Machining Parameters in Turning of Inconel-718 Using Multi Objective Optimisation Coupled with MADM" *International Journal Machining and Machinability of Materials* Vol. 8 (1/2) pp. 209–225.

13. V. M. Athawale, S. Chakraborty (2010) "A TOPSIS Method-Based Approach to Machine Tool selection" *International Conference on Industrial Engineering and Operations Management,* Dhaka, Bangladesh, January 9–10, 2010.

14. J. Kumar, G. S. Singh (2016) "Optimization of Machining Parameters of Titanium Alloy Steel Using: TOPSIS Method" *International Journal of Scientific Research in Science, Engineering and Technology* Vol. 2 pp. 1019–1022.

13 Numerical and Experimental Investigation of Additive Manufactured Cellular Lattice Structures

V. Phanindra Bogu
Vidya Jyothi Institute of Technology

Locherla Daloji
Vishnu Institute of Technology

Bangaru Babu Popuri
National Institute of Technology

CONTENTS

13.1 INTRODUCTION

The cellular lattice structures are predominantly creating impact in energy-absorbing applications for the protection of impact loads [1. The cellular lattice structures are filled with repeated unit cells (honeycomb [2],octahedral,dodecahedron, etc.) to accomplish the desired density with varying porosity. These structures are more

DOI: 10.1201/9781003154518-13

197

flexible to achieve properties like strength-weight ratio,low thermal expansion coefficient,and negative Poisson's ratio [3]. Moreover,these lattice structures are widely used in various engineering applications such as ultra-light structures,sandwich structures,energy-absorbing devices [4],heat sinks,conformal cooling channels,even in orthopaedic implants and tissue engineering.

In additive manufacturing (AM) family,the fused deposition method (FDM) is one of the manufacturing processes,which builds a 3D component from CAD data using thermoplastic filament [5]. This filament is heated and extruded layer by layer until it finishes the part. The nozzle extrudes both support and model material as per the requirement. As per layer height,the build platform is lowered in successive manner. After completion of the final part,post-processing is required to get the final part. It has advantages like to manufacture tough and durable parts,ease of use,end-use of products,and no size limitation. Typically,ABS,PLA,PC, and Nylon materials are used. Likewise,the plastics parts can be fabricated by various AM processes such as vat-photo polymerisation for polymer resins,selective laser sintering for polymer powders,and sheet lamination for polymer sheets [5]. The FDM is the most widely used [6] method among all the AM techniques due to minimum wastageand consistent prototype accuracy.

Gorguluarslan etal. [7]proposed a framework of cellular lattice structures in design and fabrication. The cellular lattice structures are incorporated in a sandwich panel instead of honeycomb structures by Dong etal. [6]. The results were compared with honeycombs;however,the cellular lattice structure has shown great potential to sustain shear and compressive loads.

Stankovićetal. studied the anisotropic properties of additive manufactured lattice structures [7,8] and observed the build orientation. The orientation is one of the most significant parameters of additive manufactured components. Maskery etal. examined body-centred cube (BCC) and BCCz (reinforced variant) lattice structures and studied the deformation and energy absorption [9]. The BCCz lattices provide high modulus and plastic collapse strength than BCC. The BCCz provides more anisotropy in mechanical properties while BCC possessesan anisotropy nature. Beyer and Figueroa studied that fabrication of cellular lattice structures with AMconsume less material [8,10]. The unit cell with vertical trusses in a cube type of design was close to the standard solid block,hexagonal designs resulted in higher yield strength. In addition,three types of structures considered such as square pyramidal,tetrahedral,and kagome. The kagome structure strength was close to a solid one.

The finite element analysis (FEA) was carried out on various AM parts to validate the results [7,11]. In this regard,Bhandari and Lopez-Anido,Ravari etal. conducted finite elemental analysis on a given lattice structure and compared with experimental data to envisage the effectsof strut diameter on the elastic modulus and other mechanical properties. These mechanical properties are able to predict with numerical simulations [2,3,11–13], and numerical simulations are able to decrease the experimental effort [14].

In this chapter, the face-centred cubic (FCC) and star-type lattice structures are fabricated through the FDM technology with polylactic acid material. The mechanical properties such as modulus of elasticity,compressive strength and strains are calculated experimentallyin $X,Y,$and Z directions. The experimental results are compared with FEA results.

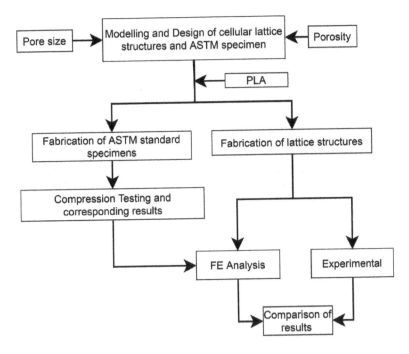

FIGURE 13.1 Flow chart of complete methodology.

TABLE 13.1
Properties of Polylactic Acid (PLA) [15]

S.No	Material Property	Units	Value
1	Density(ρ)	kg/m^3	1.25
2	Elastic modulus (E)	MPa	3500
3	Poisson's ratio(ν)	–	0.36
4	Yield strength (σ_y)	MPa	60

13.2 MATERIALS AND METHODOLOGY

The work discussed geometrical modelling,fabrication,FE analysis, and experimental testing of specimens. The total workflow is represented in Figure 13.1.

The PLA is a biodegradable and bioactive thermoplastic polymer derived from renewable sources [15]. It is currently the second most produced and consumed bioplastic in terms of volume. The PLA can accomplish the requirements of the automotive industry such as mechanical performance,heat resistance,and durability [16,17].

13.2.1 MODELLING OF LATTICE STRUCTURES AND STANDARD BLOCK

The Rhinoceros software is used to model the cellular lattice structures with two types of unit cell configurations such as FCC and star with a strut diameter of 2 mm.

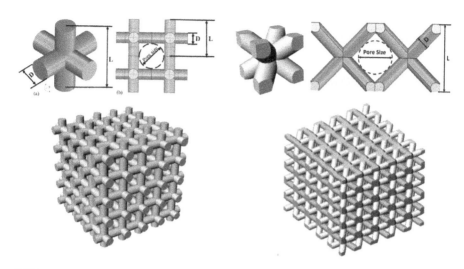

FIGURE 13.2   Unit cell representation of FCC and star lattice structures.

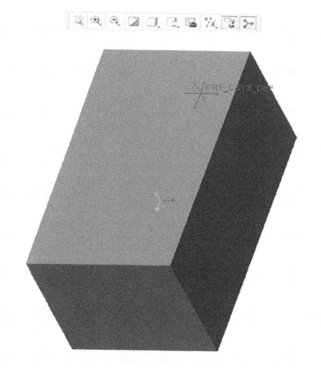

FIGURE 13.3   ASTM standard compression specimen.

Initially, the single unit cell size of 5mm³ × 5mm³ × 5mm³ ($L \times L \times L$) is modelled then patterned in X and Y directions with a distance of 5 mm i.e. distance between each unit cell. This single layer was again patterned in Z-axis [18]. The final lattice structures are obtained with 30 mm³ × 30 mm³ × 30 mm³ which means that the height of the lattice structure is 30mm in all dimensions as shown in Figure 13.2. The compressive strength of cellular lattice structures depends upon the strut diameter and cell size. In addition, the compressive standard specimen 12.7mm³ × 12.7mm³ × 25.4 mm³ is modelled as per ASTM D695 [19] shown in Figure 13.3.

13.2.2   SPECIMEN FABRICATION

The CAD model was exported to Standard Tessellation Language (STL) file [12]. It represents the surface geometry of a 3D object with triangulated facets. The accuracy and resolution of the STL areimproved with an increase of triangles. The final STL was imported into slicing software called flash print, which helps to slice the STL file and generate geometry codes (G-codes) in a machine-readable format is ".x3g". The machine is loaded with PLA filament with a diameter of 1.75 mm and the printing parameters are considered with a layer thickness is 0.1 mm, printing speed 50 mm/sec, travelling speed 40 mm/sec, infill is 100% [20] and nozzle diameter is 0.4 mm. Finally, fabricated ASTM standard specimen and lattice structures are shown in Figure 13.4.

13.2.3   MECHANICAL TESTING OF SPECIMEN

The compression test is significant in measuring the elastic and fracture behaviour of materials. The ASTM D695 standard test method is adopted for testing the standard block to observe mechanical properties of rigid plastics such as elastic modulus, proportional limit, and compressive yield strength. As per standard, the tested sample is either cylindrical or cube. In this work, the cube size 12.7mm³ × 12.7mm³ × 25.4 mm³ sample is considered for testing.

The computerised universal testing machine was set up in such a manner that the specimens rested on the bottom plate while the other plate applied compressive force from the top side. The maximum load considered for this test is 30 kN and the strain rate is maintained at 2 mm/min. The strain rate is considered relatively slow for the accuracy of data.

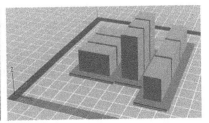

FIGURE 13.4   Lattice structure samples printed on FDM and standard block in X,Y,Z directions.

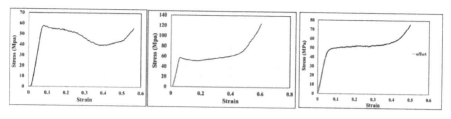

FIGURE 13.5   Stress–strain curve of ASTM standard specimen in $X, Y,$ and Z directions.

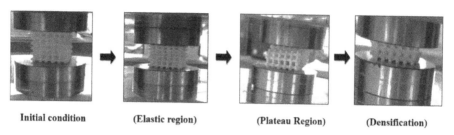

Initial condition   (Elastic region)   (Plateau Region)   (Densification)

FIGURE 13.6   Representation of different regions in FCC lattice structure.

The specimens are tested anisotropically in all directions such as $X, Y,$ and Z directions. The load vs displacement is recorded during compression testing and converted to a stress–strain curve to estimate the mechanical properties. In terms of accuracy, the lattice specimen was tested until the breaking point and three specimens were considered in each direction and averaged the value. The linear portion of the stress–strain curve is used in calculating the value of elastic modulus and 2% offset curve was drawn to determine the yield strength of the specimen, the corresponding graphs are shown in Figure 13.5. The stress–strain curve describes three stages such as elastic deformation, plastic deformation, and fracture. The average anisotropic elastic modulus of ASTM standard specimen is 1000 MPa and corresponding yield strengths in $X, Y,$ and Z directions are 57, 58, and 48 MPa as shown in Figure 13.5.

13.3   RESULTS AND DISCUSSION

The mechanical properties are strongly dependent on build direction and orientation. The specimens were printed in three directions such as $X, Y,$ and $Z,$ and the mechanical properties were calculated based on directions. While conducting the mechanical testing on specimens, three regions were observed as shown in Figures 13.6 and 13.7.

1. **Linear elastic region**: The elastic deformation is occurred due to the bending struts and this linear elasticity is characterised by elastic modulus.
2. **Plateau stress region**: The unit cell struts begin to collapse and become denser under compressive loads. Due to densification, energy absorption is more in this region.
3. **Densification region**: The stiffness of the lattice structure is increasing due to struts contact with each other.

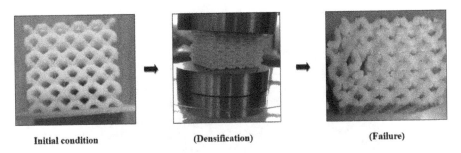

FIGURE 13.7   Representation of densification region for star lattice structure.

13.3.1   FINITE ELEMENT METHOD OF LATTICE STRUCTURES

The lattice structures are modelled in Rhinoceros software and exported to Ansys 18.0 for FEA. The elastoplastic condition is considered for FEA. The elastic modulus helps to understand the elastic behaviour of the material, whereas the tangent modulus represents the plastic behaviour of the material. The graph points were approximated and plotted in Excel in order to calculate the elastic modulus.

In Ansys software, the ten-node tetrahedral element is considered for analysis, and the material properties defined such as Elastic modulus 1000 MPa, density 1.25 kg/mm^3, and Poisson's ratio is 0.36. The model was fine-meshed and defined the boundary conditions are shown in Figure 13.8. The applied load was divided into hundred sub-steps and it was increasing to the level above which the load steps fail due to plastic deformation. The FEA results are converged with an element size of 0.1mm and the results are used to plot the load vs displacement in an excel spreadsheet.

These FEA results are analysed with experimental data. Due to the nonlinear behaviour of the material the specimen undergoes large deformation in Ansys. For this reason, the FE analysis of the lattice structure using solid elements is compared with experimental values. Typically, the lattice structure undergoes linear behaviour to nonlinear behaviour under compressive loads however linear behaviour is considered for evaluating the results. The corresponding deformation and equivalent stress results are shown in Figures 13.9 and 13.10.

13.3.2   COMPARISON OF EXPERIMENTAL AND ANALYSIS RESULTS OF FCC AND STAR LATTICE STRUCTURES

From the experimental data, the stress–strain curve follows an initial period of linear elasticity and when the structure begins to densification shows nonlinear behaviour under compressive loading. From the below graphs, it was noticed that the experimental behaviour is followed the same trend in both X and Y directions as shown in Figures 13.11 and 13.12. Whereas in the Z direction the behaviour is altered because of anisotropic in nature. When compared with experimental results a less deviation is observed in the Z direction with FEA results are shown in Figure 13.11. From Figure 13.12, it is noticed that the experimental and FEA results have a large deviation of nearly 48% in all directions.

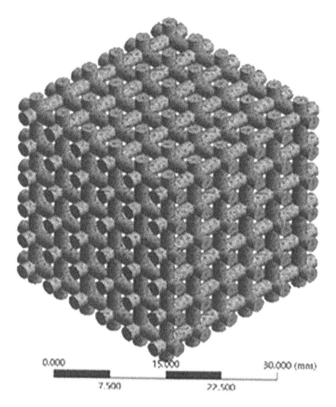

FIGURE 13.8   Mesh model of FCC lattice structure.

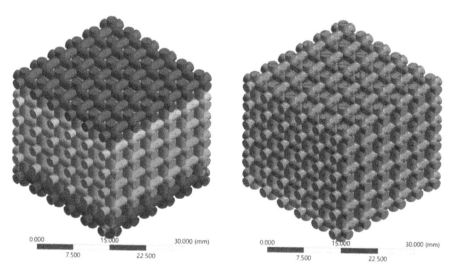

FIGURE 13.9   Total deformation and equivalent stresses of FCC lattice structure.

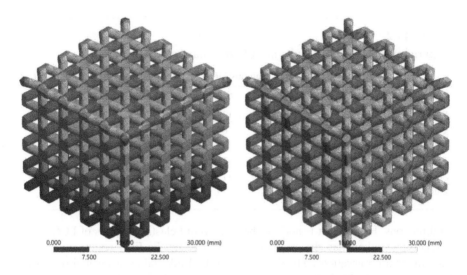

FIGURE 13.10 Total deformation and equivalent stresses of star lattice structure.

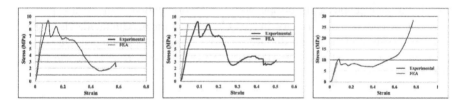

FIGURE 13.11 Comparison of experimental and FEA of FCC lattice in (a) X-direction (b) Y-direction (c) Z-direction.

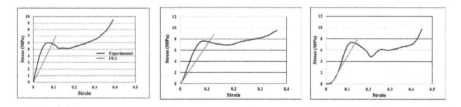

FIGURE 13.12 Comparison of experimental and FEA of star lattice in (a) X-direction (b) Y-direction (c) Z-direction.

From Table 13.2, the elastic modulus of both FCC and star lattice in the Z direction has the least value; this is because the layer is added in the Z direction while fabrication in a 3D printer. The values of elastic modulus in X and Y directions are expected to be similar, however, there is a little deviation in their elastic modulus. The FCC structure seems to be stronger than the star lattice while comparing elastic modulus, compressive yield strength, and strain.

For FE analysis, it is difficult to capture the layer-by-layer phenomenon effect in the Z direction. It is challenging to comment on the strength of a lattice structure in

TABLE 13.2
Experimental and FEA Results of FCC and Star Lattice Structures

Direction	Type	Elastic Modulus(MPa)		Compressive Yield Strength(MPa)	
		Experimental	FEA	Experimental	FEA
X-direction	FCC lattice	130	139	9.37	12.3
X-direction	Star lattice	123	67	6.1	6.2
Y-direction	FCC lattice	138	145	9.24	12.3
Y-direction	Star lattice	115	78	7.5	6.3
Z-direction	FCC lattice	122	119	9.9	12.3
Z-direction	Star lattice	110	59	7.1	6.22

all directions. However, it is noticed that the overall elastic modulus of FCC lattice is relatively higher than the star lattice structure and the FEA results are near to experimental observations. The difference in the FEA and experimental results for FCC lattice nearly 5%. In the case of star lattice, it was observed that 48% as shown in Table 13.2. The star lattice is showing the highest deviation because the FE model is considered homogenous and isotropic, however, the orientation of the strut is playing a key role in load-bearing capacity. In the FCC unitcell, the maximum load is bearing by vertical struts and the load is divided into four corners of star unitcell. Due to this maximum stress is concentrated at the meeting point of four struts in the star lattice structure.

13.4 CONCLUSION

In this study FCC and star-type lattice structures were designed with the same parameters such as strut diameter and size of the specimen and the specimen is fabricated through FDM with PLA material. Subsequently, the specimens are tested to evaluate the mechanical properties like Elastic modulus, compressive yield strength and strain. These experimental results are validated with Ansys software.

It was observed that the FCC lattice structure exhibits higher strength in both experimental and FEA results. The FEA results are relatively high with experimental values and it depends on meshing size and type of element. The finite element results are less accurate at predicting the elastic modulus values, in the case of FCC lattice structure, the difference is observed near 5% change and for star lattice up to 48% difference. Finally, it is concluded that the FCC lattice structure is more appropriate for mechanical applications.

ABBREVIATIONS

AM   Additive manufacturing
FDM   Fused deposition method
ABS   Acrylonitrile Butadiene Styrene
PLA   Polylatic acid
PC   Polycarbonate

BCC	Body-centred cube
BCCz	Reinforced variant of body-centred cube
FEA	Finite element analysis
FCC	Face-centred cubic
CAD	Computer-aided design
3D	Three dimensional
STL	Standard Tessellation Language
G-codes	Geometry codes
.x3g	File extension
ASTM	American Society for Testing and Materials

REFERENCES

1. Zuhal Ozdemir, Everth Hernandez-Nava, Andrew Tyas, James A.Warren, Stephen D.Fay, Russell Goodall, Iain Todd, Harm Askes. 2016. Energy absorption in lattice structures in dynamics. *Experiments, International Journal of Impact Engineering* 89:49–61.
2. Biranchi Panda, Marco Leite, Bibhuti Bhusan Biswal, Xiaodong Niu, Akhil Garg, 2018. Experimental and numerical modeling of mechanical properties of 3D printed honeycomb structures. *Measurement* 116:495–506.
3. Evangelos Ptochos, George Labeas. 2012. Elastic modulus and Poisson's ratio determination of micro-lattice cellular structures by analytical, numerical and homogenisation methods. *Journal of Sandwich Structures and Materials* 14:597–626.
4. Guoying Dong, Yunlong Tang, Yaoyao Fiona Zhao. 2017. Simulation of elastic properties of solid-lattice hybrid structures fabricated by additive manufacturing. *Procedia Manufacturing* 10:760–770.
5. Ian Gibson, David Rosen, Brent Stucker. 2015. *Additive Manufacturing Technologies 3D Printing, Rapid Prototyping, and Direct Digital Manufacturing.* Springer, New York.
6. Guoying Dong, Grace Wijaya, Yunlong Tang , Yaoyao Fiona Zhao. 2018. Optimizing process parameters of fused deposition modeling by Taguchi method for the fabrication of lattice structures. *Additive Manufacturing* 19:62–72.
7. Recep M. Gorguluarslan, Umesh N. Gandhi, Raghuram Mandapati, Seung-Kyum Choi. 2015. A design and fabrication framework for periodic lattice based cellular structures in additive manufacturing. *Design Engineering Technical Conference and Computers and Information in Engineering Conference*, Boston, MA.
8. R. A. Rahman Rashid, J. Mallavarapu, S. Palanisamy, S.H. Masood. 2017. A comparative study of flexural properties of additively manufactured aluminum lattice structures. *Materials: Proceedings* 4:8597–8604.
9. Ian Maskery, Alexandra Hussey, Ajit Panesar, Adedeji Aremu, Christopher Tuck, Ian Ashcroft, Richard Hague. 2016. An investigation into reinforced and functionally graded lattice structures. *Journal of Cellular Plastics* 53:151–165.
10. Christiane Beyer, Dustin Figueroa. 2016. Design and analysis of lattice structures for additive manufacturing. *Journal of Manufacturing Science and Engineering* 138:121014–121015.
11. Sunil Bhandari, Roberto Lopez-Anido. 2018. Finite element analysis of thermoplastic polymer extrusion 3D printed material for mechanical property prediction. *Additive Manufacturing* 22:187–196.
12. Mark Helou, Supachai Vongbunyong, Sami Kara. 2016. Finite element analysis and validation of cellular structures. *Procedia CIRP* 50:94–99.

13. Jie Niu, Hui Leng Choo, Wei Sun. 2016. Finite element analysis and experimental study of plastic lattice structures manufactured by selective laser sintering. *Journal of Materials: Design and Applications* 231:171–178.

14. M. R. Karamooz Ravari, M. Kadkhodaei, M. Badrossamay, R. Rezaei. 2014. Numerical investigation on mechanical properties of cellular lattice structures fabricated by fused deposition modelling. *International Journal of Mechanical Sciences* 88:154–161.

15. J. Antonio Travieso-Rodriguez, Ramon Jerez-Mesa, Jordi Llumà, Oriol Traver-Ramos, Giovanni Gomez-Gras and Joan Josep Roa Rovira. 2019. Mechanical properties of 3D-printing polylactic acid parts subjected to bending stress and fatigue testing. *Materials* 12:3859.

16. Tuan D. Ngo, Alireza Kashani, Gabriele Imbalzano, Kate T.Q. Nguyen, David Hui. 2018. Additive manufacturing (3D Printing): A review of materials, methods, applications and challenges. *Composites Part B: Engineering* 143:172–196.

17. Filipe Amarante dos Santos, H. Rebelo, M. Coutinho, L.S. Sutherland, C. Cismasiu, Ilenia Farina, F. Fraternali. 2021. Low velocity impact response of 3D printed structures formed by cellular metamaterials and stiffening plates: PLA vs. PETG. *Composite Structures* 256:113–128.

18. Tino Stanković, Jochen Mueller, Kristina Shea. 2017. The effect of anisotropy on the optimization of additively manufactured lattice structures. *Additive Manufacturing* 17:67–76.

19. Chee Kai Chua, Chee How Wong and Wai Yee Yeong. 2017. *Standards, Quality Control, and Measurement Sciences in 3D Printing and Additive Manufacturing.* Academic Press, London.

20. Pushpendra Yadav, Pushpendra Yadav, Ankit Sahai & Rahul Swarup Sharma. 2019. Experimental investigations for effects of raster orientation and infill design on mechanical properties in additive manufacturing by fused deposition modelling. In *Lecture Notes on Multidisciplinary Industrial Engineering*, ed. R.G. Narayanan, S. N. Joshi and U. S. Dixit, 415–424. Springer, Singapore.

14 Wear Measurement by Real-Time Condition Monitoring Using Ferrography

Swati Kamble and Rajiv B.
College of Engineering Pune (COEP)

CONTENTS

14.1 INTRODUCTION

For health improvement of machines,their maintenance as per directions is very necessary. Throughcondition monitoring as a part of preventive maintenance [1], the life of machine components can be increased. Any component failure of machine results in machine breakdown which results in financial loss as well as loss of time. This leads to a bad effect on production. Hence condition monitoring [2,3] is used to identify the probable failure of components and rectify it as early as possible before they get failed.

Different condition monitoring techniques [4–6] used for maintenance are shown in Figure 14.1. Characteristics thatare used by these condition monitoring methods are shown in Table 14.1.

Some of these methods are as follows:

- **Vibration monitoring**: The analysis of vibrations [7,8] generated while the machine is in operating condition gives the health of the machine condition. If the vibration level is high,automatically life of machine will be reduced. Hence, it is important to detect small variations also in the pattern of vibration, and reasons foroccurrence must be diagnosed.
- **Noise monitoring**:Sound waves are monitored considering a particular situation. If high sound waves are produced, then there is a problem of masking.

DOI: 10.1201/9781003154518-14

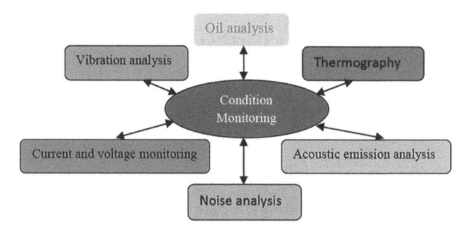

FIGURE 14.1 Condition monitoring techniques.

TABLE 14.1

Condition Monitoring Methods and Their Characteristics Used for Analysis

Technique	Characteristics
Vibration analysis	Monitoring frequency, amplitude, acceleration
Thermography	Analyses infrared images
Noise analysis	Monitoring sound waves
Oil analysis	Ferrographic oil analysis and image processing for finding wear particles
Acoustic emission analysis	Monitoring crack transmission, insufficient lubrication
Current and voltage monitoring	*Analyses* electrical signals like *current & voltage*

- **Oil analysis**: Oil analysis is used as lubricant examination done for detecting wear particles [9–12] as shown in Figure 14.2.
- In wear debris [13] collection large wear particles [14,15] are collected by filter and magnetic chip detector as shown in Figure 14.3. This examination indicatesabout wear of parts thatare moving. Sometimes electric chip detectors are also used which consists of the electric circuit with detectors. Alarm is also there to indicate if the rate of wear particles is high.
- Smaller wear particles will be collected from floating oil. Thisexamination gives an early warning about part failure.For this two methods are used:
  - **SOAP (Spectroscopic Oil Analysis Procedure)**: In this method,the concentration of wear particles can be found rapidly. One drawback of this method is it will not give information regarding the shape of particles.
  - **Ferrographic oil analysis**: In this method, wear particles [16–18] are deposited on ferrogram [19] accordingly to their sizes after oil passesthrough a magnetic chip detector [20]. This ferrogram [21,22] is then examined for wear particles' shape,size, and concentration.

- Used oil condition is monitored for its colour change, viscosity change, whether there is the formation of foam, and increased or decreased water content.

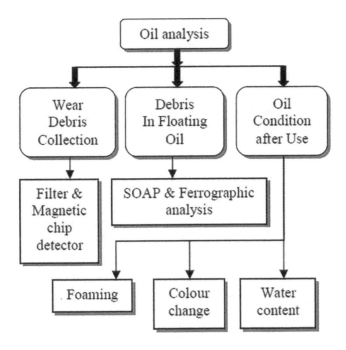

FIGURE 14.2 Oil analysis.

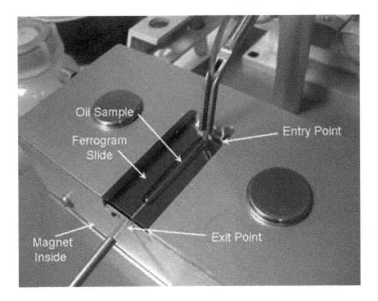

FIGURE 14.3 Magnetic separation of particles [13].

14.2   WEAR MEASUREMENT

For wear measurement, some important parameters are considered, as shown in Figure 14.4. By varying these parameters, wear characteristics are analysed by using appropriate arrangement.

- Geometry and material of contacting surfaces:
  There are commonly used tribo-pairs instruments along with their motions like sliding or rotary motion as shown in Figure 14.5. From these most frequently used test rigs are pin on disk and four ball tester in tribology for various applications arrangements.
- **Mode of lubrication**: According to application requirements,wear measurement can be done under dry [23] lubrication (no lubricant), moderate

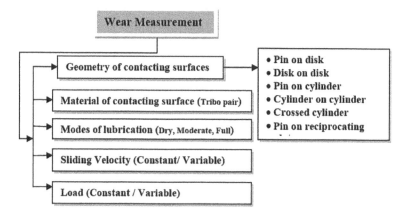

FIGURE 14.4   Wear measurement parameters.

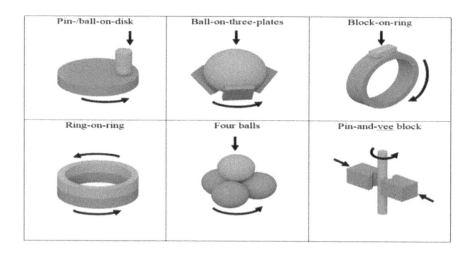

FIGURE 14.5   Some arrangements of tribo pairs.

[24] lubrication (quantity of lubricant is sufficient) or full lubrication (all parts are fully immersed in lubricant bath) mode.

- **Sliding velocity**: Velocity of moving parts [25] is constant or variable which is decided as per application. Generally, wear will be more in case of variable velocity of sliding.
- **Load**: Load acting on parts will be constant or variable [26].

Before wear measurement, these parameters must be taken into account for accurate detection regarding wear characteristics.

14.3   WEAR DEBRIS ANALYSIS

Used lubricating oil [27,28] from operating machines parts contains various metallic and non-metallic wear debris particles,due to friction and wear of components [28].

Figure 14.6 shows various characteristics considered for the wear debris analysis. Wear measurement is done from the contacting surfaces, chemical composition of particles [29], heat generation (formation of oxidation), and change in the condition of lubrication. Also in this figure, various methods used for this analysis are indicated.

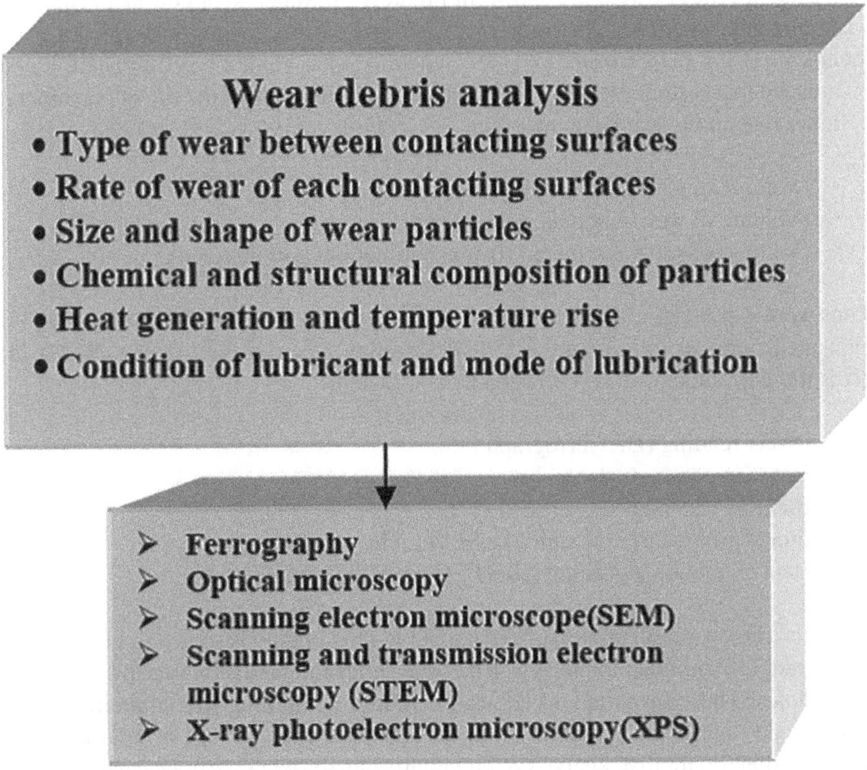

Wear debris analysis
- Type of wear between contacting surfaces
- Rate of wear of each contacting surfaces
- Size and shape of wear particles
- Chemical and structural composition of particles
- Heat generation and temperature rise
- Condition of lubricant and mode of lubrication

➢ Ferrography
➢ Optical microscopy
➢ Scanning electron microscope(SEM)
➢ Scanning and transmission electron microscopy (STEM)
➢ X-ray photoelectron microscopy(XPS)

FIGURE 14.6   Wear debris analysis characteristics & instruments used for analysis.

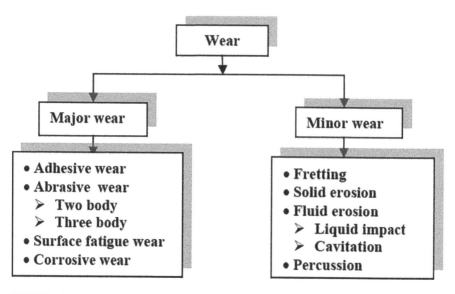

FIGURE 14.7 Types of wear.

Different types of wear are shown in Figure 14.7. Major wear considers adhesive wear, abrasive wear [30], corrosion [31] wear and surface fatigue wear. Minor wear includes fretting [32], erosion [33] etc. Generally wear cannot be eliminated. It can be reduced to a certain extent by different strategies to improve the life of machinery.

Laws related to wear state that:

- (Volume of wear) α (travel distance),
- (Volume of worn-out material) α (load),
- (Volume of worn-out material) 1/α (hardness of soft material).

Thus worn-out material particle characterictics were found by using ferrography [34] along with optical microscopy [35] and scanning electron microscope (SEM) [2] gives more accurate results. Ferrography consists of:

- Direct reading (DR) ferrograph [36],
- Dual ferrogram analyser,
- Bichromatic microscope/SEM [37],
- Image processing software like MATLAB,
- Data extraction algorithms like FECNN [38], BPNN [39].

Flow diagram of actual processes carried out in ferrography is shown in Figure 14.8. Ferrographic condition monitoring [40] is preventive maintenance done by collecting oil samples. These oil samples [41] are monitored by making ferrogram and under microscope images are captured. From these images analysis [35] of wear particles identification (qualitative analysis & quantitative analysis) [42] can be carried out.

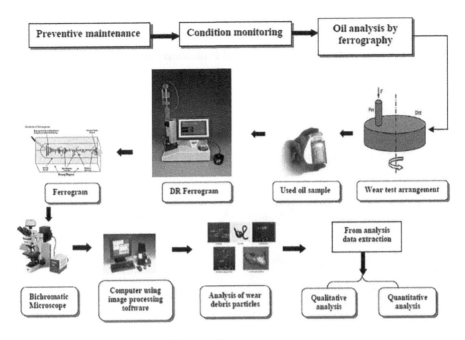

FIGURE 14.8   Flow diagram of ferrography.

By using this method,type of wear,its severity,wear characteristics such as particles size, their shape [43,44], distribution and concentration [45] can be found.

In ferrography [46] which type of wear occurred can be detected accurately. Wear severity [47] is calculated by the following formulae:

L: Reading of large particles quantity,
S: Reading of small particles quantity,
$(L+S)$ gives concentration of wear particles.
$(L-S)$ gives size distribution of particles.

- Wear Severity Index (WSI) = (L^2-S^2),
- Wear Particle Concentration (WPC) = $(L + S)$,
- Percentage of Large Particles (PLP) = $(L/L + S) \times 100\%$.

If quantity of L and S is high, it will result in abnormal wear.

- Risk Priority Number (RPN) = (Severity × occurrences × Detection)

RPN defines failure will occur or not,also it states failure effect. In Table 14.2, failure severity on machine health with its % occurrence and probability of detection is summarised. RPM must be as low as possible to avoid failure of parts of machines. Thus health and reliability of components can be increased.

TABLE 14.2

Failure Severity with % Occurence and Probability of Detection

Failure	Severity	Occurrences(%)	Probability of Detection
No or minor failure, not significant	1	0	0–5
Minor failure, slight effect	2–3	0.001–0.005	6–25
Moderate failure	4–6	0.005–0.05	26–55
High failure causing problems	7–8	>0.20	56–75
Sufficient high failure effect on safety	9–10	10%–50% or more	76–100

Engine Specifications

Engine:- 4 Stroke Single cylinder air cooled

Stroke length:- 49.5 mm

Displacement:- 97.2 cc

Bore:- 50 mm

Compression:- 9:1

Fuel tank capacity:- 10.5 litre

Oil tank capacity:- 1 litre

Maximum Power:- 5.74 KW at 7500 rpm

Maximum torque:- 8.04 N-m at 4500 rpm

FIGURE 14.9   Bike engine with specifications used for oil analysis [7].

Severity of wear is indicated from 1 to 10 scale. As severity increases, a large quantity of wear occur. Hence, to increase the life of machine components, severity must be as low as possible.

14.4   CASE STUDY

Ferrographic oil analysis method is used for I. C. engine wear Debris Analysis [40]. In this study, ferrography was used for the detection of wear particles by using Hero HF Deluxe bike engine oil. Used bike engine along with specifications are shown in Figure 14.9. By ferrographic analysis of wear particles, both qualitative and quantitative parameters can be found.

In the experimentation, five oil samples were collected at the interval of 520, 2800, 5156, 9500, and 10,144 km. Then wear particles obtained from the collected oil are analysed and the graphs are drawn for the comparative analysis. The results obtained from the collected oil sample after the predefined kilometres are shown in Figure 14.10.

In these graphs:

(a) Wear particle concentration (WPC),
(b) Wear particles generated in normal rubbing and
(c) Maximum size of particles generated in bearing, are shown for five collected samples.

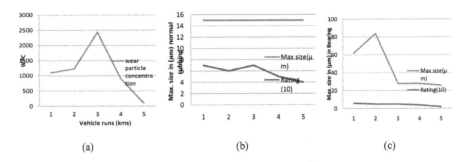

FIGURE 14.10 (a) Graph showing WPC. (b) Wear particles in normal rubbing. (c) Wear particles in bearing [7].

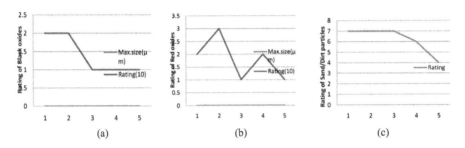

FIGURE 14.11 (a) Rating of black oxide. (b) Rating of red oxide. (c) Rating of dirt/dust/sand particles [7].

Wear particles rating also known as wear severity,is shown in Figure 14.11. The darkness of particles indicates oxidation. In the collected oil fine particles of minor size are seen. As shown in graph, (a) rating is ranging between 1 and 2, which shows the normal condition, (b) red oxides appear as a beach of red sandand the rating of these oxide particles is also very small which lies between normal ranges (c) sand/dirt/dust particles appearance will not get changed after heat treatment.If the quantity of these collected particles is high then wear severity will get changed from normal to critical condition.

Thus from this analysis, it is concluded thatwear particles are larger in size initially. After continuous use, size of wear particles gets reduced, but the quantity of small particles gets increased. Hence condition monitoring by ferrography is necessary after specific time for identifying real-time wear measurement of components.

14.5 CONCLUSION

This paper mainly emphasised the importance of ferrographic method which is used for condition monitoring for the health of machines resulting in an improved lifetime of the machine which reduces downtime of plant. In this method, analysis basically includes three steps:

- Decide the required size of debris group (large particles or small particles) for analysis;

- Focus on the characteristics of wear debris particles accordingly from ferrographic analysis;
- Set up a correlation between parameters of wear particles characteristics and severity of wear by suitable mathematical tools as well as with data extraction algorithms.

ABBREVIATIONS

DR   Direct reading
AI   Artificial Intelligence
HEMM Heavy earth moving machines
SOAP   Spectroscopic Oil Analysis Procedure
SEM   Scanning electron Microscope
WSI   Wear Severity Index
WPC   Wear Particle Concentration
PLP   Percentage of Large Particle
RPN   Risk Priority Number

REFERENCES

1. Ping Lu, Honor E. Powrie, Robert J.K. Wood, Terry J. Harvey, Nicholas R. Harris, "Early wear detection and its significance for condition monitoring", *Tribology International*159 (2021) 106946.
2. Peng Peng, Jiugen Wang, "Wear particle classification considering particle overlapping", *Wear*422–423 (2019) 119–127.
3. Po Zhang, Wenlong Lu, Xiaojun Liu, Wenzheng Zhai, Mingzhuo Zhou, Xiangqian (Jane) Jiang, "A comparative study on torsional fretting and torsional sliding wear of CuNiAl under different lubricated conditions", *Tribology International* 117 (2018) 78–86.
4. Jingqiu Wang, Xiaolei Wang, "A wear particle identification method by combining principal component analysis and grey relational analysis", *Wear* 304 (2013) 96–102.
5. V. Macian, R. Payri, B. TormosL, Montoro, "Applying analytical ferrography as a technique to detect failures in Diesel engine fuel injection systems", *Wear* 260 (2006) 562–566.
6. Lv Wenxiu, Wang Liyong, Chen Tao, "Ferrographic analysis in wear fault diagnosis for the confluent planetary gear mechanism", *2017 13th IEEE International Conference on Electronic Measurement & Instruments (ICEMI)*, IEEE, Yangzhou, 978-1-5090-5035-2, 2017.
7. Yoshiro Iwai, Tomomi Honda, Toshiro Miyajima, Shigeki Yoshinaga, M. Higashi, Yoshio Fuwa, "Quantitative estimation of wear amounts by real time measurement of wear debris in lubricating oil", *Tribology International* 43 (2010) 388–394.
8. Zhe Geng, Debashis Puhan, Tom Reddyhoff, "Using acoustic emission to characterize friction and wear in dry sliding steel contacts", *Tribology International* 134 (2019) 394–407.
9. S.J. Eder, C. Ielchici, S. Krenn, D. Brandtner, "An experimental framework for determining wear in porous journal bearings operated in the mixed lubrication regime", *Tribology International* 123 (2018) 1–9.

10. O. O. Ayodele, M. A. Awotunde, M. B. Shongwe, A. O. Adegbenjo, B. J. Babalola, B.A.Obadela, and P. AOlubambi, "Evaluation of wear and corrosion behaviour of hybrid sintered Ti6Al4V alloy", *Key Engineering Materials* 821 (2019) 321–326. ISSN: 1662-9795.

11. Qingfei He, Guiming Chen, Xiaohu Chen, Chunjiang Yao, "Application of oil analysis to the condition monitoring of large engineering machinery", *2009 8th International Conference on Reliability, Maintainability and Safety*, IEEE, Chengdu, 978-1-4244-4905-7, 2009.

12. Xianzhong Tian, Tongsen Hu, Jian Zhang, "Application to recognition of ferrography image with fractal neural network", *MIPPR 2005 SAR and Multispectral Image Processing*, 2005.

13. Gwidon P. Stachowiak, Gwidon W. Stachowiak, Pawel Podsiadlo, "Automated classification of wear particles based on their surface texture and shape features", *Tribology International* 41 (2008) 34–43.

14. Mohammed Ahmed Al-Bukhaiti, Ahmed Abouel Kasem Mohamad, Karam Mosa Emara,Shemy M. Ahmed, "Effect of slurry concentration on erosion wear behavior of AISI 5117 steel and high-chromium white cast iron", *Industrial Lubrication and Tribology* 70(4)(2018)628–638.

15. Harpreet Singh, Hiralal Bhowmick, "Lubrication characteristics and wear mechanism mapping for hybrid aluminium metal matrix composite sliding under surfactant functionalized MWCNT-oil", *Tribology International* 145 (2020) 106152.

16. Jiufei Luo, Song Feng, Guang Qiu, Leng Han, "Segmentation of Wear Debris Based on Edge Detection and Contour Classification", *2018 International Conference on Sensing, Diagnostics, Prognostics, and Control (SDPC)*, IEEE, Xi'an, 978-1-5386-6057-7, 2018.

17. Mahde C. Isa, Hasril Nain, Nik H. Yusoff, Mohd Subhi Din Yati, M.M. Muhammad, Irwan Mohd Nor, "Ferrographic analysis of wear particles of various machinery systems of a commercial marine ship", *Procedia Engineering* 68 (2013) 345–351.

18. Peng Peng, Jiugen Wang, "FECNN: A promising model for wear particle recognition", *Wear* 432–433 (2019) 202968.

19. Mengyan Nie, Ling Wang, "Review of condition monitoring and fault diagnosis technologies for wind turbine gearbox", *Procedia CIRP* 11 (2013) 287–290.

20. Yimeng Li, Jing Wu, Qiang Guo, "Electromagnetic sensor for detecting wear debris in lubricating oil", *IEEE Transactions on Instrumentation and Measurement* 69(5)(2020) 2533–2541.

21. Bin Fan, Song Feng, Yitong Che, Junhong Mao, Youbai Xie, "An oil monitoring method of wear evaluation for engine hot tests", *International Journal of Advanced Manufacturing Technology* 94(2018):3199–3207.

22. Wei Yuan, Song Feng, Zhiwen Wang, Qianjian Guo, Jie Yu, "Tribology analysis of spherical-surface contact sliding pairs under fluctuating loads", *Micro and Nanosystems* 12 (2020)23–32.

23. Ashesh Tiwari, Suraj Kumar Sharma, "Wear debris analysis of internal combustion engine by ferrography technique", *International Journal Of Engineering Sciences & Research Technology* 3(7) (2014) 788–793.

24. Sanjay Kumara, Deepam Goyalb, Rajeev K. Dangc, Sukhdeep S. Dhamib, B.S. Pablab, "Condition based maintenance of bearings and gears for fault detection – A review", *Materials Today: Proceedings* 5 (2018) 6128–6137.

25. O. Levi, N. Eliaz, "failure analysis and condition monitoring of an open-loop oil system using ferrography", *Tribology Letters* 36(2009) 17–29.

26. Xingjian Dai, Yong Wang, Shiqiang Yu, "Ferrographic analysis of pivot jewel bearing in oil-bath lubrication", *Wear* 376–377 (2017) 843–850.

27. Kenji Matsumoto, Tatsuya Tokunaga, Masahiko Kawabata, "Engine seizure monitoring system using wear debris analysis and particle measurement", SAE Technical Paper 2016-01-0888, 2016. doi:10.4271/2016-01-0888.

28. Aniket Magar, Shreekant Kshirsagar, "Weardebris analysis of machines using ferrography", *International Journal for Research in Applied Science & Engineering Technology (IJRASET)* 7(I) (2019).

29. Shuo Wang, Tonghai Wu, Kunpeng Wang, Thompson Sarkodie-Gyan, "Ferrograph analysis with improved particle segmentation and classification methods", *Journal of Computing and Information Science in Engineering* 20 (2020) 021001–021002.

30. Lv Wenxiu, Wang Liyong, Chen Tao, "Ferrographic analysis in wear fault diagnosis for the confluent planetary gear mechanism", *2017 13th IEEE International Conference on Electronic Measurement & Instruments (ICEMI)*, IEEE, Yangzhou, 978-1-5090-5035-2, 2017.

31. Wei Hong, Shaoping Wang, Mileta M. Tomovic, Haokuo Liu, Jian Shi, Xingjian Wang, "A novel indicator for mechanical failure and life prediction based on debris monitoring", *IEEE Transactions on Reliability* 66(1)(2017) 161–169.

32. Sontinan Intasonti, Tadpon Kullawong, Surapol Raadnui, "A novel concept for solid debris extraction technique from used lubricants for predictive maintenance", *Proceedings of the 2018 IEEE*, Bangkok, 2018.

33. Liu Tonggang, Wu Jian, Tang Xiaohang,Yang Zhiyi, "Qualitative ferrographic analysis method by quantitative parameters of wear debris characteristics", *Industrial Lubrication and Tribology* 64 (6) (2012) 367–375.

34. Robin Kumar Biswas, M. C. Majumdar, S. K. Basu, "Vibration and oil analysis by ferrography for condition monitoring", *Journal of The Institution of Engineers (India): Series C* 94(3) (2013) 267–274.

35. Xin Pei, Wei Pu, Ying Zhang, Lu Huang, "Surface topography and friction coefficient evolution during sliding wear in a mixed lubricated rolling-sliding contact", *Tribology International* 137 (2019) 303–312.

36. W. Hoffmann, "Some experience with ferrography in monitoring the condition of aircraft engines", *Wear* 65 (1981) 307–313.

37. Ashwani Kumar, Subrata Kumar Ghosh, "Size distribution analysis of wear debris generated in HEMM engine oil for reliability assessment: A statistical approach", *Measurement* 131 (2019) 412–418.

38. Alan Hase, Masaki Wada, Hiroshi Mishina, "Scanning electron microscope observation study for identification of wear mechanism using acoustic emission technique", *Tribology International* 72 (2014) 51–57.

39. Shuo Wang, Tonghai Wu, Tao Shao, Zhongxiao Peng, "Integrated model of BP neural network and CNN algorithm for automatic wear debris classification", *Wear* 426–427 (2019) 1761–1770.

40. M. H. Jones, "Ferrography applied to diesel engine oil analysis", *Wear* 56 (1979) 93–103.

41. Chandan Kumar, Manoj Kumar, "Wear debris analysis using ferrography", *International Journal of Recent Trends in Engineering & Research (IJRTER)* 2(8)(2016) 1455–1457.

42. Jingqiu Wang, Xiaolei Wang, "The segmentation of ferrography images: A brief survey", *Materials Science Forum* 770 (2014) 427–432.

43. Xiuqin Bai, Hanliang Xiao, Lu Zhang, "The condition monitoring of large slewing bearing based on oil analysis method", *Engineering Materials* 474–476 (2011) 716–719.

44. Xufeng Jiang, Fang Liu, Pengcheng Zhao, "Gearbox Non-ferrous metal bearing wear condition monitoring based on oil analysis", *Applied Mechanics and Materials* 164 (2012) 73–76.

45. Zhongyu Huang, Zhiqiang Yu, Zhixiong Li, Yuancheng Geng, "A fault diagnosis method of rolling bearing through wear particle and vibration analyses", *Applied Mechanics and Materials* 26–28 (2010) 676–681.

46. Weiping Chen, "Effect of free abrasive on sub-surface damage in rolling friction contact of optical lens", *The International Journal of Advanced Manufacturing Technology* 100 (2019) 1243–1251.

47. Matt McMahon, "Analytical ferrography: A powerful diagnostic tool", *Maintenance and Engineering* (2017) 1–9.

15 Design, Modelling and Comparative Analysis of a Horizontal Axis Wind Turbine

Ninad Vaidya and Shivprakash B. Barve
Dr. Vishwanath Karad MIT World Peace University

CONTENTS

15.1 INTRODUCTION

The amount of energy produced from harnessing wind power has surpassed many milestones. From a small amount of 159 GW in 2009 to a colossal leap of 650 GW in 2019 [1], wind energy has become the personification of renewable energy and it is apparent by this paradigm shift observable today. It is estimated that exposure to particulate matter is responsible for 18.8% of global deaths in the year 2018. Global wind energy production expanded approximately 20% in 2019, with around 60 GW production capability added to the global production. India added 2.5 GW of wind power in the year 2019 [2–3].

Designing, developing and simulating an energy-producing wind turbine is a multiplex procedure. Multiple speculations are considered while designing a turbine. The most important speculation is the Blade Element Momentum Theory (BEM)

DOI: 10.1201/9781003154518-15

[4–7]. Multiple materials are used for the production of new wind turbines. It was concluded that composite materials such as carbon nanotubes, carbon fibre, fibre-glass impregnated with polyester or alternatives like epoxy resin greatly improve efficiency over conventional materials [8–14].

Qblade is an explicitly designed software for the analysis of wind turbine blades [15–18]. Qblade aids in validating the numerical design's accuracy by providing real-world simulation values. The use of models using Computer Aided Drafting (CAD) software was analysed in finite element analysis (FEA) software to determine various structural parameters such as tower thickness and blade thickness for structural assurance [19–25].

15.2   ANALYTICAL DESIGN

Wind energy observations from over four locations were recorded by using a vane anemometer.

15.2.1   Wind Observations (m/sec)

a. $V_{avg} = 6.5$
b. $V_{design} = 8.5$
c. Cut in velocity = 4.5
d. Cut out velocity = 18

15.2.2   Design Considerations

a. Power Required = 1 KW
b. Coefficient of Performance $(C_p) = 45\%$
c. Mechanical Efficiency $(\eta_{mech}) = 85\%$
d. Tip Speed Ratio = 6

15.2.3   Rotor Design

Rotor =1.5 m
  Swept Area = 7.068 m²
  Wind Power = 2658.63 W
  Efficiency of Energy Transformation = 38.25%
  Angular Speed ω = 34 Rad/s
  Rotor Speed = 325 rpm
  Torque τ = 29.38 Nm
  Tower Height H_t = 4.5 m

15.3   SOFTWARE MODELLING AND ANALYSIS

15.3.1   Solidworks CAD Models and Renders

CAD model of rotor was designed in solidworks, and it is shown in Figure 15.1.

FIGURE 15.1   CAD model of rotor.

15.3.2   MATERIAL ASSIGNMENT

The various material was assigned for various parts of rotor. Material AISI4130 was assigned to Hub, Hub rear, Yaw Rods and for Tower. A-Glass Fibre was assigned to Blade and PVC was assigned to Yaw.

15.3.3   STRUCTURAL ANALYSIS

The tower is stress analysed in an FEA software ANSYS, and it is shown in Figure 15.2. It was illustrated that,

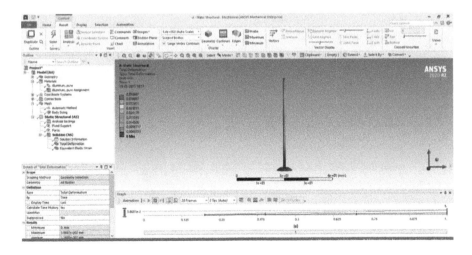

FIGURE 15.2   Structural analysis in ANSYS.

The force applied = 5600 N

    Maximum deformation observed = 0.034 mm

    Thus, the results confirm that the design is safe.

15.3.4 AERODYNAMIC ANALYSIS

The wind turbine simulation and design framework were developed with the soft-ware Qblade. Simulation of horizontal axis was utilized the BEM method and a Double Multiple Stream (DMS) algorithm is utilized in Qblade for the simulation of wind turbine performance. The data of Cl and Cd over numerous angles of attacks were required for simulation. The comparison of results of various air foil in relations of their Cl and Cd and Cl/Cd and angle of attack is shown via Figure 15.3.

15.3.5 ROTOR DESIGN

Qblade is required to input the various design considerations of the blade for rotor design. Once the basic blade shape is completed, sectional twist and air foil are to be assigned to each individual section. The blade design module is used for theh efficient design of rotors and blades. This rotor design is used in the final simulation. It is shown in Figure 15.4.

15.4 QBLADE AERODYNAMIC SIMULATIONS

The design of the blades and the turbine form were specified. Various parame-ters, such as form of power regulation, rotational speed, cut in and out velocity or generator efficiency, were specified. With specified setup, turbine was simulated.

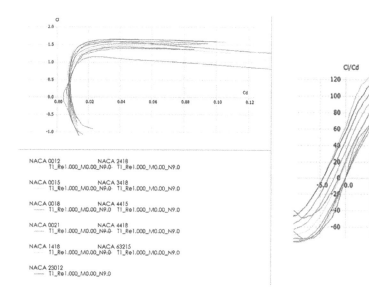

FIGURE 15.3 Airfoil comparison results in Qblade.

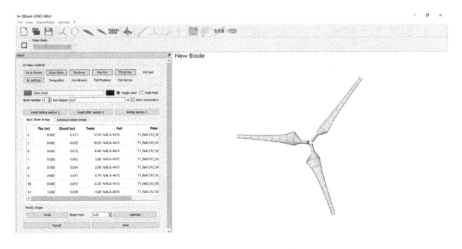

FIGURE 15.4 Rotor design in Qblade.

With different tip speed ratios, dimensionless simulation was carried out. It was useful for the comparison of different rotor geometries. Various parameters were simulated with different blade pitch variations, rotational speeds, and incoming velocity. It was helpful to investigate turbine characteristics. Simulations results were available in the post-processor module.

The power results considering the wake loss, tip loss, wind drag, weight action of rotor and wind compressive force are shown in Figures 15.5 and 15.6.

15.5 RESULTS AND DISCUSSIONS

The amount of power generated at the corresponding speed of rotation of the turbine. Upon creating a varying wind field from 4 to 8.5 m/sec, Qblade performs a

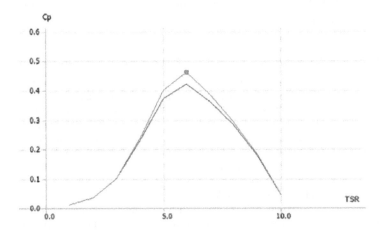

FIGURE 15.5 Verification of analytically found C_p in Qblade.

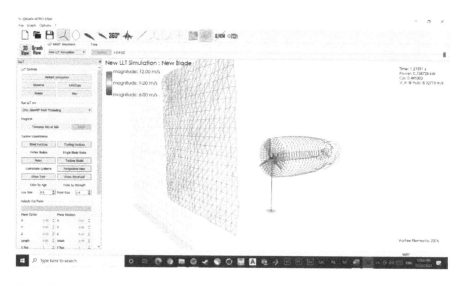

FIGURE 15.6   Qblade simulation.

simulation of the turbine in the generated wind field. Qblade aerodynamic simulation proves that in real-world conditions, the turbine can produce about 760 W/h of power under varying conditions.

15.6   CONCLUSIONS

The wind turbine is analytically designed and results are verified using multiple simulation software. The structural analysis was done using ANSYS. The environmental flow analysis was done using solidworks flow. The Aerodynamic analysis was done using Qblade.

The theoretical efficiency was found to be 38.45% which is a 7.25% improvement over standard HAWT efficiency. The simulation results determined power of 760W at mean speed, including losses.

REFERENCES

1. REN21 (2020). *Renewables 2020 Global Status Report*. Paris: REN21 Secretariat, p. 131.
2. L. Burrows (2021). Deaths from fossil fuel emissions higher than previously thought, Harvard John A. Paulson School of Engineering and Applied Sciences, February 2021.
3. S. Saji, N. Kuldeep, A. Tyagi (2019). *A Second Wind for India's Wind Energy Sector: Pathways to Achieve 60 GW*. New Delhi: Council on Energy, Environment and Water, pp. 1–64.
4. S. Gundtoft (2012). Wind turbines, University College of Aarhus, January, pp. 1–22.
5. J. A. Karlsen (2009). Performance calculations for a model turbine, Master's thesis, Institutt for energi-og prosessteknikk, June.
6. N. Tenguria, N. D. Mittal, S. J. Ahmed (2010). Investigation of blade performance of horizontal axis wind turbine based on blade element momentum theory (BEMT) using NACA airfoils. *International Journal of Engineering, Science and Technology*. 2 (12). doi: 10.4314/ijest.v2i12.64565.
7. G. Ingram (2011). Wind turbine blade analysis using the blade element momentum method, 18 October, pp. 1–21.

8. L. Mishnaevsky, K. Branner, H. N. Petersen, J. Beauson, M. McGugan, B. F. Sørensen . Materials for wind turbine blades: An overview. *Materials (Basel).* 10 (11): 1285. doi: 10.3390/ma10111285.

9. L. Thomas, M. Ramachandra (2018). Advanced materials for wind turbine blade – A review. *Materials Today: Proceedings.* 5 (1): 2635–2640. doi: 10.1016/j.matpr. 2018.01.043.

10. B. Attaf (2013). *Recent Advances in Composite Materials for Wind Turbine Blades, Chapter 1.* Hong Kong: World Academic Publishing, pp. 1–24.

11. S. A. AlBat'hi, Y. F. Buys, M. H. Hadzari, M. Othman (2015). A light material for wind turbine blades. *Advanced Materials Research.* 1115: 308–313. doi: 10.4028/www.scientific.net/AMR.1115.308.

12. V. Paul, A. Thomas, S. Herbert, L. Daniel, L. Donald, G. Dayton, M. John, W. Musial, J. Kevin, Z. Michael, M. Antonio, W. Tsai Stephen, J. Richmond (2003). Trends in the design, manufacture and evaluation of wind turbine blades. *Wind Energy.* 6 (3): 245–259. doi: 10.1002/we.90.

13. M. Jureczko, M. Pawlak, A. Mężyk (2005). Optimisation of wind turbine blades. *Journal of Materials Processing Technology.* 167: 463–471. doi: 10.1016/j.jmatprotec. 2005.06.055.

14. M. Alaskari et al. (2019). Analysis of wind turbine using QBlade software. *2nd International Conference on Sustainable Engineering Techniques (ICSET 2019), IOP Conf. Series: Materials Science and Engineering*, Vol. 518, pp. 1–11. doi:10.1088/1757-899X/518/3/032020.

15. M. R. Islam, L. Bin Bashar, N. S. Rafi (2019), Design and simulation of a small wind turbine blade with QBlade and validation with MATLAB. *4th International Conference on Electrical Information and Communication Technology (EICT)*, pp. 1–6. doi: 10.1109/ EICT48899.2019.9068762.

16. D. Marten, J. Peukert, G. Pechlivanoglou, C. Nayeri, C. Paschereit (2013). QBLADE: An open-source tool for design and simulation of horizontal and vertical axis wind turbines. *International Journal of Emerging Technology and Advanced Engineering.* 3 (Special Issue 3): 264–269.

17. V. R. Ponakala, D. G. Kumar (2017). Design and simulation of small wind turbine blades in Q-Blade. *International Journal of Engineering Development and Research.* 5 (4): 1095–1103.

18. D. Marten (2014). *QBlade Short Manual*, pp. 1–17. doi: 10.13140/RG.2.1.4015.0241.

19. G. D. Tsega, B. S. Yigezu (2019). Upwind 2MW horizontal axis wind turbine tower design and analysis, automation. *Control and Intelligent Systems.* 7 (5): 111–131. doi: 10.11648/j.acis.20190705.11.

20. P. Gulve, S. B. Barve (2014). Design and construction of vertical axis wind turbine. *International Journal of Mechanical Engineering and Technology (IJMET).* 5 (10): 148–155.

21. H. Cao (2011). Aerodynamics analysis of small horizontal axis wind turbine blades by using 2D and 3D CFD modelling. Master's thesis, University of Central Lancashire, pp. 1–93.

22. J. F. Manwell, J. G. McGowan, A. L. Rogers (2009). *Wind Energy Explained: Theory, Design and Application*, Second Edition. Chichester: Wiley, pp. 91–153.

23. B. D. Agarkar, S. B. Barve (2016). A review on hybrid solar/wind/hydro power generation system. *International Journal of Current Engineering and Technology.* 4 (4): 188.

24. D. S. Shah, S. B. Barve (2021). Design, analysis and simulation of a Darrieus (Eggbeater type) wind turbine. *International Journal of Engineering and Technology (IRJET).* 8 (10): 1655–1660.

25. N. Karwa, S. B. Barve (2021). Design, modelling and analysis of savonius vertical axis wind turbine. *International Journal of Engineering and Technology (IRJET).* 8 (11): 351–357.

Index